The American Association of Teachers of French

A Celebration of FLES*

Sequential *FLES,*

FLEX,

and

Immersion

Gladys C. Lipton
Editor

National Textbook Company
a division of NTC/CONTEMPORARY PUBLISHING GROUP
Lincolnwood, Illinois USA

DEDICATION

This book is dedicated to **FLES*** (K–8) students and teachers who demonstrate the reality and the importance of teaching and learning foreign language, before the age of ten.

G.C.L.

Publisher: Steve VanThournout
Editorial Director: Cindy Krejcsi
Executive Editor: Mary Jane Maples
Senior Editor: Elizabeth Millán
Director, World Languages Publishing: Keith Fry
Art Director: Ophelia M. Chambliss
Production Manager: Margo Goia

Cover Design: Larry Cope; **Interior Design:** Think Design

ISBN: 0-8442-9343-1

Published by National Textbook Company,
a division of NTC/Contemporary Publishing Group, Inc.
4255 West Touhy Avenue,
Lincolnwood (Chicago), Illinois 60646-1975 U.S.A.
© 1998 NTC/Contemporary Publishing Group, Inc.
All rights reserved. No part of this book may be reproduced,
stored in a retrieval system, or transmitted in any form or by any means,
electronic, mechanical, photocopying, recording, or otherwise,
without prior permission of the publisher.
Manufactured in the United States of America.

Library of Congress Catalog Card Number: 98-91257

890 VP 0987654321

Contents

FOREWORD by Paul Simon   vii

INTRODUCTION   ix

PART 1

FOCUS ON **FLES*** PROGRAMS: MULTIPLE INTERFACES   1

Public Education in America and the Implications of
Foreign Language and Second Language Acquisition   2
    Peter Negroni

The People Factor in the Glastonbury Public Schools   7
    Christine Brown

Public Relations: Inside and Outside   13
    Kathleen Riordan

The Georgia PTA Foreign Language Resolution   15
    Lynne B. Bryan

Guidelines for **FLES*** Programs   18
    Gladys C. Lipton

ICAL: Variation on a FLEX Theme   24
    Dora F. Kennedy and Pat Barr-Harrison

Allegro Sostenuto: A Baker's Dozen of Challenges
for the Immersion Administrator   29
    Paul A. García

A Teacher's View of Advocacy   45
    Harriet Saxon

PART 2

FOCUS ON **FLES*** LEARNERS   49

A Salad of Language Learners   50
    Elizabeth Miller

The Northern Kentucky University **FLES*** Troupe:
Reaching Foreign Language Learners of Today and Tomorrow   57
    Katherine C. Kurk

Differing Abilities in the Sequential FLES Class Virginia L. Gramer	61
We Can Teach All Students: **FLES*** *Students Rarely Fail!* Gladys C. Lipton	69
Mon Parcours: Letting Them Tell Their Story Lena L. Lucietto	73
Reaching Them All via Multiple Intelligences: Floor Mapping Patricia R. Duggar	77

PART 3

FOCUS ON **FLES*** METHODOLOGY   81

Reading in Second Language Acquisition Virginia L. Gramer	82
Bridging the Gap in **FLES***: *Suggestions for the Transition to the Written Word* Juliette Eastwick and Elizabeth Tomlinson	88
A Kaleidoscope of Discovery: The Sequential FLES Program in Rutherford, New Jersey Harriet Saxon	94
Reading the World: **FLES*** *and Global Education* Katherine C. Kurk and Hilary W. Landwehr	101
Is There Life after "Simon Dit"?: Expanding Your **FLES*** *Classroom through the Use of Learning Centers* Astrid M. DeBuhr	111
Let the Theme Draw Them In Suzanne Cane	116
Linking Language and Context: An Example of an Interdisciplinary Approach Lena L. Lucietto	128

PART 4

EXPANDING THE FOCUS OF **FLES***   135

A "French-ship" with the Community Harriet Saxon	136
Of Tapestries, Tortillas, and Mulberry Bushes Lena L. Lucietto	142
From Sukiyaki to Croissants: Global Education at Work in the Elementary School Astrid M. DeBuhr	147

The Jewel in Our Crown Alan S. Wax, Lydia Hurst, Kathleen Durkin, and Diane Merenda	151
Summer Language Immersion Day Camps Evelyne Cella Armstrong	154
All the World's a Stage (You and Your Students the Actors) Elizabeth Miller	161

PART 5

EVAULATING FLES* PROGRAMS   167

Using Class Quizzes to Promote the Linguistic Accuracy of Younger Learners Rebecca M. Valette	168
Portfolio Assessment of Second Languages in the Elementary Classroom Philip Korfe	175
Assessment, Evaluation, and Accountability: Why Bother Evaluating FLES* Programs? Gladys C. Lipton	178
Making the Grade: Continuous Evaluation in the FLES* Classroom Maureen Regan-Baker	184
He or She That Tooteth Not His or Her Own Horn . . . That Horn Goeth Untooteth Elizabeth Miller	189
Celebrating the Successes of FLES* through Evaluation Deborah Wilburn-Robinson	193

APPENDIXES

A. Definitions	206
B. The Five Cs of the Standards for Foreign Language Learning	207
C. **FLES*** Teacher Competencies	209
D. Focus on **FLES***	211
E. Suggestions for Attracting French **FLES*** Students	215
F. Basic **FLES*** Mini-Bibliography	222
G. Mini-Biographies of the Contributors to This Volume	224

Foreword

Slowly, slowly we are learning the importance of foreign language education to our security, to our ability to provide world leadership, to our economy, and to our culture.

Gladys Lipton has compiled a book—*A Celebration of FLES**—that is practical, but is not so buried in practicality that it does not require us to dream a little. I like the comment of Peter Negroni, the Superintendent of Schools of Springfield, Massachusetts, who writes: "I see a place where people dream in more than one language."

I want that too—but before that is achieved we have to simply dream. Readers should ask themselves two basic questions: What kind of a world do I want? What am I willing to do to achieve it?

The realistic answer that most people give to the second question is: not much. At least until they are challenged. And that's what this book does. It gives practical insights from a French class, for example, that can be applied to a Spanish or a German or a Chinese class.

Having served both as a senator and now as a teacher, I can say candidly that in both professions (and all others) there is a tendency to get into a rut, to do things in the same manner, over and over. "We always have done it that way," is the defense mechanism. When the first matches were produced to create fire, I am sure there were those who still wanted to rub two sticks together to start a flame.

A Celebration of FLES* is a tactful call on people who understand the importance of foreign language instruction to improve their work. I hope the word spreads about the importance of this book.

A decade ago the great threat to the world was nuclear destruction. Thanks to the fall of the Berlin Wall and unbelievable developments in Central and Eastern Europe, that threat has been reduced dramatically. Today the great threat is instability. Sometimes people who speak the same language fight each other, as in Somalia. But frequently the barrier to understanding is language. As I write this, I recall a few hours ago meeting a student from Poland on the Southern Illinois University campus. I was able to sum up my total knowledge of Polish, about four phrases, and she beamed. My few words were a small gesture that acknowledged her culture and its importance.

Our culture is weak in doing that. *A Celebration of FLES** will not solve the problem, but it will put one important piece into a mosaic that we must create.

Paul Simon
Southern Illinois University
Carbondale

Introduction

For the past twelve years, **FLES*** has been characterized by rebirth, tremendous growth of programs, increasing enrollments, and much-needed new scientific and research-based information about the rationale for beginning foreign language study before the age of ten.

The members of the National **FLES*** Commission of the American Association of Teachers of French take pride in the multifaceted services the commission provides for **FLES*** teachers of French—services that, in fact, impact all **FLES*** teachers. For over thirty years, **FLES*** practitioners (elementary school foreign language teachers) and supporters, including FL middle school teachers, FL high school teachers, university faculty, superintendents, principals, curriculum directors, administrators, parents, teacher-trainers, coordinators, supervisors, methods instructors, and other **FLES*** advocates, have written articles in the *Reports of the National FLES* Commission of AATF,* relating practical ideas, suggestions, successful experiences, and comments that have been in the forefront of the profession.

FLES*, the overall term for all types of elementary school foreign language programs, was a term I created during an address I delivered to a large group of superintendents and principals. They pointed out that it was misleading to use one term, "FLES," for two different things: that is, for both the overall term describing all types of elementary school foreign language programs and the specific term describing one program model of FLES. In response to this constructive criticism, I devised two new terms. **FLES*** (pronounced FLESTAR) is the overall term for all types of elementary school foreign language programs. It incorporates the three program models: Sequential FLES, FLEX, and Immersion. Sequential FLES is the name of the specific program model formerly known as "FLES."

This volume, *A Celebration of FLES*,* is offered as a celebration of **FLES*** teachers across the country for their enthusiasm, their teaching skills, their creativity, their resourcefulness, and their outstanding results! It is also offered as a celebration of **FLES*** students in K–8 classes who view the **FLES*** experience as an exciting first step in becoming familiar with the world and who, in turn, will become **FLES*** supporters. It is also offered as a celebration of the countless supporters of **FLES***—

parents, school board members, counselors, administrators, principals, supervisors, curriculum directors, teacher-trainers, and **FLES*** advocates in the social, business, and political arenas of the community who have enthusiastically supported **FLES*** programs over the years in hundreds of schools and school communities, in countless budget hearings, in numerous curriculum meetings, in press conferences and interviews, and everywhere else **FLES*** has come under discussion.

The articles in this volume, which were selected from the twelve most recent years of Reports of the National **FLES*** Commission of AAFT, treat a wide variety of topics and themes. In Section 1, "Focus on **FLES*** Programs: Multiple Interfaces," the authors deal with how the three program models of **FLES*** are organized and the important roles of the various players in Sequential FLES, FLEX, and Immersion. In Section 2, "Focus on **FLES*** Learners," many classroom-oriented suggestions are given in hopes of reaching **FLES*** learners who have differing abilities, learning styles, intelligences, and preferences. In Section 3, "Focus on **FLES*** Methodology," the authors present a broad range of basic, practical procedures for teaching **FLES***. In Section 4, "Expanding the Focus on **FLES***," many creative and innovative suggestions are offered for practical applications of **FLES*** in the community, in camps, in travel abroad, and in other settings. In Section 5, "Evaluating **FLES*** Programs," the authors identify effective ways of assessing and evaluating **FLES*** students and programs. Several useful appendixes complete the volume.

A *Celebration of FLES** is also a celebration of the past and present officers and members of the Executive Council of the American Association of Teachers of French; the past Executive Director, Fred Jenkins; and the present Executive Director, Jayne Abrate, who have supported and encouraged the work of the National **FLES*** Commission of AATF.

We are particularly endebted to Mark Pattis, Keith Fry, and Elizabeth Millán of NTC/Contemporary Publishing Group, Inc., for their interest in working collaboratively with AATF on this volume.

Gladys C. Lipton, Editor

PART 1

Focus on **FLES*** Programs: Multiple Interfaces

Public Education in America and the Implications of Foreign Language and Second Language Acquisition

Peter Negroni
Superintendent of Schools
Springfield, Massachusetts

I would like to share my thoughts on public education in America and the implications of foreign language and second language acquisition. I am fortunate in that I speak to hundreds of groups all over the country. I must admit that second language educators are my favorite group to address. Indeed I bring a bias to this article, for while I am presently a superintendent, I see myself as a second language teacher. This was my first love in teaching and continues to be what I love to do most.

In all of my thirty-one years of experience I have found second language teachers to be a very special breed. We have a certain commitment and caring. We simply love what we do, and it shows in the way we work with children. All you have to do is enter any second language class in America and you will see that what I say is true.

Why is it that second language teachers are such a caring and committed group? I suppose it's because you cannot be a second language teacher without caring about other cultures and people. We indeed go beyond the interest in subject matter. We are interested in literature, customs, how people live, traditions, and values of others. We are all interested in something that is different than we are. We are open to learning about others and see value in differences. In fact, we are enchanted by these differences. And we have a very unique perspective that monolingual people do not have. We can look at things from more than one point of view because language is such a powerful tool. It allows us these multiperspectives.

Just think about this a minute. Not only can we think in more than one language, but because we understand and respect the culture of that language we have a different perspective. Furthermore, I am joyful of the fact that I can dream in Spanish.

What I ask you to think about are the implications of this unique perspective of second language educators on current conditions in education in America. How do we fit into the major reforms that are taking place in this country? Why is it that I believe that second language educators and second language acquisition programs can become the cornerstone—the centerpiece—of the new efforts to reform public education?

Let us consider for a moment where we are in America today. For the first time in this experiment called "The American Democracy," we have significantly altered our expectations for the public schools. We are now expected to teach equally well all the children. This indeed is a new demand. In the past we were ready to accept that some would fail, but not today. In this increasingly complex world, the new demand is in the area of human resources. People have become important because we have moved from an industrial society to an information society.

This new expectation to educate all is occurring at a most curious time in our history. The demographics of this country are changing more rapidly than ever before in our history. The number of people who come to this country not speaking English is dramatically increasing.

What are the challenges before us as educators? The challenge is the need to educate all in an increasingly diverse population.

What, again I ask, are the implications specifically for second language educators? They are enormous—we have an opportunity before us unlike any other in the history of this country. Second language educators can be at the center of the reform efforts in this country. We can use what we believe about the importance of culture and people to create schools that work for all children.

If America is to survive as a nation, it must naturally respect diversity as an asset. It must see bilingualism and biculturalism as assets and not liabilities. Well, we, the second language educators of America, already believe this, and we can become the implementors of programs that use culture and bilingualism as assets. We can be the pioneers of reforms needed in America under the conditions that presently exist.

What stands in our way from taking center stage? Indeed, very little. However, we must recognize that there are problems that face us as educators. Everyone in America is still not convinced as we are that diversity is an asset.

We still have some old ideas and old notions to conquer, such as:

1. **English is enough.** There are forces in our country that believe that everyone else should learn to speak English. We still send people as ambassadors to foreign countries who do not speak the language of the country they are going to. Imagine it in the reverse; it just does not happen. Everyone who comes here to represent another country speaks English.

2. **Language teaching is an extra.** We still have school systems in America that offer language to fewer than 10 percent of the students. There are some school systems and colleges that graduate students who have had no foreign language exposure. How can anyone be considered educated and speak only one language? This is unthinkable in other countries. You are not educated unless you speak more than one language.
3. **Language programs are the first to be cut in hard times.** Because language programs are viewed as an extra, they are the first to be cut. People view language as a frill. In fact, our own colleagues who are not language teachers are the first to say, "But you have to have science, math, and social studies. You can get along without language teaching."
4. **Language is for the best and the brightest.** All across America we have entrance requirements to take a language that render a large portion of our population ineligible. Some of us as language teachers have fallen prey to this one. We want only the best students. There is a strong connection here to the reform movement in America today. If you believe as I do that we must teach all children and that we must switch the paradigm from teaching the children to the best of their potential to teaching the children to the best of our potential, then you will see the enormous implication for second language acquisition.

The one thing that over 98 percent of all human beings have in common is language. Over 98 percent of people are able to speak a language. This means that human beings have the inherent capacity to learn a language. I believe that all of these people—over 98 percent of human beings—can learn a second, a third, as many languages as they are exposed to.

Unfortunately, not all agree. I was working with a principal on school effectiveness who said to me, "Dr. Negroni, I don't care what you say about the fact that all kids can learn. These kids can't learn French." My response to this educator was, "Aren't these children lucky that they were not born in France or in Quebec City or in Martinique?"

Language is the natural vehicle to prove that all children can learn, and it can be used as a powerful part of the pedagogy needed to transform our schools as well as our belief system about teaching and learning. The children in America all have the capacity to speak more than one language. They are limited only by the people who refuse to believe they can.

In addition to the facts I have presented, I believe there are some very strong economic reasons for second language acquisition to be at the cornerstone of the reform effort in America. We have seen in the last three years some of the most important historical events of this century.

The composition of today's world is very different. Communism has fallen and we have to move to a global economy. In order to be successful as a nation, we must be able to compete in this new smaller world. Language, communication, and education have become the national defense of the year 2000. Language and communication are integral to our being successful in this new global economy. Language and understanding of others' cultures will be more critical than ever in this new world.

I do not believe, as some do, that computers that instantly translate letters and conversations will be the answer. Yes, these are helpful tools, but they will never replace human interaction. They will never replace the bond that understanding another language and culture will bring. It is time that Americans and America's teachers understand what is before them.

When we, the teachers of America, look at a child who speaks a language other than English, we must look at that language as an asset and not as a hindrance—as a gift the child brings with him or her. We must never tell children—as I was told in school—"Forget your Spanish and learn English." Yes, learn English, but never forget your Spanish. We must never tell children to forget their culture.

An experience of mine illustrates the point. I recently spoke with a church group in a nearby wealthy suburb. During the question period, a man raised the issue of bilingualism and bilingual education. Prior to responding, I asked him if he thought it would be good if all the students in his community learned to speak a second language. His response was an enthusiastic "Yes, of course." I suggested to him that 30 percent of the children in my schools already had that advantage.

I know that you see my point, but I am not sure that he did. In hundreds, if not thousands of classrooms across America, children are being told to forget the language they bring to school because the only language that counts is English. Of course, all of us in this room clearly understand the importance of English and that all children must master English. However, this should not be at the expense of another language. We, as foreign language teachers, must be the strongest advocates for this position.

Foreign language teachers are not so silly as to believe that English is not critically important for our children to succeed—but we are silly enough to believe that it is better, in addition to English, to speak one or more languages. Unfortunately, there are not enough people in America who believe this. So it is incumbent upon us—and on every teacher in America—to begin to make the connections I have just emphasized.

Walls are tumbling down. Whoever believed the statues of Lenin would crash to the ground? If communism could fall, why can't every child in America learn to speak Russian? We all know that for communism to fall was much harder than for American children to learn to speak Russian. What we have before us is a decade of opportunities for foreign language teachers. The time is right for us, and we cannot allow this opportunity to pass us by.

I would like to end by discussing vision. *Vision* has become a popular word. I become worried when I ask someone about their vision and they say they have to find it in their desk. Imagine your vision being locked up in a desk. You see, for me, vision is not something you write on a piece of paper. Vision, for me, is what you have in your heart. What you believe deeply inside of you with conviction. YOU carry it with you every day. You act it out every day. Your behavior is what demonstrates your vision, not what you write on a piece of paper.

What, I ask you, is our vision as the foreign language teachers of America? It's quite simple. For vision is what I call the preferred future. It is what we want for ourselves, our families, and our country.

A vision of the preferred future is more important than anything else. Over and over we are learning that when children have a belief in themselves and when they believe they have a positive place in the future, they will strive for that future.

How about a snapshot of the future that has in it every single American speaking a minimum of three languages? I believe that foreign language teachers have the capacity to make that snapshot come alive. Foreign language teachers can help develop for America this preferred vision.

My snapshot of the preferred future has in it an America that respects its diversity and allows for a flourishing democracy where all people support and work with each other. But most of all, *I see a place where people dream in more than one language.*

The People Factor in the Glastonbury Public Schools

Christine Brown
Glastonbury Public Schools
Glastonbury, Connecticut

The success of the FLES program in the Glastonbury (CT) Public Schools is a direct result of not only those who work today with youngsters, but also of those administrators, parents, school board members, and students who have supported the program for more than thirty years.

In 1956, Glastonbury was fortunate to appoint a new superintendent, Dr. Laurence Paquin. Dr. Paquin believed that foreign languages were a necessary component of any academic program. In his previous school district (Fairfield, CT), he had supervised the implementation of one of the nation's first FLES programs, and he felt that Glastonbury was the kind of community that would support an early language program as well as an expansion of offerings at the junior and senior high levels. Dr. Paquin hired a former foreign language director, Mary Thompson, to be director of curriculum in Glastonbury. Mary Thompson, a legend in her own time, was dedicated to establishing an excellent language program. Mary, along with professors from Yale University, wrote a proposal, later funded by a generous grant from the National Defense Education Act, to adapt the Army Language Teaching Method for secondary school students. She also knew that to develop oral proficiency, students had to have the opportunity to begin language learning at an early age. In 1956, she began the Glastonbury FLES program.

From 1956 to the present, the FLES program has continued to serve all students in our community. Although the methodology has changed significantly (from primarily audio-lingual to more proficiency-based), the support of many individuals continues to be the essential component to maintaining an excellent, properly funded, and well-articulated program.

First, if one is to implement a new program, school administrators must support the concept of early language learning. Without a supportive superintendent and curriculum director, it is difficult to convince principals and classroom teachers to give the time necessary in an already crowded elementary-school curriculum. Second, without the support of parents, administrators are reluctant to add more subjects to the school day. Even reluctant administrators will change their minds about FLES if informed parents put enough pressure on them. Those interested in beginning programs must cultivate community support and provide up-to-date and accurate information to school decision makers.

Certainly, parents must also pressure school board members to consider seriously the possibility of beginning early language programs. Although board members may themselves be quite supportive of the concept, they are prohibited from lobbying as individuals with their own educational agendas. They must act as a board and their reelection or reappointment generally depends on whether they represent the views of the parent community. Active, vocal, and well-informed parents can sway the opinions of unconvinced board members.

Classroom teachers, special-area teachers, and principals are all potential supporters of language programs in the elementary schools. Although classroom teachers or principals may not have studied languages themselves, most are at least aware of the importance of geography and the need for international competitiveness. In order to convince these individuals that a knowledge of foreign language is essential in today's world, FLES advocates must show the connections between language learning and global awareness. Skeptics can be invited to visit FLES teachers in other districts to meet with administrators and classroom teachers who do support FLES for its value in heightening both linguistics and global awareness. Present students and graduates of FLES programs are also great advocates for early language programs. In Glastonbury, we often seek testimony even from high school graduates.

In 1985, we surveyed 1,200 graduates from our high school to solicit their opinions of our program in grades 3 through 12. We received three hundred responses from our survey. Our graduates indicated strong support for our FLES program (they ranked FLES as *the* most favorite component) and suggested we move the program to kindergarten. Both board members and our superintendent were overjoyed at these responses.

Once a program is in place, it is important to continue to cultivate advocates. Our elementary teachers hold annual FLES demonstration classes during Foreign Language Week. Parents and grandparents are invited and turn out in droves for the events. This year, several parents videotaped lessons in which their youngsters participated. Systemwide events also help cultivate support from the community. We hold annual Spanish Spelling Bees and International Nights to which parents, grandparents, and the community are invited to see exhibits, sample foods, and watch students at all levels perform.

In conclusion, we encourage administrators, classroom teachers, and parents to become active supporters of our programs. When we face potential budget cuts, we can call upon those individuals who have seen and experienced the fruits of our labor.

The support of people interested in foreign languages is the most important element of any public relations effort. Following are comments from some of our best supporters:

> My daughter, Jessica, has been in the FLES language program since she was in the third grade. The small dose of daily Spanish was instrumental in developing an appreciation for foreign languages. Now that she is in the seventh grade she has chosen to continue with Spanish and is thinking about Russian for high school.
>
> I feel the exposure to any foreign language at an early age can develop an awareness and appreciation of different cultures.

Marilyn Hamlin
Marilyn Hamlin
First-grade teacher

> I feel that elementary school is a great time to start to learn a foreign language. At this age, children are still uninhibited and playful. Thus, teaching language through the use of games (telephone games) and puppets makes learning fun and real to the children. Just as children enjoy speaking Pig Latin, it can be a game for them to speak a foreign language.

Barbara Solomon
Barbara Solomon
Elementary art teacher
Glastonbury Public Schools

> FLES increases children's awareness, interest, and understanding of diverse countries and cultures. Students eagerly learn songs and dances of other countries and especially enjoy singing in foreign languages.

Eleanor Vivona
Eleanor Vivona
Elementary music teacher

Research tells us that children are best able to acquire a second language before their eleventh birthday. Recognizing this, students in Glastonbury are introduced to Spanish as they enter third grade. They are then encouraged to pursue a foreign language throughout their elementary and secondary years. With this strong emphasis on a second language, we are giving the students of Glastonbury an increased knowledge of other cultures as well as a broader perspective on their own. We are enhancing their listening and speaking skills. We are increasing their employment opportunities, and we are preparing them to live in a rapidly shrinking world where English will not necessarily be the dominant language. Most importantly, we are opening doors to the multilingual, multicultural twenty-first century.

Mary Ann Manchester
Mary Ann Manchester
Principal, Hebron Avenue School
Glastonbury, CT

I have been asked to comment on my feelings about the FLES program as I see it functioning in the Glastonbury Public School System. I am delighted to have this opportunity since I have seen this program work on several different levels.

My own children are now eighteen and sixteen. My son was in fourth grade and my daughter was in third grade when this program was moved from a fifth-grade to a third-grade level within the school system. My husband and I have often spoken of how fortunate we feel to have had the children involved in such a program.

Our son is an average foreign language student. He has no fear of language and has excellent pronunciation in Spanish. We are sure this is due to his early exposure. Our daughter is an excellent language student. She is now a sophomore at Glastonbury High School and is doing A-quality work in a high-ability Spanish IV course. She is totally comfortable with the language. Last year, Glastonbury had an exchange graduate student from Spain. He worked with our daughter, and he told us that she has a better accent than many of the teachers whom he has met in the United States. We feel that our son is a student who would have met little success if he had waited until high school to become acquainted with a language. Although our daughter would have almost certainly done well, she would never have had the opportunity to learn as much about the Spanish language as she has had due to Glastonbury's program.

In addition to being a parent, I am a second-grade teacher at the Eastbury School in Glastonbury. My second graders are first introduced to Spanish through a social studies unit on Mexico. We are "taught" Spanish names, numbers, colors, and greetings by fifth-grade "teachers" who are under the supervision of the school Spanish teacher. The children think of Spanish as a treat. They love their time with the fifth graders and "Señora." By the time that we finish Mexico, the children are looking forward to Spanish in the classroom the following year. I love the end of the year assemblies where I get to see many of my class "alumni" receive awards or Spanish recognition that I knew they would be given.

During the past three years, I have been finishing my master's degree at Central Connecticut State University. Of course the inevitable teacher comparison of curriculum has occurred again and again. One place where I find consistent peer ENVY is with the Glastonbury elementary foreign language program. I hear that same type of program admiration when I work with parent groups within the town. It is one program area where parents agree that Glastonbury is very fortunate. Everybody seems to feel we are definitely doing something right. We are giving our children a definite learning advantage in the foreign language curriculum area.

It was a pleasure to talk to teachers from Maine who visited our school last fall to look at our Spanish program. It is my sincere hope that other schools will follow in our footsteps.

Sincerely,

Janet L. Asikainen

Janet L. Asikainen
Second-grade teacher

Comments from Students

Studying a foreign language is _____ because _____ .

Tobalito: Studying a foreign language is challenging because of the sounds and words.

Amata: Studying a foreign language is fun because you get to learn a language you don't understand.

Rosa: Studying a foreign language is good because if you go to a foreign country you could speak their language.

Susita: Studying a foreign language is in a way interesting because it puts a little "variety" in your life.

Karin: Studying a foreign language is hard because it takes a lot of time, practice, and patience.

Chris: Studying a foreign language is important because if you travel when you get older or are in a business that travels frequently, you need to know other languages.

Alicia: Studying a foreign language is interesting because you learn another language, other customs, and everyday living. You know something that a lot of other people don't know.

Heather: Studying a foreign language is fun and interesting because you find out things you never knew about the country, and once you really know the language you can talk to your friends and to other people in that language.

Public Relations: Inside and Outside

Kathleen Riordan
Springfield Public Schools
Springfield, Massachusetts

Addressing the topic of public relations for **FLES*** often leads to a discussion of newsletters, newspapers, radio, and television coverage. All of these are important and must be included if any program is to win support from the general public. It is possible, however, to forget the school public, the department public, and the administration public if one speaks only to the general public. This report will focus on successful practices of public relations on the inside.

If a **FLES*** program is to be successful, the **FLES*** teachers must be team members—of the **FLES*** team and of the school's or schools' team. Team members cooperate and share ideas, time, expertise, and hard work. **FLES*** teachers need to seize opportunities to participate in total school activities. This participation is important to them personally and professionally. A **FLES*** teacher can easily feel isolated and alone if he or she does not share in schoolwide social and academic events. These events are often very important in school team building because they often lead to discussions where the **FLES*** teacher has the opportunity to learn about trends in elementary education and to share language trends with colleagues. One should never underestimate the importance of such informal interactions for personal growth and professional development and for the chance they provide to build understanding and support for the concept of early language experiences. The more **FLES*** teachers know about developments in elementary education, the more successful they will be in their language classes.

Is the job of a **FLES*** teacher ever done? The answer from all practitioners is a resounding no. There is always yet another constituency. A crucial group in this category is the school administration. The support of the principals and assistant principals is crucial to the success of any **FLES*** program. How does one relate to this public? The answer is fairly obvious—by keeping them informed about all aspects of the program. This may seem obvious. Yet, it is often ignored. The school administration needs to know about the **FLES*** program in order to be supportive. The **FLES*** teacher should make some time to talk regularly with the administration about the program, class activities, expectations of students in the areas of homework and attendance, and materials needed for the program. These informed administrators will be better able to answer questions from parents, other teachers, or the general public. A **FLES*** teacher should not assume that administrators understand the ins and outs of the program. An informed administrator can be a supportive and valuable ally. An informed school administrator can speak with pride about the **FLES*** program to a wide group of constituents who may never know the **FLES*** teacher.

Beyond the school building one finds the central administration at the superintendent level. On his or her own, or with the support of the school administration, the **FLES*** teacher should keep the central administrative superintendents informed of the goals, activities, and special events associated with the program. These administrators should be invited to regular classes and any special events. Materials created by the children can be sent to them. These practices create good exposure for the program and, at the same time, help administrators to understand the goals and activities associated with the **FLES*** program.

Are all foreign language teachers supportive of **FLES*** programs? It would be wonderful if the answer were a resounding yes. We know that it is not. Why is this the case? In some cases, the answer can be found in a lack of knowledge about **FLES*** and its goals and activities. No articulated foreign language program can be truly successful if its segments exist in isolation. The entire program is only as strong as its segments. A secondary school foreign language teacher who does not support **FLES*** can be very damaging to a program because he or she is viewed as an expert by the general public and other educators. People cannot really support what they do not understand. **FLES*** teachers need to interact with other language teachers in the system or district. Joint meetings or informal sharing times when the entire staff has the opportunity to see student work or videos of students in **FLES*** classes can do much to bridge any knowledge or misinformation gap that may exist. Secondary school language teachers are generally supportive of **FLES*** programs when they understand them. Personal contact with them is also important for team building.

Of course, all of these personal and professional interactions take time above and beyond the time committed to preparing for and teaching classes. Are they important to the care and sustenance of a successful **FLES*** program? Yes, of course! Are they optional activities? No, they are essential!

Is a **FLES*** teacher's job ever done? No, not really! Is a **FLES*** teacher's job rewarding and satisfying? Yes, definitely!

The Georgia PTA Foreign Language Resolution

Lynne B. Bryan
Macon College, Georgia

In 1993, the chair of the AATF **FLES*** Commission and the AATSP **FLES*** Committee, Gladys Lipton, contacted all members of both groups and requested our assistance in approaching the Parents and Teachers Association (PTA) in our respective states to request that a resolution be adopted at the state level in support of foreign language instruction on the elementary-school level.

Lynne Bryan spearheaded the effort in Georgia. First a draft was composed that elaborated and expanded on the topics submitted by Gladys Lipton. It was deemed critical to write a document that would support foreign language efforts on all levels and would stress continuation and articulation from one level to the next. Lynne Bryan then enlisted the assistance of the consultant for elementary-school foreign language programs in the Georgia State Department of Education, Marcia Speilberger, as well as that of the president and the immediate past president of the Foreign Language Association of Georgia, Donna Myers and Lynne McClendon. The document that had been drafted was shared and edited before it was forwarded to the Georgia PTA.

Since it had been suggested that the members of the national **FLES*** groups approach a local PTA chapter and then assist that chapter in taking the resolution to the state chapter, Lynne Bryan contacted an area school and was given the name of Pat Blascovich, a parent who was on the state PTA board. Pat Blascovich immediately gave support and urged that we contact the state PTA office. On the state level, the resolutions chair, Leana Roach, was instrumental in assisting the foreign language representatives in rewording the document in "PTA resolution terminology." The state PTA president, Janice West, was supportive of this foreign language resolution, and it was taken, in revised form, to the PTA Board of Managers meeting, where it was passed. The Board of Managers then presented the document to the membership, and it was adopted at the state convention of the Georgia PTA on April 28, 1994. Lynne Bryan has been sharing information about the process with colleagues in many other states and at regional and national foreign language conventions.

Since the adoption of the Georgia PTA foreign language resolution, efforts have been made to have a national PTA foreign language resolution adopted. When such a resolution was first presented to the national organization, it was felt that more time and information were needed. The Georgia PTA is planning to present the national resolution again, and it is hoped that, with the additional information supplied and with the support of additional states, it will be adopted in the near future.

Georgia Congress of Parents and Teachers
114 Baker Street, NE, Atlanta, Georgia 30308

RESOLUTION

Foreign Language Programs

1) Whereas, Children have the ability to learn and excel in the pronunciation and comprehension of a foreign language; and

2) Whereas, Children who have studied a foreign language in elementary school achieve expected gains and even have higher scores on standardized tests in reading, language arts and mathematics than those who have not; and

3) Whereas, Children who have studied a foreign language show greater flexibility, creativity, divergent thinking and higher order thinking skills; and

4) Whereas, Children who have studied a foreign language develop a sense of cultural pluralism (openness to and appreciation of other cultures); and

5) Whereas, Children studying a foreign language have an improved self-concept and sense of achievement in school; and

6) Whereas, Elementary foreign language study has a favorable effect on foreign language study later on in high school and college; and

7) Whereas, The possession of foreign language skills and the ability to communicate across cultures, both within the United States and abroad, enhances the employability of our citizens and their career success; and

8) Whereas, The possession of foreign language skills enhances the ability of United States citizens to do business in a global economy, and

9) Whereas, The ability to use foreign languages in the socio-political arena is critical in promoting a democratic way of life; now, therefore be it

Resolved, That the National PTA and its constituent bodies support the inclusion of foreign language programs in our elementary (K–5) and middle schools; and be it further

| Resolved, | That the National PTA and constituent bodies encourage the implementation of these foreign language programs to begin as early as possible and provide the longest possible sequence of instruction; and be it further |
| Resolved, | That the National PTA and its constituent bodies promote articulated foreign language study from early childhood through high school, college and university levels. |

Adopted by the Georgia PTA Board of Managers
April 29, 1994

Guidelines for **FLES*** Programs

Gladys C. Lipton
University of Maryland, Baltimore County
Baltimore, Maryland

The administration of all types of **FLES*** programs can be creative, innovative, and effective, and need not be unduly burdensome. Nonetheless, many pressured administrators do not welcome the thought of adding a foreign language program to an already crowded curriculum. Usually, they have no problem in accepting the benefits of foreign language study for students in elementary and middle schools. Rather, the first reaction I typically get when the subject of **FLES*** is broached is: "Oh no—more uncertainty about getting qualified teachers! More hassles about materials of instruction! More . . . everything!"

Most administrators are in favor of some type of elementary school foreign language program. They know that if the program is successful, it will help children to understand and adapt to today's and tomorrow's world. The key question for them is: What type of program is appropriate to the needs of the local community?

Each and every school community has specific needs and constraints, which is why each and every school community must go through the arduous task of examining needs, anticipating problems, and planning both short- and long-term goals. There are no shortcuts!

Interest in elementary school foreign language programs is high—in fact, higher than ever—as new options become available to decision makers. Although it is clear that interest and support are there, it is equally clear that we must take great care to deliver what we promise in the goals of any program we undertake and that we document the quality of the program. The big question for **FLES*** supporters is how to deliver the benefits of **FLES*** to our communities.

The goal of this article is to identify the ways in which decision makers, administrators, principals, and supervisors can maximize the effectiveness of all types of **FLES*** programs. (See definitions in Appendix A.)

QUESTIONS

When a **FLES*** program is first considered, many basic questions arise. They cover a wide range of topics, such as: What is the optimum age to introduce a foreign language? What research supports early foreign language study? How expensive is a **FLES*** program? Who should be involved? Where do we find trained teachers? Which program model is best? How can we fit **FLES*** into our crowded schedule? Is **FLES*** worth while even if done on a limited basis?

Such questions need to be discussed by a **FLES*** advisory committee in the local school or school district. Other questions and procedures are documented elsewhere (see Appendix E), but a thorough discussion of the goals and outcomes of the program needs to be conducted by a committee consisting of administrators, teachers, parents, other school community members, university and business people, and other interested parties.

THE RESEARCH RATIONALE FOR **FLES***

In the last twelve years, a number of exciting research findings have come to the public's attention, which has provided new impetus for starting all types of **FLES*** programs. Among those findings are the following:

1. Children have the ability to learn a foreign language easily and excel in authentic pronunciation.
2. Children who have studied a foreign language before the age of ten show greater cognitive development, such as mental flexibility, creativity, divergent thinking, and higher-order thinking skills.
3. Children who have studied a foreign language achieve expected gains and even earn higher scores on standardized tests in reading, language arts, and mathematics than do children who have not studied a foreign language.
4. Children who have studied a foreign language before the age of ten develop a sense of cultural pluralism (openness to and appreciation of other cultures).
5. Children studying a foreign language develop an improved self-image and sense of achievement in school.
6. According to brain surgeons and researchers, the study of foreign languages before the age of ten offers an optimum "window of opportunity" for learning.
7. On the 1995 Advanced Placement French Language Examination, high school students who started their study of French in grades 1–3 or 4–6 outperformed students who started foreign language study later.

(For further information, send for "The **FLES*** Research Packet," listed in Appendix E.)

GUIDING PRINCIPLES FOR THE PLANNING OF ANY TYPE OF FLES* PROGRAM

- All K–8 elementary school students should have the opportunity to start the study of a foreign language before the age of ten.
- All three program models (Sequential FLES, FLEX, and Immersion) are valid foreign language programs, provided that they fulfill their goals.
- Each of the program models can contribute, in different ways, to the K–12 foreign language sequence, in consonance with national foreign language standards. (See Appendix B.)
- There is no one best way to provide **FLES*** instruction, nor is there only one best method of **FLES*** instruction.

PLANNING SUGGESTIONS

Because the study of a foreign language before the age of ten is important for all students, plans, procedures, and budgets should provide the kind of program that offers foreign language study to all students in the school or school district. No child should be deprived of this opportunity to view the world from different perspectives! Schools and school districts should plan for programs that take the following factors into consideration:

- Long-range planning and commitment
- Opportunities for long-term funding
- Development of a broad base of support from the various constituencies within the school or school district community, including parents and others, in the creation of a foreign language advisory committee
- Development of goals and student outcomes for the program in accordance with national foreign language standards
- Availability of fluent, trained teachers
- Development of a realistic, written curriculum, reinforcing the elementary school program, and articulated with the K–12 foreign language sequence

- Availability of age-appropriate materials of instruction
- Development of an evaluation design based on the goals of the program
- Planning that addresses the rationale for the program, articulation plans, decisions about beginning grade, language choices, student participants (**FLES*** offered to all students before the age of ten), schedule, and other issues specific to the community

Matching the goals of the program with the budgetary constraints calls for consensus-building, resourcefulness, creativity, and flexibility.

Key Questions

- Are we convinced that the study of a foreign language and culture can add an important dimension to the children's educational program that they cannot get elsewhere?
- Who is opposed to the program? Why?
- Are our goals realistic? Does everyone understand the goals?
- Are we better off with the program than without it?

(For further information about the implementation of **FLES*** programs, see *Elementary Foreign Language Programs, FLES*: An Administrator's Guide*, by Gladys Lipton. Lincolnwood, IL: National Textbook Company.)

OPTIONS WHEN ESTABLISHING A FLES* PROGRAM

- Explore long-term funding from foundations, government grants, and contributions by local businesses.
- If faced with a restricted budget, adapt the goals of the program to be less demanding, but make sure that everyone understands that outcomes will be limited.
- Explore long-term hiring practices that will facilitate the recruitment of effective elementary school teachers with strong backgrounds in foreign language.
- Explore in-service development programs that offer incentives to elementary school teachers for foreign language study and study abroad.

- Seek the cooperation of local and/or state universities that might be interested in training **FLES*** teachers.
- Encourage local high school students who excel in foreign languages to think about a career in teaching at the elementary school level.
- Explore research on the use of video programs, satellite programs, mini language laboratories, computer programs, and other forms of technology in the elementary school classroom.
- Explore the use of foreign teachers (native speakers) in your **FLES*** program.
- Encourage teachers to become familiar with new teaching approaches and techniques, such as TPR (total physical response), cooperative learning, content-based instruction, the higher-order thinking skills approach, the real-life situations approach, and many others. (See **FLES*** Teacher Competencies, Appendix C.)
- Investigate the foreign language skills of the current staff so that a team-teaching approach can be organized.
- Plan for the integration of foreign language with other subjects. For example; in social studies it is important to explore all aspects of different countries, and the language spoken by a people is an important component of their life. Foreign language can be integrated with other subjects as well.
- Foreign language programs that meet before or after school are not optimally effective because they lead children to view foreign language study as an adjunct to the school day rather than an integral part of it. They can be used as a "foot in the door" approach, however, for a relatively short period of time.
- When the classroom teacher is also the foreign language teacher, the question of scheduling is not a problem. Such a setup can work well in all three program models—Sequential FLES, FLEX, and Immersion.

WHAT ARE THE BENEFITS OF FLES* TO CHILDREN?

Any form of **FLES*** program should help students to develop a wide range of skills, abilities, and positive attitudes. Children who have participated in **FLES*** should:

- Enjoy studying a foreign language and culture
- Demonstrate linguistic abilities (and others) in accordance with performance indicators of the national foreign language standards (the five C's)

- Appreciate cultural aspects of the people(s) who speak the foreign language
- Experience the success of foreign language learning
- Demonstrate achievement of the linguistic and cultural goals of their programs
- Show an awareness of and sensitivity to people from different cultures who speak a foreign language
- Be prepared to continue their study of the foreign language and be ready for new challenges in that study
- Display near-native pronunciation of the foreign language, if they started participating in **FLES*** before the age of ten
- Recognize the importance of knowing a foreign language in today's and tomorrow's world
- Demonstrate listening and speaking (and other) abilities in the foreign language in real-life situations
- Display reading and writing abilities in the foreign language
- Know how to follow directions in the foreign language and perform a variety of real-life tasks
- Use the foreign language in meaningful, age-appropriate, real-life situations

(Adapted from Gladys Lipton, 1996. "The Many Benefits of All Types of **FLES*** Programs. *Northeast Conference Newsletter (Fall):* 56–57.)

For information about evaluation of **FLES*** programs, see Part 5.

ICAL: Variation on a FLEX Theme

Dora F. Kennedy
University of Maryland
College Park, Maryland

and

Pat Barr-Harrison
Prince George's County Public Schools, Maryland

ICAL (International Culture and Language) is an exploratory program model originated in the public schools of Prince George's County, Maryland. The exploratory concept may be implemented in a variety of contexts, particularly in K–8 levels. Whereas in middle school it usually takes the form of a separate interdisciplinary course, scheduled in different possible time frames (e.g., a semester, nine weeks, a year), in the elementary school it is desirable to weave FLEX experiences into the fabric of the interrelated curriculum. The two areas most suited to FLEX enrichment are language arts and social studies.

The ICAL program in Prince George's County was designed to enhance the social studies program in certain magnet schools. However, the model is adaptable to any elementary school, provided that it has a foreign language teacher, age-appropriate materials, and in-service support.

In general, FLEX programs introduce students to languages and cultures and offer some awareness of language relationships. Under this umbrella, the ICAL goals are as follows:

- Learn to say several basic expressions in the target language, such as greetings, counting, and geographic names (the sophistication of these items being affected by the age and grade level of the students).
- Recognize the language when it is seen and heard.
- Participate in limited imitative writing in context, depending on the nature of the target language (alphabetic or nonalphabetic).
- Experience music and songs from the target culture.
- Identify the areas of the world where the language is spoken.

- Acquire basic knowledge about the culture.
- Hear or read a representative folktale or legend (in English).
- Acquire the above skills and knowledge as a reinforcement of social studies skills and as an expansion of linguistic development.

These goals are achieved through thematic units about the countries being studied at particular grade levels in the social studies program. The ICAL program spans grades 2, 3, and 4.

The countries involved are as follows:
Grade 2: Japan and France
Grade 3: Italy, Germany, and China
Grade 4: Spanish-speaking areas and Russia

In this model, students go into a conventional Exploratory course in grade 5, followed by a Sequential FLES program in grade 6 that articulates with the middle schools that receive these students in grade 7. The foreign language teacher in each elementary school teaches the entire program for that school (i.e., ICAL, Exploratory, and Sequential FLES).

ICAL requires close collaboration and planning between the foreign language teacher and the grade level teachers. Each thematic unit is four to six weeks' duration. The units are taught in keeping with the social studies schedule of each grade level involved. They are taught three times a week, whereas the Exploratory program in grade 5 and the Sequential FLES program in grade 6 are taught daily.

CONTENTS OF EACH THEMATIC LANGUAGE EXPERIENCE UNIT

Each unit (e.g., Japanese, German) contains four weekly lesson topics. Each lesson may cover two to four instructional periods. Typical contents include

- Greetings that are practiced orally in meaningful exchanges
- New vocabulary, phrases, and geographic names introduced through thematic topics, such as family, numbers, food, clothing, etc.
- Folktales and songs that students listen to and participate in
- Other interesting cultural material that is particularly child-oriented

Teaching ICAL Units

Each lesson includes objectives, language practice including limited writing, cultural discussion, film, video, songs, realia, and so forth, as reflected in the specially created age-appropriate student packet for each language in the program.

Basic Materials for Each ICAL Unit

- Student activity packets (one per student, bound, to be used as an activity book)
- A teacher's version of the unit, with methodology
- A reference book on the target language, with practice cassettes, for the teacher
- Visuals, such as maps, videos, realia, and posters
- Audiocassettes of songs (may include practice phrases for the students)
- A culturgram that includes a map of each country and current cultural information (see list of references)
- Children's trade books in English about the country or countries (The school library is a good source.)

A distinguishing feature of the ICAL program is its many activities offering hands-on experiences, including field trips.

Teacher Qualifications/In-Service

The teachers in the ICAL program are language majors who have also been exposed to various other languages formally or informally. The school system's policy is to give preference to applicants who know more than one language, particularly for the middle school and elementary levels.

Since the ICAL teachers also teach the Sequential FLES program in grades 5 and 6, they are mostly French and Spanish majors with some knowledge of other languages. Selected high school teachers in the system have been consultants and in-service providers for Japanese, Russian, German, and Italian. A consultant from outside the system has assisted in the development of the Chinese ICAL, helped teachers with pronunciation of the material in the unit, and provided additional cultural information and products.

SUMMARY

Q. ICAL: What is it?

A. ICAL is a variation on FLEX at elementary school level. It is associated with and enhances the social studies curriculum.

Q. How is it implemented?

A. ICAL is implemented as an extension of the social studies program. (It may be adapted to the language arts program by some systems.)

Q. In what grade levels is ICAL presented?

A. In Prince George's County, it is presented in grades 2, 3, and 4. (This type of program is ideal for K–1 also.)

Q. Who teaches it?

A. Certified foreign language teachers.

Q. What about materials?

A. System-created thematic units are used, plus hands-on or manipulative materials available from commercial firms.

Q. What is the difference between the usual FLEX programs and ICAL?

A. ICAL includes several languages over the span of three grade levels. Its curriculum must be integrated with social studies, which requires close collaboration between the foreign language teacher and classroom teachers.

The ICAL model does not interfere with a long-sequence program that may already be in place in an elementary school. It broadens the horizons of the children by adding another dimension to the social studies program in keeping with the goals of global education.

REFERENCES

Barr-Harrison, P., D. Davis, et al. 1994–1998. *ICAL Thematic Units (French, Spanish, German, Russian, Japanese)*. Prince George's County Schools, Dept. of Instruction and Curriculum, Stern Bldg., E. Hampton Drive, Capitol Heights, MD 20743.

Culturgrams. Kennedy Center Publications, Brigham Young University, P.O. Box 24538; Provo, Utah 84602. WEB site: http://www.byu.edu/culturgrams. Pamphlets on all countries, including maps, cultural information, and language samples. Revised each year.

De Lorenzo, W., and D. Kennedy. 1994. "Point Counter Point: The Case for Exploratory Programs in Middle/Junior High School (K–8)." *Foreign Language Annals* (spring): 70–88.

Lipton, G. 1996. "The Many Benefits of All Types of **FLES*** Programs." *Northeast Conference Newsletter* 40, (Fall): 54–57.

Marcos, K. 1996. "Foreign Language Exploratory Programs: Introduction to Language Learning." *Eric Digest*, Washington DC: ERIC Clearing House of Languages and Linguistics. (Update of a 1985 *Digest* article by D. Kennedy.)

Sheeren, J., and P. McCarthy. 1991. "Foreign Language Study Spurs Growth in FLEX Programs." *EMC Foreign Language Newsletter (fall):* 2–3.

Wing, B. 1996. "Starting Early: Foreign Languages in the Elementary and Middle Schools." *Northeast Conference Newsletter* 40 (fall): 21–53.

Allegro Sostenuto: A Baker's Dozen of Challenges for the Immersion Administrator

Paul A. García
School District of Kansas City, Missouri

OVERTURE: INTRODUCTION TO A BAKER'S DOZEN

No one, neither those in education nor those outside our profession, ever promised that school programs would be "easy to assemble," despite "batteries" of time, talent, and resources being more or less included. **FLES*** managers whose programs traditionally and generally are found at the periphery of the "real school day" of core subjects accept as given that for them the notion of a level playing field upon which they may confront an array of concerns and programmatic issues simply does not exist. Despite the uneven, uphill battles, more than a few similarities are discernible that do not vary locally. A baker's dozen of such managerial issues for Immersion projects is the topic of this report. They are taken from the author's own experiences in establishing and implementing the Immersion language programs of the Kansas City, MO, schools since their inception in 1986–1987 (nine schools, K–8, with over 2,000 students in French, German, and Spanish), as well as a collage of challenges observed and reported on elsewhere in this country by teachers and administrators. A reconsideration of and reflection on these challenges may suggest alternatives or options to others faced with similar concerns.

An abbreviated conceptual framework is necessary for the administrator to be mindful of:

1. Endorse and espouse the notion that people—children and adults—make and break the program.
2. Maintain and occasionally modify the "vision" of the program.

3. Think "small" rather than "big."
4. Expect the unexpected.
5. The issues considered have been selected from both the "big picture" and the "small picture" domains. No attempt has been made to establish priorities—their random appearance is precisely how these and other concerns present themselves—they simply "happen."

Upbeats, Rhythms, Rif(t)s, and Resolutions

Challenge 1: The new Immersion teacher, fresh from abroad, has no knowledge of or experience in the American school culture.

The new Immersion teacher must have a substantive, mid-August opening staff development program and a school-year follow-up, despite the dangers of overwork and fatigue that the other 10- or 10.5-month employees display when faced with an extended contract year. In an early AATF **FLES*** Commission Report (García 1990), we proposed a support net that seeks to aid in the emotional and intellectual adjustment of the foreign national teacher. That advice has been followed, in Kansas City and elsewhere, with consequent benefits that timely and ongoing staff preparation (and emotional, physical stability—housing, transportation, friendships) bring to an Immersion program. Partner teachers, bilingual aides and administrators, and appropriately scheduled workshops dealing with Immersion classroom activities combined with individual feedback are essential to successful integration of the teacher into the program.

But they come about only if adjustment to the school culture can be made. Administrators who tire of the plaintive rejoinder, "But this is not the way we do it in my country," and thereupon acquiesce to divergent and divisive behaviors (such as deciding not to attend the next immersion staff meeting) that damage the program integrity or perceptions thereof by decision makers, simply to avoid dissension, are mistaken, from both the program and the staff development perspectives. New Immersion staff need staff development on a variety of topics, despite their disclaimers. As chief managers of a program fraught with many in-born difficulties (books, materials, staff members who often are foreign to the community as well as to the nation, and even community apathy are a few of these), school leaders must learn how to acculturate the foreign national to the local conditions as rapidly and as effectively as possible—often during the first three or four months of their stay. In effect, leadership says, "This is the United States, and here, in our program, be it better or worse than your way, this is different. And you, as the teacher with no present 'ownership' of the program or the community, will follow my lead." This straightforward, and possibly harsh-sounding recommendation is a distillation of the change process that the supportive administrator, working with Immersion staff, can produce for an effective workplace for Immersion and non-Immersion staff. No one wishes to damage the program because of an unwillingness to understand the broader implications of the teacher's role beyond the classroom confines.

Challenge 2: The building principal, staff, and students are overcome by the layering effect of too many, many program pieces.

"Layering," in this context, means placing one program (Immersion) into the matrix of ongoing, continuing activities. Usually this does not work, even on paper. Root causes for program layering need review before introducing the Immersion structure into a school. An example of layering that threatens the viability and efficacy of an Immersion program would be scheduling an upper-elementary site (say, grades 4–5) for total and partial Immersion in three languages. Scheduling the twelve different groups (three languages x two strands x two grades) for support services—art, music, p.e., for instance—creates structural havoc: Students and staff have incoherent frameworks. By dint of time/scheduling/staff number constraints, the sequences for content instruction become choppy, diluted experiences rather than the sustained, linking times they should be. Although the best way, obviously, to avoid the layering effect is to avoid it in the planning phase, even experienced Immersion administrators cannot foresee every contingency.

Challenge 3: The immersion teacher has little background in the areas of language acquisition and Immersion methodology.

As in the case of our first challenge, it is imperative that planned in-service opportunities for Immersion staff concentrate on management and school culture issues while developing critical insights into Immersion teacher strategies and language acquisition. Immersion programs in their planning stages have a number of solutions from which to choose workshop topics. There are print and video formats (such as from Montgomery County, MD) that are available, and local Immersion teachers willingly share their expertise. While historically Immersion school programs rely heavily on colleagues to serve as presenters for such seminars, it is worth while for administrators to seek out persons within the Immersion network to provide other perspectives. Organizations such as Advocates for Language Learning (ALL), AATFk, AATG, AATSP, and NNELL (National Network for Early Language Learning) have developed listings of resource persons and/or products for such an endeavor.

Language acquisition for the elementary Immersion child (K–2) must be formulated on the basis of several considerations. Among them, and foremost, are play activities (music, games, kinetic experiences), content-related language (while not foremost during early stages), and a blending with what may be called "social language." An effective discourse ambiance must be developed for the classroom so that the child makes use of the teacher's language output and can utilize student responses for support. The ability of the Immersion teacher to consider the implications of basic precepts of language acquisition (García 1987) is an often-forgotten feature of Immersion staff development; this comes about because the number of persons involved in the decision-making process often do not have the expertise in that area.

Challenge 4: Recruitment policies for the Immersion program allow children with no second language skills to enter an Immersion class at grade 2 and above.

Late-entry Immersion children who are placed into what is essentially a closed system after grade 1 are recruited for placement by those who cannot acknowledge the linguistic and affective domain benefits of "seat time" for immersion students. If, for example, a child in Total Immersion has a 200-minute language/content experience daily in both kindergarten and first grade, then those (approximately) 1,200 hours of exposure to a purposefully organized second language experience cannot be discounted or negated by casually asserting that a child new to immersion in grade 2 or grade 4 will be coached by teachers and assisted by peers, thus "learning to sink or swim as if dropped into a foreign country," as one recruiter suggested. Examining the causes for such a placement policy uncovers one or more of the following: a good-will attempt to have business as usual, since Immersion is a district or school program; an ignorant or naive perspective that Immersion is just like a regular school except in another language; an intramural justification, such as a court order endorsing a magnet plan that was meant to be a changing and developing document but instead is interpreted as though it were written on a petrified tablet; and finally, a fear that student attrition will mar official class size or teacher/student ratios. Resolution of placement issues necessitates the usual tasks of leadership, parental support, credibility, and, lamentably, precious time away from other tasks. Immersion programs that do not limit entry points face an end-product, in language and content-acquisition terms, that is diluted and that provides little satisfaction and some stress to staff and parents.

Challenge 5: Parents and staff are at odds with district policies that mandate standardized English-language testing of Immersion students on content that has not been learned in English.

Standardized testing of Immersion students is a concern that will not soon disappear from American schools. Because our society is so measurement-oriented and statistics-reliant, there exist state education agencies, local school boards, administrators, and parents who want and need to demonstrate that their charges have "measured up" to "objective, reliable criteria." Testing is not an invalid concept. Children who are to mature and become productive, contributing adults must learn how to deal with testing and comparisons. We who are managers in education must review what is done with test results, rather, for it seems that inappropriate comparisons and listings say less about what a child has acquired in a German-language context and more about the inability of an organization to cope with a different paradigm. While some testing documents exist for Spanish and French and none for German, normal scores for large populations of Immersion students do not exist and would provide, we believe, unreliable achievement data. Indeed, children need to be cognizant of test-taking and academic performance activities; they should not be told to take a lengthy battery of tests "for fun"—it isn't. Nor can "testwiseness" preparations have great value if the activities practiced are linguistically inappropriate and interfere with language arts learning (reading, sound systems, etc.) in the Immersion tongue.

Partial resolution on this issue to the satisfaction of stakeholders came to Kansas City several years into its Immersion program, in February 1990 and in April 1993. In 1990, Total Immersion students in K–2 were granted a waiver of all sections of testing with the exception of the math sections of the ITBS. Thereupon, a 1994 court order allowed the district to exempt students from any testing through grade 3—and this came as a rider to a larger issue, the founding of an Immersion middle school. On the debit side, principals are still required to plan for test score gains in English reading by another district division, and pressures about raising test scores continue unabated (and, in some quarters, have risen in decibel strength, becoming a metric to judge teacher and principal efficacy). The consequent behavior exhibited by adults impedes and, at times, imperils the intersecting paradigms (English-language testing for English-language education with Immersion instruction) and causes dysfunctions in staff-student work, parent-school relations, and adult-to-adult relationships. If a compromise between testing and not testing can succeed, it is important that one review the issues and possible consequences within the framework of Immersion instruction and the locally used delivery model.

Such decisiveness has to come from strong upper-level leadership. The author believes that a full waiver of English-language test batteries should be created. Finally, nonstandardized testing tools can be developed, as was done with a language assessment model locally developed by the author and several colleagues in 1993–1995 for Immersion students in grade 2. Locally developed measures aligned with district-approved curriculum objectives and a realization of the limits of an Immersion curriculum (which includes language instruction as well as content instruction) can give evaluators a picture of what students know and how they might use that knowledge. Such measures also give educators and parents an opportunity to review curriculum decisions and coverage or goals of what can be expected in the classroom over the course of a school year. Research findings from the United States and Canada indicate that Immersion students do succeed at peer-comparable levels by grades 5 and 6. Those who honorably are concerned about students not being tested early and thereby "falling through the cracks" without early remediation might pose their concern—our common concern—another way: "How can support structures be properly set into place to ensure Immersion students that the transfer of knowledge from one language to English occurs?" And further, "What suggested structures support the goals of Immersion education for all students?" A model for the introduction of English to Immersion, for the introduction of test-taking, and for the maintenance of a series of assessment instruments are not lofty goals that may not be reached. Rather, it should be understood that such structures can be put into place by administrators and staff members whose trust levels and confidence are unshaken by the political aspects of test-score reporting so prevalent in our society. Kansas City, which has been no stranger to political strife and civil court matters relating to education and its magnet program, was able to develop a series of teacher committees called together during 1992–1995 by this writer for the purposes of English language arts development. The purpose was quite straightforward: how to assist the English teacher in delivering appropriate instruction to students who were taught to read in French, German, or Spanish, and how to use the students' transfer skills to develop and maintain a high level of literacy in English.

Challenge 6: Staff who need or are required to undergo in-service do not want in-service programs.

Staff not wishing to participate in in-service usually cite as their reasonable arguments the obligatory nature of the program itself and their repetitive, irrelevant, and nonparticipatory nature as actors. At the secondary level, where subject-specific programs are costly, process-related staff programs dominate the schedule for professional development. Subject-matter specialists consider themselves intellectually famished. Whether true or not, the perception of in-service as an unnecessary evil will continue, because its acceptance is symbolic of the changing academic and educational topography that is in conflict with the traditional structure of the school day and our definitions of "school time" and "teacher contract time" and the attendant philosophical implications.

Essential, well-prepared in-service programs with teacher-directed input and decision making will be more successful during these years of transition than top-down planning. There will, unfortunately, continue to be a shortfall between knowledge-giving programs and their in-class application, however; the notion of change as a slow or even undesired process is well-ingrained in our psyche. For Kansas City, MO, staff, in-service is a court-mandated program that few avoid for fear of unwanted consequences. In the case of the Immersion schools, this writer put together a steering committee that designs and carries out programs based upon questionnaires and informal polling of Immersion teachers' needs. Building administrators are part of the committee as well (although many do not participate except through reading the circulated memoranda that give a record of the decisions) and may, of course, reserve part of the week's work of local, on-site needs and initiatives. Staff development and curriculum development have often been kept apart, needlessly, we think, since the hands-on aspect of materials development appeals to teachers who learn to plan in groups as effectively as they plan for instruction in their own classrooms. Among the results of the cooperative activities that became a characteristic of the Immersion in-service programs for Kansas City teachers are the concrete results of the sessions: praise and actively involved individuals who understand the role they must play in the success of their students. One item that was not fixable, unfortunately, was the compressed time that was allocated to the program: forty hours of work in one week in August. Others would do well to determine how to offer an adequate preparation and education experience that is continual but on a less (temporally) bulky basis.

Challenge 7: The ordering or purchasing system cannot process needed materials for Immersion within reasonable periods.

A purchasing division that deals with foreign vendors, yet where the entire purchasing staff is resolutely monolingual, needs to be coaxed and assisted on its way to greater global business acumen. Other Immersion program directors have recognized that ordering books and materials from abroad (Kansas City has used over twelve vendors from six nations) requires an in-house education program. Identifying the key person in the internal section of purchasing that makes contacts with publishers and being of assistance in establishing supportive procedures ensures that the little things that can go wrong in a big way during the ordering period are reduced. Examples of such dysfunctions abound and can be corrected. It is not too early to educate purchasing agents that it is not a good idea to wait until late July to process orders destined for August-vacation-bound Belgian firms. Nor is it impossible to assist a buyer with the implications of time differences between the United States and Europe. (Yes, one does get an answering machine at 4 P.M. in Kansas City, because it's 11 P.M. in Europe. And, yes, the answering machine of a textbook firm in Germany does have a monolingual recording—German—because American purchasers are few and far between.) Attempts should be made to identify one or two individuals to be charged with the ordering of materials for Immersion programs. Making friends before one needs them, to restate a political maxim of Lyndon Johnson, again proves invaluable.

Even more worthy of consideration than the ordering process is a continual need to develop flexibility in how one acquires materials for Immersion. It is very important, for instance, for the Spanish Immersion teacher to be aware of the late-November Feria Internacional del Libro in Guadalajara, which is the exposition for books for children that are published throughout the Spanish-speaking world. Similarly, the French Immersion teacher may need to be part of a buying trip/conference trip to the Canadian Immersion teachers' conference that is held yearly at the beginning of November. Having funds available for on-site purchases can happen and should.

Challenge 8: Community members are neutral or negatively inclined toward the Immersion program.

Community representatives who do not know what an Immersion program is about are truly grist for the mill of the entire Immersion family. All efforts that produce public awareness are mandatory in such a scenario. Children's programs, business organization luncheons, foreign language adult evening classes, and similar events are consistent with producing the "overnight success" that an Immersion program can be, even if, as is often the case, that process takes five or six years! A caveat: Political factors that have nothing to do with the concept of Immersion can often play a role in the demise of a successful activity, despite the interest of parents and staff. Local conditions must be continually considered. Cautions regarding the elitist perception of immersion or the importance of neighbors who cannot send their children to the local magnet school and therefore want a return to neighborhood schools cannot be raised often enough everywhere. In summary, it makes sense and may mean survival to a program if the staff is convinced of its mission and vision and can convey the egalitarian nature that Immersion education provides to the stakeholders as it actively and responsibly counters the attacks from beyond.

Challenge 9: Foreign national staff from countries that have a tax treaty with the United States thus receive pay that is substantially higher than that of their American counterparts. A non-national may complain about the American "consumer way of life" even as he or she makes plans to use two or three days of sick leave at Christmas to vacation in the Bahamas and thus extend the holiday period. Parents and colleagues are not happy.

For this writer, the concerns of foreign nationals in Immersion—including identifying appropriate personnel, getting visas, easing adjustment to the new school, and mediating staff-staff relations—are the stuff of anecdotes, of melodrama, and, occasionally, of tragedy. For years to come, Immersion education will remain a market in which the teacher has the market advantage. More so than Spanish Immersion, French, German, and other language projects in our country will continue to rely upon non-American staff trained in another nation. People being people, a variety of relationships will be established between colleagues, including those of the friction-dominant variety. The Immersion administrator is obligated to assist the incoming staff member in that person's initial encounter with the diversity of U.S. culture and its microcosm, the school, while also assisting in the encounters with American bureaucratic demands. Granting an Immersion teacher sick-leave time to return early to South America may seem to be a prudent course of action in one setting and wholly unacceptable in another. It depends on the individual set of circumstances, and, thus, it is the astute principal who works closely at the beginning of the school year with new and returning staff to explain what we call the "unwritten work rules" that are not illegal but simply unspoken.

Before late October, that building leader lets the individual Immersion teachers know the expectation of harmony and cooperation, and, if they exist, the formal consequences of actions that hamper smooth relationships. The American teacher in a Partial Immersion setting, for example, has to be a willing, active partner of the Immersion language colleague in so many ways—a shared management and discipline philosophy being foremost—and, consequently, any actions, patterns, or perceived lack of commitment (always leaving school immediately upon the close of the contract day or consciously padding the holiday period) will deflect from program and school goals. Perhaps it would be beneficial for administrators confronted with raw relations between Immersion and non-Immersion staff to declare certain conversations (such as taxes) taboo and certain activities (such as extending the winter holiday by three weeks except in true emergency situations) ill-advised. All this must be accomplished, of course, while one is simultaneously working toward establishing an atmosphere of meaningful sharing. Support structures and understanding Immersion goals mandate that justifiable complaints be dealt with promptly and appropriately. Actions that promote pettiness or divisiveness also need to be dealt with. Knowing the second language and understanding the cultural background of the foreign Immersion teacher are not necessary prerequisites for empowering the administrator to review the big picture in an individual instance and act accordingly.

Challenge 10: The building principal sees the local big picture (his or her school, district goals) and neglects or ignores the big picture of what Immersion is.

Seeing the "vision" of an Immersion project denotes many different (and all valid) perspectives, especially for those individuals who are charged with developing multischool programs and assisting several building leaders. Districtwide officials, as they promote site-based control and initiatives, need to pay special attention to producing a team of Immersion principals whose first response to concerns is the query "What is best for Immersion and the Immersion student?" rather than "What is best for my school?" In this regard, Immersion experience in our country has varied, due in part to the lack of continuity in high-level administrative positions and due in part to educational exigencies such as improving test scores (that often—ironically—conflict with improving learning and achievement). Administrators who come to a school or district after an Immersion program has been well established frequently have little regard for the dynamics of an Immersion program and its local origins. Additionally, they have a high need for putting their personal imprint on an event. If an educational bureaucracy is under continual attack because of a historical lack of credibility, energies are dissipated by many who choose to attempt to educate newcomers. It is accurate to say that some leaders with trust-level or teamsmanship qualities vis-à-vis parents, community members, and teachers are in need of maturing formation. As a consequence of competing forces in a school system, a "recessive genetic code" among administrators is often detectable—that "my school first" idea that disregards, perhaps, issues of articulation ("Lend my fourth-grade teacher to the Immersion middle school for a year or two—no way! "What—a meeting of third-grade Immersion teachers from the four schools during the work day? I won't have my teacher there!") as it takes a short-term approach to challenges and thus creates the possibility of long-term program truncation ("That middle school immersion program won't get off the ground").

Parents, for example, may be unwilling to have a child attend the appropriate middle school for Immersion for a variety of spoken and unspoken reasons. Percentages of student-body integration at the next school level if an Immersion program has been established as a desegregative tool, the loss of an Immersion setting, or a sudden loss of interest in languages are given as causes for not continuing Immersion (García, Lorenz, and Robison 1995). Here is where the relationship of the principal and other administrators on behalf of the project in its K–12 entirety has a direct bearing on what is good for Immersion and Immersion students. Reflection upon strategies to overcome parent and student hesitation must be founded on a global impact—the K–12 expanse of the program. Similarly, in the recruitment of new staff, the persons who interview candidates must maintain a broad view of a candidate's potential worth to the entire program rather than to the more parochial determination of where the candidate would fit into one site. Every Immersion teacher in a multiple-site program should be an excellent candidate for any site. Differences of style between professionals need not damage the value that a teacher has for the program; there is probably no school that hasn't had a teacher whose work elsewhere wasn't as exemplary as it became within a new set of relationships. The conceptual frame of reference here is to assist decision makers to become team members who have a tangible loyalty to their program and where success moves from singular to plural in terms of sites and activities that must cross specific school boundaries or locations.

Challenge 11: Parents know what a magnet school is, but do not know what the requirements for admission mean.

Ignorance of language immersion is a many-layered characteristic among parents and others; it manifests itself in several forms. One example might be the parent who informs the Kansas City placement office that the child will accept placement at the French magnet school and thereupon calls the school principal to say, "Your school was my third choice, so can my child be exempted from taking French? She's more interested in art. Can she have an extended art period instead?" Or the administrator who says, "Let's put this child in fifth-grade Immersion; her mother says she knows her numbers to ten as well as the alphabet in Spanish, and her babysitter is her grandmother, who speaks some Spanish." One lesson to be derived from either scenario, which we considered in an earlier challenge (number 8), is that activities keyed to improving the public's conception of what we do be sustained over a long period of time—years, in fact. Public-awareness activities are time-consuming, budget-sensitive, and labor-intensive (how many people can do so much for so little!). Immersion administrators must develop an appropriate action plan that is both person-to-person or door-to-door in character and even broader in scope. Activities such as open houses, programs at churches and community centers, information tables at neighborhood rallies, parent-provided leads, and newspaper and radio interviews must somehow be fitted into the working day and night. Popularizing an Immersion program depends more on the team effort, ultimately, than on the fiscal effort, and maintaining that program over a long period (which, lamentably, often flies into headwinds of change and newer initiatives) is a vocation that calls for extraordinary people skills.

Challenge 12: A high-level administrator suggests eliminating either the Total Immersion or the Partial Immersion program, or the middle school or the high school portion of Immersion.

In a time of economic constraints such as the 1990s have become, program success, especially in an endeavor such as immersion, may not be enough to save a program from elimination. The potential for savings exists everywhere in Immersion, if one takes on the cost cutter's perspective. Foreign travel for recruitment is costly, visa matters are not inexpensive, materials development during extended work-year seminars cost money, and the hidden costs of helping the foreign national teacher adjust to life in the United States become less hidden, for example, when the last volunteers to house new Immersion teachers say "Not this year." Elimination of Total Immersion in favor of Partial Immersion would, to provide another scenario, reduce the aggregate staff needed from elsewhere. Or, finally, reducing the Immersion program to one language (presumably, to many, Spanish) and to a K–5 option rather than the needed K–12 program might also be ideas that suggest themselves during times of funding crises. Such scenarios are too numerous and too mind-boggling for the Immersion advocate to contemplate. But one must. Averting such nightmates depends in large part on the "people who count" factor in a school system. One must plan for the unexpected budget crisis as one becomes a successful lobbyist for Immersion at all levels. Programs that are successful also get cut, unfortunately. It is the task of many, especially the parents, to convince the decision makers that the budget cutting become a pruning rather than an amputation. An Immersion middle school program the size of Kansas City's does not exist in many places (about 240 children are eligible to go into grade 6; most schools with Immersion programs have fewer than 60 students in grade 5 [García, Lorenz, and Robison 1996, 42]. Advocates of significant number and persistent, ethical pressures can make common cause and effectively deny the decimation of a different program that is assuredly difficult to implement and maintain. Many parent members of Advocates for Language Learning (ALL) have recounted at national meetings the heroic efforts that they had to undertake to ensure that a program need was met, from matters of administrative direction to matters of testing to matters of siting a continuing program into the middle school. As investors in their community and their own children's future, parents have the most to lose if a program is slated for dismantling. No one wishes to risk justifiable parental uproar if a child's educational future is at risk. And one of the reasons is the subtle sensibility that active and numerous parents exert, especially in a multischool operation. Immersion parents include among their number a modestly high percentage of risk takers from the perspective of non-Immersion parents, at least, persons, that is, who are willing to try out an educational program that proposes to deliver a product that is multicultural and multilingual and that thus speaks to our society's future. The "people count" component of the complex of Immersion challenges and concerns plays a role in preparing for the unforeseen.

Challenge 13: All five Immersion teachers are foreign nationals, and all, for different reasons and at different times, decide not to extend their contracts beyond their first year.

An Immersion staff turnover rate of 100 percent is as unlucky as the traditional connotation attributed to the number of this challenge. No program, Immersion or traditional, can achieve stability and continuity—and success and support—if an inordinately high teacher-attrition rate exists. While some might think that the 100 percent figure may seem symbolic of a worst-case scenario, it can happen (and did, twice, to two French Immersion schools in Kansas City, in 1988 and 1990). The writer compiled attrition data for the Kansas City Immersion schools during their first years of operation. (The numbers follow.) Fortunately, by 1992, the rate of resignations was below 15 percent, which was closer to the district average of 12 percent for non-Immersion programs.

Year	Number of Immersion Staff	Number Who Resigned	Number of U.S. Staff Who Resigned	Number of Foreign National Staff Who Resigned	Percentage of Staff Who Resigned
1987–1988	32 (3 languages)	13	2	11	40.6%
1988–1989	46 (3 languages)	21	1	20	45.7
1989–1990	76 (3 languages)	18	1	17	23.7

During interviews and informal conversations, staff members who resigned most often cited the following reasons:

1. Family obligations at home, homesickness
2. Return to a permanent teaching post in one's home country
3. Dissatisfaction with the school, the district, or the Immersion program

4. A belief that the Immersion program's work ethic was too demanding
5. A better employment offer elsewhere
6. Incompatibility with the elementary school setting
7. Personal educational opportunities elsewhere

In addition to reviewing departure rates and reasons, reflection upon the single factor of foreign Immersion staff dependence is critical. (For Kansas City, this was 64 percent of staff in 1991. By 1995, the number was reduced to about 50 percent of staff, thanks to a change in the immigration status of several individuals who obtained green cards and an aggressive policy of employing Immersion colleagues from Puerto Rico. Again, there were wide variations between the Immersion languages: Spanish Immersion has our most stable faculty, French and German alternate for second place.) Further, one must conclude that parents, administrators, and others have much less control over the quality of Immersion programs than they have over other programs that are not so labor-market dependent. Visa status, economic stability in the home country and the attendant job possibilities, and, finally, the lack of "roots" in the local community directly influence Immersion staff attrition more than they perhaps should. But that is the reality that confronts us if we continue to establish and expand Immersion programs, regardless of their value. This writer's position has been to recommend that Immersion administrators begin, first, to plan a smaller program while they provide for actual additional staff (above the approved teacher-student ratios) at the outset to offset the "early burn-out, sudden resignation" syndrome that occurs. (This has worked well in Kansas City; it took almost seven years [1987–1994] for parties to agree to the quality of this proposal and less than two [1996] for it to be challenged by a different group of stakeholders.) Second, the administrators must work with staff members to develop as much program continuity as possible: curriculum objectives, copies of planning outlines, videotaped lessons, and files, files, files of developed units and materials that enable the succeeding generations of Immersion teachers to avoid starting from scratch. Third, we must determine if local contractual considerations allow for multiple-year contracts to be offered (and appropriate contents/rewards/penalties for early departures, as determined). Last, a review of the Immersion teachers' home countries—in terms of which nations provide both quality staff for Immersion and staying power—is in order during the time one makes recruitment decisions.

These recommendations do not mean that substantive issues of attrition will disappear after the first two years of a program's establishment. Our hope is that the program's growth, as it stabilizes, will be matched by diminished faculty attrition and increased attention to those support structures (aides, co-teachers, extended contracts, etc.) that are needed. During spare time (!), outreach to teacher education institutions must be made to ensure that appropriate information and employment opportunities for American Immersion teachers come into existence.

Coda

The report has examined the typical challenges of an Immersion program administrator. It is predicated on the basis that Immersion programs, despite their very low frequency of occurrence in our country, are an important contribution to increased linguistic and cultural awareness and skills for our young people for the twenty-first century. It follows, therefore, that heroic measures and considerable thought must be undertaken to keep afloat an enterprise that at first view is deemed eminently sinkable because of the ungainly superstructures that its educational core requires. The issues selected for discussion from the perspectives of parents, students, teachers, administrators, and community members attempt to display, ultimately, what all good programs are characterized by: a clearly stated vision that is widely and honestly disseminated; a willingness to espouse, nurture, and celebrate the emergence of Immersion among other education programs; a requirement to produce and sustain teamwork and compassion; and, finally, the ability to recognize and act upon the truth of Barry Commoner's postulate from a generation ago. In the context of the environment, he said in an interview, "Nothing ever disappears completely, and everything is connected." In the diverse school structures that may sail parallel to that "bridge to the twenty-first century" and provide an alternative vehicle for reaching our future, model Immersion projects can be exemplars of divergent paradigms housed in a multifaceted school system.

References

Curtain, Helena Anderson, and Carol Ann Pesola. 1994. *Languages and Children: Making the Match.* 2nd ed. Reading, MA: Addison Wesley.

García, Paul A. 1987. "Basic Precepts of Language Acquisition." Unpublished document for in-service programs.

———. 1989. "Paradigm Shift: The Future Is Now," in *National FLES* Commission Report*, ed. Gladys C. Lipton, 83–88. Urbana, IL: AATF.

———. 1990. "Five Easy Pieces: Considerations on the In-Service Needs of **FLES*** Teachers," in *Innovations in FLES* Programs*, ed. G. Lipton, 22–32. Urbana, IL: Commission of AATF.

———. 1995. "A Delicate Balance: Continuing Immersion in U.S. Middle and High Schools." University of Minnesota Symposium on Immersion (October).

García, Paul. A., Eileen Lorenz, and Robert Robison. 1995. "Immersion Programs Enter the Middle School: Research, Strategies, and Considerations," in *Foreign Languages: The Journey of a Lifetime,* eds. Richard Donato and Robert Terry, 37–74. Lincolnwood, IL: National Textbook Company.

Grittner, Frank M. 1990. "Bandwagons Revisited: A Perspective on Movements in Foreign Language Education," in *New Perspectives and New Directions in Foreign Language Education,* ed., Diane W. Birckbichler, 9–43. Lincolnwood, IL: National Textbook Co.

Lange, Dale L. 1990. "Sketching the Crisis and Exploring Different Perspectives in Foreign Language Curriculum," in *New Perspectives and New Directions in Foreign Language Education,* ed. Diane W. Birchbichler, 77–109. Lincolnwood, IL: National Textbook Co.

Lipton, Gladys C. 1998. *Practical Handbook to Elementary Foreign Language Programs,* 3rd ed. Lincolnwood, IL: NTC/Contemporary Publishing Co.

———. 1990. "**FLES*** Programs: Today and Tomorrow," *AATF National Bulletin* 16 (Nov.) 7–10.

Montgomery County Schools, MD. 1989. *Videotapes for Immersion Teacher Training,* Rockville, MD: Montgomery County School.

A Teacher's View of Advocacy

Harriet Saxon
*Pierrepont School
Rutherford, New Jersey*

Mesdames et messieurs, as you walk along tree-lined Park Avenue in the center of Rutherford, please note on your left, the charming, informative, and creative library window. Of course, it's about French! Stop and look! Enjoy the projects, posters, decorations, paper figurines, and the exciting colors of a young person's world of learning French. Visit the Rutherford Library and enjoy the three-dimensional mural of Paris with its streets, monuments, parks, museums, cafes, and Parisians strolling along flower-lined cobblestone streets. The students from all the French classes helped to re-create Paris in the heart of Rutherford.

Continue your promenade along Union Avenue and, directly in front of Union School, you may cool yourself in the shade of the linden tree that was planted to celebrate the bicentennial of *la Révolution française.* The dignitaries of the town and school communities joined in the planting of this historic tree while students sang *La Marseillaise.* Students joined the Memorial Day parade festivities dressed in the costumes of *les sans-culottes* and the dresses of the Revolution. Their felt banners, flags, and garlands of flowers, *bleu, blanc et rouge,* were a sensation!

Visit our Kipp Senior Center. Students this morning are presenting a program on "Little Known Facts to Fascinate About *la Statue de la Liberté.*" Last year, the seniors enjoyed a "trip" to Québec with slides and films presented by the eighth-grade French class. Come back and visit in June, when the seventh-grade French students will present a mini-concert of French music and poetry.

Continue your walk through Rutherford to the Pierrepont School and enjoy *Le Petit Jardin de Claude Monet,* which the students planted in front of the school. You may see young French artists sketching and painting the daffodils and tulips and petunias in the style of the impressionists! Many thanks are given to the art teachers who advise and teach the students to "Make an Impression." Attractive bulletin boards exhibit the work of the French students surrounded by pastel flowers trimmed in silver glitter!

Stay for the afternoon and enjoy lunch *au café* at *Le Marché aux Puces,* the annual French fundraiser, organized by the students and parents of the eighth-grade class, who will visit Québec for four days in May. Students, parents, and friends return each year to serve and cook at the café, sell things at the flea market tables, and welcome friends to their *confiserie, salon de coiffure,* manicure shop, flower shop, and other activities that display a bit of Paris at Pierrepont School. Enjoy and laugh at the antics of Guignol at *Le Thèâtre de Guignol* and the songs, comic scenes, and presentation of *Le Petit Chaperon Rouge.* At the café, enjoy a *café, quiche, crêpes, soupe à l'oignon, mousse au chocolat, beignets,* and *salade niçoise* for a perfect *déjeuner français.*

And for the evening? *Mes amis,* you have a choice! You may enjoy a serious and beautiful *soirée* at a performance of *Le Rossignol Chante au Clair de Lune.* This evening of poetry and music features excerpts of poetry from Madame de Sévigné, Paul Verlaine, and Rimbaud. Students present comments about the composers whose works are performed. A ballerina delights with her interpretation of a court dance from the Versailles court of Louis XV. This *soirée* was presented for the Parents and Teachers Association, with the superintendent of schools and the president of the board of education in attendance.

If you would like to enjoy a bit of *la joie de vivre,* come to the Cabaret. Relax and enjoy songs and dances from *Carnival, La Belle et la Bête, Gigi, Camelot, Les Misérables, Phantom of the Opera,* and the songs of Chevalier and Piaf. Costumes! Lights! Music! *Bon appétit!* The *chefs* have prepared a splendid *souper* of delicate French sandwiches and *fromage,* fruit kebabs, and cream puffs with delicious French vanilla ice cream. Spring has arrived at the Cabaret, with pastel banners, matching table covers, and walls transformed into the flower gardens of Camelot.

For visitors who would like to stay the night, we suggest the French hotel, Le Novotel, which is located five minutes from the Pierrepont School in Lyndhurst, New Jersey. Please mention that you were sent by the French Program in Rutherford. Students from our school have been welcomed many times by the French management, and have decorated the lobby of this hotel during the Christmas holidays. They also have enjoyed an informative day with the different staff members of Le Novotel, where they spend a French Career Day.

Now, we invite you to spend a French Day in New York City with us. We plan to leave early in the morning to visit the Metropolitan Museum of Art and discover the treasures of the French Sculpture Garden. We also have a scavenger hunt through the Impressionist Galleries and special French exhibits. We divide into prearranged groups and try to find the paintings for each clue listed, such as: "Name at least three different varieties of flowers that Monet liked to paint" or "Which painting would you most like to own and why?" We enjoy lunch at a French restaurant (we like *les sans-culottes*, which continues the theme of the French Revolution, which the class studied last year), and then conclude the day with a matinee performance of *Les Misérables.*

National Foreign Language Week provides a perfect time for French students on all levels to present programs for the promotion of language study to the mayor and town council and to members of the board of education. Last year, the presentation included skits, songs, stories, verse, and dance, with costumes, posters, and music. The mayor presented a proclamation that declared the month of March World Languages Month in Rutherford, New Jersey. The president of the board of education complimented both students and teachers for their dedication in learning a second language and for providing students the opportunities that lead to the understanding of different cultures.

French is alive and well in Rutherford, New Jersey, but it takes the effort and cooperation of many people: administrators, teachers, parents, community members, businesspeople, and, especially, marvelous students who really get into the "swing of French." The activities described above may be expanded or adapted to meet local needs and can be adapted to other languages as well. *Bonne chance!*

PART 2

Focus on **FLES*** Learners

A Salad of Language Learners

Elizabeth Miller
Crystal Springs Uplands School
Hillsborough, California

A **FLES*** teacher who walks into an elementary school classroom of twenty-five children is confronted with a veritable salad of different learning styles—at least twenty-five varieties—including a mixture of learning problems from mild perceptual difficulties to serious learning disabilities. The effective teacher must create, therefore, at least twenty-five different teaching strategies for reaching each student and providing him or her with some measure of success. The teacher who relies on the comfort of one approach fails all of his or her students—from the most capable to the most severely learning disabled. What is not surprising is that **FLES*** teachers, by instinct (and by unfathomable creativity, which is the nature of the beast) are already providing the variety of teaching styles that the diversity of the classroom demands. I would like to briefly address the challenges facing the **FLES*** teacher today, including students with dyslexia and attention deficit disorder, techniques to ensure such students' positive participation, and the importance of keeping all students, even those with learning problems, in the foreign language program.

The **FLES*** teacher of the 1990s faces a different student than he or she may recall from his or her own elementary school experience. Traditional text- or vocabulary-oriented language instruction will fall very flat today, and for the child with a learning problem, it is a disaster. Even in the most filtered situation of high academic achievers, it still isn't enough. Coloring *la Tour Eiffel* or listing the parts of the body in French or conjugating the verb *avoir* hardly re-creates communication. Nor do such activities provide adequate foundation in the language-learning process to enhance foreign language study at the secondary level. Unfortunately, what this type of activity does provide for the teacher is a quiet and orderly classroom. Given the increasing number of perceptual problems, learning disorders, and attention dysfunctions in our classrooms, a desire for quiet and order is understandable. However, the needs of children with such difficulties can be recognized and better served with some changes or additions to the **FLES*** teacher's "bag of tricks."

Two buzzwords of educators these days are definitely *dyslexia* and *attention deficit disorder*. Teachers are becoming better educated in identifying student learning problems as something other than laziness or poor discipline, and parents are more willing to have their children "officially" diagnosed with learning problems as more and more states mandate positive support for such students (untimed testing, individual testing environments, separate college admission criteria, and support tutoring). Both parents and students need to see diagnosis as a facilitating step rather than the labeling of a handicap—and then we can get on with the task of teaching.

DYSLEXIA

Dyslexic children are being identified earlier and earlier, which salvages the self-esteem of many who would otherwise have been dismissed as "dumb" or discipline problems. Quite often the phenomenon doesn't surface until the written symbol comes into play. Until then, the child assumes that everyone thinks the way he or she does. For the dyslexic child, the inability to grasp symbols creates frustration, self-doubt, and a fatiguing experience of disorientation that can lead to the quick abandonment of any activity related to written words or numbers. Writing is a painful process, and the results are often illegible because for the dyslexic, the words seem to float around and sometimes swim right off the paper. Keeping a word sitting on a line is next to impossible. The concentration that may click in to help the child focus can become so intense that it causes headaches or stomachaches. Daydreaming helps to relieve the tension, but it has obvious consequences. Spelling is a primary problem because the dyslexic often cannot see any difference between a correct and an incorrect form. All three-letter words look the same. The letters could go forward or backward or inside out—to the dyslexic, they would not look any different. Traditional classroom activities of reading and writing wear these children down. However, quite often, dyslexic children are the stars in **FLES*** listening comprehension activities! Stronger auditory skills often take over and compensate for symbol-based frustration.

It is important to look at some of the advantages of being a dyslexic. These individuals come with some special talents—as evidenced by such famous dyslexic people as Albert Einstein, Thomas Edison, Walt Disney, Winston Churchill, and Whoopi Goldberg (see *The Gift of Dyslexia*, by Ronald Davis, Ability Workshop Press, Burlingame, CA). They think mainly in pictures, they are highly insightful, they are more aware of their environment (which is why they seem to be more easily distracted), and they have wonderful imaginations! The main reason they can be successful in early **FLES*** classrooms is that the process of "thinking in pictures" is how we present language. We don't start with the symbol (the word) written on the board; we start with the object itself. We take out an apple and pass it around: *C'est la pomme.* Those sounds are directly associated with the real thing—the letters in a book do not intervene. We associate an activity—*J'ouvre la porte*—with actually going over and opening the door. It isn't important where one word ends and the next begins; it's the total sound that accompanies the movement. **FLES*** teachers have long been doing this to teach language, and it is what "modern" specialists are now advising to all teachers who are trying to reach dyslexic children.

Some of the "symptoms" that appear when the dyslexic starts to have difficulty in the classroom are related to written language: letter reversal, inconsistent spelling, words or letters skipped when reading or writing. But other problems translate into other behaviors: inability to sit still, problems with balance, excessive daydreaming, no concept of time (which includes telling time and doing things within a realistic time frame), distractiveness, hyperactivity, or hypoactivity (being underactive). Sequencing of anything becomes a gargantuan task—numbers, days of the week, and so forth. But this does NOT mean the dyslexic should be removed from the foreign language classroom! Some specific suggestions will follow about handling the dyslexic child within the framework of your **FLES*** classroom, but the very first step is to redefine what is important for this language learner. Does a nine-year-old need to write everything in order to communicate in a foreign language? Must he or she be able to read everything he or she can say? Does he or she need to know initially that in the sentence *Je ne sais pas*, the part that is the verb is *sais*? We need to remember that our role in the **FLES*** classroom is three-fold: First, we are to establish a set of sounds that may be unfamiliar within the hearing center of the children so that they may accurately reproduce those sounds in speech. Second, we are to familiarize the children with the process of learning a foreign language, a process that is initially based on auditory cues and requires unself-conscious risk taking and an ability to accept the ambiguous. Third, we are to create a love for language learning and appeal to the curiosity of the children for other cultures, engendering respect and tolerance for those aspects of human culture that are different from our own. The dyslexic can reach each of these goals—and do so successfully. It has been shown that deciding it is "too hard" to learn a foreign language and removing the child from the foreign language classroom so that he or she can take a foreign language later in high school, "when he or she is ready," leads to failure. Even a small amount of early exposure to foreign language learning—the process, the language patterns, and the sounds—permits the child to have some measure of success at the secondary level, but when there is no early exposure, the child lacks a familiar base from which to work, and repeated failure is the result. Even right brain/left brain researchers have found that those students whose dominant side renders language learning difficult can find success if there has been some consistent foreign language in the elementary school experience. Hoping that language proficiency will fall into place with more maturity is wishful, if not dangerous, thinking.

ATTENTION DEFICIT DISORDER

The characteristics are familiar. These are children incapable of following through on any task assigned. They respond to someone's question on the other side of the classroom. They sabotage any group project and can cause collapse of any activity that is not highly structured. They can start off well with a test, but the slightest sneeze can destroy their concentration and the rest of their answers become gibberish. They are unrealistically optimistic about their own abilities, but can lose self-confidence quickly and give up. They are forgetful, disorganized, frequently late, and impatient with peers. Their focus is so limited that they end up being labeled low-ability students, when in fact many are exceedingly bright. They can be fantastically creative, but their inattention to detail keeps them at the low end of the conventional grading scale. Whether you are comfortable with the term "ADD" or not, whether you embrace it as a legitimate learning disorder or a chemical breakdown is almost irrelevant. The behavior is there in the classroom and needs to be dealt with by the teacher—and, even better, by the student and teacher in partnership.

It is the creativity of the **FLES*** teacher that captures the focus of the ADD child. A **FLES*** teacher sails into the classroom with something different from the ordinary academic demands and with a variety of activities to capture the student's attention. These children hold little tolerance for boredom, so the **FLES*** teacher is a welcome relief! Perhaps the first step is to permit the term "ADD" and encourage the child to think of himself or herself as a capable student, although you and the child need to work together to keep him or her on task. If the child knows there is support from you, he or she will be motivated to focus. If we take such children out of the foreign language classroom because they need more "maturity to handle the load," we have destroyed a valuable part of them.

If we can look at the symptoms and behaviors of dyslexia and ADD as learning "difficulties" rather than "disorders," we can weave our programs in ways that provide success for every child. Some specific suggestions follow.

Classroom Management Techniques

1. Place pupils with learning problems at desks where there is the least interference. Front rows, away from windows, are best. Avoid large tables with several students—they inevitably invite distraction.
2. The multisensory approach is essential—but **FLES*** teachers have been doing this for years! The student must interact with the language in as many ways a possible: auditory, visual, touch, taste, kinesthetic. Save the symbol (the written word) for later—as "later" as possible! Once a word or idea is well-established orally, its sound can be paired with the graphic.
3. Frequent review is essential to deal with retention weaknesses.
4. Save two or three minutes at the end of a class to summarize and underline what was introduced, what was drilled, what was reviewed. This constant reinforcement is essential.
5. Class structure is important because internal disorganization is distracting to the ADD and dyslexic. However, this does NOT mean a classroom should be silent! The more moving around there is in conjunction with manipulating the language, the better. But you need to establish systems to keep the direction of the class in view. Many specialists suggest creating private signals with your learning problem student to bring him or her back on task.
6. Peer tutors have been successful in many classes. Provide incentives for the peer teachers to ensure the success of their teaching.
7. Do one thing at a time. Children with any form of learning problem will have difficulty listening and writing at the same time.
8. When presenting new material, be sure to start with the familiar and concrete—something the student can see, touch, act out. For those who think through pictures, this is mandatory.
9. Pause often so that the child may process new concepts.
10. Interact often with the student. Encourage frequent choral repetition followed by individual repetition or response as reinforcement.

Managing the Written Word

1. For students with visual perceptual problems, color-coding has worked, if used consistently. For example, assign one color to feminine gender and another to masculine. Or, in advanced **FLES*** classes, color the verb endings to identify verb forms.

2. If a child has excessive perceptual disorders, contract with him or her that internal spelling will not count, but that you will look for verb endings (which would be a grammatical issue) and spellings that are *phonetically* accurate enough that the child would be understood orally. Remember, communication is the goal.
3. Post-its may enable children to deal with papers and textbooks if they cannot underline or highlight.
4. Keep the presentation of your hand-outs and other papers as clear as possible. Avoid too many pictures and extraneous decorations. Some foreign language textbooks, although wonderful for most youngsters, can be too distracting for these children to follow. Use larger type—and bold where possible—keeping some part of the page blank.
5. Provide extra time. States are now requiring that teachers provide extra time for assignments and testing of "identified" learning disabled students. Teachers themselves can determine what is realistic, and it helps to ask students how much time they think they need. In severe cases, a child may need a separate quiet room for testing—something that shortages of space, time, and personnel may restrict in most of our elementary schools—but it is still worth considering. A special space in the classroom with carrel sides could suffice.
6. Give directions in more than one way. If directions are written on paper, read them aloud too, and ask your student to read them to be sure he or she understands the task.
7. Provide practice tests.
8. Give frequent quizzes rather than long tests.
9. Keep assignments short, allowing students to concentrate on mastering one or two items.
10. Draw a simple border around material you want emphasized.
11. Use a multiple-choice format whenever possible.
12. Avoid any testing activity that requires the child to copy from one place to another (from board to paper or from book to paper).

Managing Behavior

1. Stand by the desk of your special student to help him or her stay on task, especially when you are giving directions. Refer to his or her paper often to provide individual reinforcement and use the student's work as a positive example whenever possible to build the student's confidence.

2. Establish a signal with your student to remind him or her to stay on task.
3. Change activities often so you don't lose the attention of your student. Punctuate often with some kind of physical movement. (For example, *Toutes les filles, levez-vous.*)
4. Praise *specific* behaviors because a vague compliment will not reinforce anything.
5. Require the student to keep an assignment book in which you can monitor the writing down of homework—and make sure that due dates are recorded.
6. Include special students frequently in dramatizations using the language. Special students often enjoy the safe format of dramatizations (rather than the uncomfortable uncertainty of question-answer), and they often are your most creative actors!

There are many reasons to keep children with learning difficulties in the foreign language classroom, and I urge you to pressure administrators to permit them this very special opportunity. Colleges are not yet required to waive the foreign language entrance requirement for students with learning difficulties (although a small percentage of colleges and universities are doing this voluntarily), so these students will have to fulfill two years of a foreign language before high school graduation. If these students wait to start their foreign language experience as fifteen- or sixteen-year-olds, they will be up for disappointment. To succeed in foreign language study, they need some foundation before the age of ten or eleven to hear the sounds and expose their auditory memory to the phonetic spectrum outside the American register. They will suffer less self-consciousness if they learn at an early age that languages can be conquered and that making mistakes is not a tragedy. The process of listening, repeating, understanding, responding, and then manipulating becomes automatic with youngsters, but can be fraught with terror for the uninitiated, especially for students who have discovered they have academic problems. Being comfortable with a foreign language as a communication tool is the greatest gift a **FLES*** teacher can offer, and children who have discovered they can achieve success as fourth graders will be more willing to take some risks in the high school classroom.

Undeniably, the cultural implications of providing **FLES*** to all students are also numerous, although I have concentrated on the language-learning process itself. All students need to see another culture through its language, to discover cultural differences, and to respect those differences and, one hopes, be fascinated by them—to promote tolerance of differences in our own classrooms and communities as well as in the global community. Fight for these children. They deserve every chance we can give them to prove their special skills and talents, and a foreign language is not beyond their reach.

The Northern Kentucky University FLES* Troupe: Reaching Foreign Language Learners of Today and Tomorrow

Katherine C. Kurk
Northern Kentucky University
Highland Heights, Kentucky

The new Kentucky Education Reform Act has mandated sweeping changes in K–16 curricula across the state, and one of the most promising is the promotion of foreign language learning in the earliest grades. However, while most schools embrace the concept, their budgets have left little room to maneuver, and finding qualified instructors has also been a serious problem. At Northern Kentucky University we have been addressing these concerns with service to our community via **FLES*** education for almost a decade. **FLES*** may stand for "Foreign Languages in the Elementary Schools," but to us it also means KU! Our language minors and majors have traveled to various preschools, after-school enrichment programs, and regular and gifted classrooms to teach eager beginning language students at the same time that they receive valuable methodological and pedagogical training and college credit for themselves.

Participants in the **FLES*** Troupe are usually language majors and minors (from programs in French, Spanish, and German) who have previously completed one three-hour methods course. That class has included a special **FLES*** unit: Kentucky certification in foreign languages is now granted for K–12. However, not all the students who take methods are necessarily working on certification. Some want the skills that the course provides for employment reasons; others think it will enhance their potential for a teaching assistantship in graduate school. In any case, they have had a healthy introduction to **FLES*** and to such methodologies as TPR. Then they sign up for a second, advanced methods course that involves going into a teaching situation one or two days a week for the entire academic year; making their own curriculum, worksheets, realia, assessment tools; keeping a journal of their experience that includes samples from their students' work and self-evaluation of each teaching day; working with and having observations from a mentor teacher, and even more! To enter this course, they must have the approval of both the supervising instructor and the teachers and administrators of their respective learning centers, which is based on interviews and evaluation of previous class work. Upon successful completion of the course, the student receives three hours' credit at the 400 (advanced) level and a letter grade.

Each member of the KU **FLES*** Troupe has provided foreign language instruction to children who otherwise would not have had access to a carefully articulated plan or to an instructor with both **FLES*** and target language training. We use several references for our curricular development, but our core comes from the "Indicators of Competence for grades K–4" from *Acquiring Cross-Cultural Competence*, a study of the National Commission on Cultural Competence of The American Association of Teachers of French, since our emphasis is on cultural awareness and appreciation of ethnic and identity group differences. Our students have included native and non-native speakers, and they have all benefited from one another. The journals, worksheets, and realia are all copied and on file to share from year to year. Initially our placements were usually in preschool and kindergarten situations; then we moved into after-school programs in parochial, private, and public settings. Most recently, we have placed a troupe member in a gifted program for grades 4, 5, and 6 with students who have previously had a FLEX experience and are now pursuing a single language.

Our university students have been delighted to find how receptive their young counterparts are to global education and to foreign language learning. Their eagerness and their ability to mimic sounds well, without embarrassment or hesitation, prompt the college level student-teacher to study pronunciation tapes and to search for new vocabulary with equal enthusiasm. Both teachers and learners find the joy of communication, and Northern's **FLES*** Troupe has found that their experience gives them confidence in their own abilities. One journal entry reveals: "I like seeing what I have learned put into practice, whether by speaking or by teaching others. It gives me a great sense of accomplishment to share what I know." Another trouper writes: "It is fun for me, too! Nothing stretches the imagination more than having to translate 'Mighty Morphin Power Rangers' or 'Teenage Mutant Ninja Turtles' on the spot!"

Three of our troupers for 1995 (Jill, Mark, and Tracie) were all placed at a preschool–K center: Children's Campus and Care in Crestview Hills, Kentucky. They rotated throughout the year from the three-year-olds to the four-year-olds to the "experienced" kindergartners of five and six. In her journal, Jill noted that there was "nothing" that was "too hard" to teach her young pupils since they seemed to be interested in everything. But their attention spans were limited and the pre–K crowd was an active bunch, so the instructors used a lot of Total Physical Response within a user-friendly, Lozanov surrounding. Mark, for example, had his class jump, *sauter*, when learning about the grasshopper, *la sauterelle*. He also used a worksheet, *"Les Animaux et leurs sons"*: "I went around the room as the children colored, making the animal noises and going over the animals' names. We finished by going through the animals and sounds together, pointing out their pictures on the walls, acting them out—it was fun, quite a lot of racket!" In order to teach the song *"Alouette,"* Mark used a poster board bird with detachable parts for *la tête, le bec, le cou, le dos*, and *les pattes*. "When I took apart the bird, everyone went nuts—it was enjoyable and it helped the image-to-word relationship become apparent." To celebrate *Noël*, Mark entered the classroom wearing antlers and a big red nose. Soon everyone was wearing *un nez rouge*, too.

Tracie had a particular challenge working with the three-year-olds, but she, too , used a combination of crafts and TPR to teach counting and colors. One day the class made French flags out of *bleu, blanc*, and *rouge* construction paper and straws. "Then we repeated the colors, stood in line, and marched around the room. They loved this more than anything we've done." And one day she brought in eighteen stuffed animals: *les chiens, les chats, les lapins*, and *les souris*, one for each child. The pupils identified with their animals, counted the members of their groups, made French animal sounds, and introduced themselves.

Jill also used stuffed animals with the four-year-olds in her class: "After a while, the children did not want what they had, but rather what the child next to them had. So I decided that it was time to color." The first thing the **FLES*** instructor learns is to adapt! Jill had much success using card games to teach *les couleurs*. "I took two regular decks of cards and pasted pieces of colored paper on them. Each of the children received four cards. I called out the colors in French, and if they had the color in their hand, they had to place it face down on the floor. Then we flipped them over to see if everyone got the right color. They caught on really well."

Tracie and Jill have both returned to their preschool for a second year of the **FLES*** Troupe, and they are involved in the creation of a fully articulated curriculum for ages three through six. Tracie is also using video to record and assess, and she is sending her classes' performances to share with French children in Autun. Tracie is, in fact, working on teacher certification K–12, and this experience adds nine hours of methods to the education coursework, practicums, student teaching, and French classes required for her degree. It also gives her a valuable experience to add to her dossier. Jill, however, is not planning a teaching career at all. She has added her nine hours of methods to a double major in French and in aviation, and she plans a career in international travel. Nonetheless she sees her teaching as an integral part of her learning, and she hopes some day to have all of her young students on an international flight. Mark graduated at the year's end and is currently pursuing graduate study in French. Like all the troupers before them, Tracie, Jill, and Mark agree that there are no rewards comparable to the smiles, hugs, and *mercis* they have received.

In the future, the KU **FLES*** Troupe plans to expand to include a lesser-taught language, most probably Japanese, and to help with more FLEX programs in grades 4, 5, and 6. While at first it was difficult to find students who were willing to work for a whole year for their three hours, we now have no trouble finding eager teachers, and more preschools and elementary schools are calling us for help when they incorporate global education in their curriculums. Via our **FLES*** Troupe we demonstrate to administrators, faculty, and parents that nothing takes the place of good training in both target language and methodology, and we show how much fun learning a foreign language can be. Those troupers who have graduated with certification have had multiple teaching job offers. The Northern Kentucky **FLES*** Troupe is indeed reaching the foreign language learners of today and tomorrow.

References

Lipton, Gladys C. 1998. *Practical Handbook to Elementary Foreign Language Programs.* 3rd ed. Lincolnwood, IL: NTC/Contemporary Publishing Co.

Lozano, Patti. 1991. *Guide to Successful After-School Elementary Foreign Language Programs.* Lincolnwood, IL: National Textbook Co.

Olliphant, Jo Ann. 1993. *Total Physical Fun.* Tacoma, WA: Sahmarsh Publishing.

Singerman, Alan J. 1996. *Acquiring Cross-Cultural Competence: Four Stages for Students of French.* Lincolnwood, IL: National Textbook Co. (See particularly: Kurk, Katherine C. "Part IV. Cultural Competence: Kindergarten through Eighth Grade," 65–73.)

Wiley, Patricia Davis. 1988. Rural FLES Models: Teachers and Students Learning a Foreign Language, in ed. *Shaping the Future of Foreign Language Education: FLES, Articulation, and Proficiency,* ed. John F. Laland, 82–90. Lincolnwood, IL: National Textbook Co.

Differing Abilities in the Sequential FLES Class

Virginia L. Gramer
Hinsdale Elementary School
Hinsdale, Illinois

IQ tests and teacher observation are quickly, though not always accurately, used to identify those who are and who will be skillful and knowledgeable in specific academic areas. Identifying students of differing abilities for foreign language classes has traditionally resulted in lists based on academic achievement in other disciplines, but it is interesting to look at differing abilities in a broader sense. For the young foreign language learner, the abilities required to be successful are more than cognitive, as all teachers know. Students need to be able to listen and to focus their attention for a period of time appropriate to their age level, to function as active members of large and small groups without becoming either domineering or passive observers, to seek attention in positive and acceptable ways, and to bring tasks and assignments to completion. It is not unusual for students who may have the potential to be successful in academic areas to be low achievers in reality because they have little ability in these classroom coping skills. Therefore, dealing successfully with the differing abilities of students requires a teacher to find techniques to cope with those who have a variety of behavioral and attention characteristics superimposed on low, average, and high cognitive abilities—and all of this in classes of twenty-five or more.

An elementary school teacher of foreign language may have more potential for achieving success in the Herculean task than a regular classroom teacher. The very nature of the elementary school foreign language class with its rapid flow, frequent changes of pace, and emphasis on student involvement and physical activity often succeeds with students who have behavioral and attention difficulties. In the initial years of an elementary school foreign language program almost all students achieve well. The problem seems to arise when those elements diminish that make the foreign language class fertile ground for success. After the first year or two, do we always continue the techniques that we used with younger learners and beginning students, the methods that maintained the class as a cohesive whole and kept the attention of even the most wayward students? Perhaps not. In attempting to determine at what point and for what reason the gap between success and the lack of it widens, we have observed that the increased emphasis on reading and writing pinpoints the line. Though reading and writing are components of the beginning elementary school foreign language curriculum, they are primarily adjuncts and supports of the listening and speaking skills. As students progress and graphic skills occupy a more pivotal role in the foreign language class, at whatever grade this occurs, when simple elements of grammar are introduced, then we see students experiencing a struggle to keep up. Is it because the skills of reading and writing pose a problem with these students, or is it because the techniques used to teach these children do not suit their needs, talents, or learning problems?

By following the pattern set in the regular classroom of increasing the more formal and sedentary modes of student involvement as students progress in the grades, the foreign language teacher may be programming certain students for failure. When reading and writing in the target language are emphasized more, it appears that teachers tend to focus for longer periods of class time on fewer items. It is not as easy to switch from one activity to another, and changes of pace come less often. Generally, as reading and writing increase, consistent physical activity on the part of the student decreases. With the need to focus attention for longer periods of time, some of those students who are mental nomads drift away. Though some alteration in the typical elementary school foreign language lesson design may be desirable when more time is devoted to reading and writing, it is also necessary to provide respites from the graphic skills, breaks that require significant activity on the part of the student.

Dealing with students of differing abilities in a K–5/6 setting poses one set of problems, but the problems become even more complex when different grade level organizational structures fall into play. Students accustomed to the easy give-and-take of the elementary school foreign language class are often subjected to curricular shock when they run head on into a traditional departmentalized middle school or junior high class. Even those classes that maintain an emphasis on listening and speaking skills are, more often than not, built around the accomplishment of a specific number of units, often from a high school text. The requirement of having students fit neatly into a particular level, usually level 2 or 3, when they reach high school exerts pressure on the middle school teachers to place time constraints on learning and also to cover material not easily absorbed by young preadolescents. Students whose maturity factors or learning styles are not compatible with the text-oriented, spelling-grammar curriculum fall by the wayside.

This scenario is not always inevitable. There are exceptional middle grade teachers who are able to carry off an approach that focuses on the formal text elements, preparing students to fit eventually into a level 2 or 3 high school course and that still provides worthwhile experiences for students who cannot achieve that goal. Such teachers are to be admired and revered as national treasures. Until their number increases considerably, alternative methods of providing for the differing needs of students seem to be necessary.

On the surface, the solution seems obvious. If students were able to succeed in their elementary school foreign language classes and are not now achieving, place them in a class that maintains the focus that suits their learning style and their needs, namely that of the Sequential FLES class. There are middle and junior high schools that have managed to have an alternative or parallel foreign language class as well as special classes in math and language arts. In this nontraditional course, the Sequential FLES experience is extended. If there is a text, it serves as a resource; reading and writing are just as important as in a traditional class and are perhaps even more emphasized because students with learning problems need as much input from as many sources as they can get. It is important to note, however, that in these classes, spelling and grammar are not as critical and are not the primary criteria for success. Multisensory experiences are carefully planned, and many of the techniques that work with a Sequential FLES class are adapted to the middle and junior high student. The same cultural goals are as applicable to this group as they are to any foreign language class. It is still a foreign language class, however—a vague potpourri of songs and readings about holidays and folk heroes.

In heterogeneous grouping, it is not as easy to suit the needs of the student at risk and still provide for the students who achieve well. It is difficult, but it is not impossible. Good teachers have always provided many different paths to reach a goal. Some of the techniques that allow students of differing abilities to achieve are standard, such as "chunking," "linking," and "rhythm." Other ways to cope with differing abilities, for the right and left brained, for different intelligences, for visual and auditory learners, and so on, might include some of the following.

Make connections and linkages if none exist naturally.
- String the names of three to five items together, pointing to the items themselves or to pictures of them, with a chant: "the door, the window, the chalk, the table; the door, the window, the chalk, the table." Repeat the chain several times, each time it is presented.
- Litanies, prescribed sets of statements, rejoinders, or questions and answers between teacher and student, and between student and student, are also useful and enjoyable.
- A two- or three-minute "Round Robin" at any time during a period can provide a break as well as reinforce and review. Students have a

two- to four-sentence exchange that flows from student to student as they ask or answer, one to another:

Student A: Hello, how are you?   *or*   **Student A:** Where are you going after school?

Student B: Fine, thanks, and you?   **Student B:** To town, and you?

Student A: Not bad, thank you.   **Student A:** I'm going to the pool.

Then student B turns to student C and repeats the first line:

Student B: Hello, how are you?   **Student B:** Where are you going after school?

Student C: So-so, and you?   **Student C:** To the library, and you?

Student B: Fine, thanks.   **Student B:** I'm going to the pool.

- Chants or raps are popular and one can be invented for almost any sequence. Here is one in French that students seem to remember years later:

    Un, deux, trois, quatre, cinq, OH, OH.
    Six, sept, huit, neuf, dix, LA, LA
    (Repeat again, placing fingers in a circle around eyes for OH, OH, and giving a wave of each hand for LA, LA.)
    Onze, douze, treize (clap, clap).
    Quatorze, quinze, seize (clap, clap).
    (Repeat.)
    Dix-sept, dix-huit, dix-neuf (tap, tap, on the desk.)
    Dix-sept, dix-huit, dix-neuf (tap, tap, on the desk.)
    Dix-sept, dix-huit, dix-neuf (tap, tap, on the desk.)
    VINGT!

Create as many forms of sensory input as possible. Whenever possible, add visualization to abstractions.

- On the top of a sheet for practicing negatives in French, make a "verb sandwich":

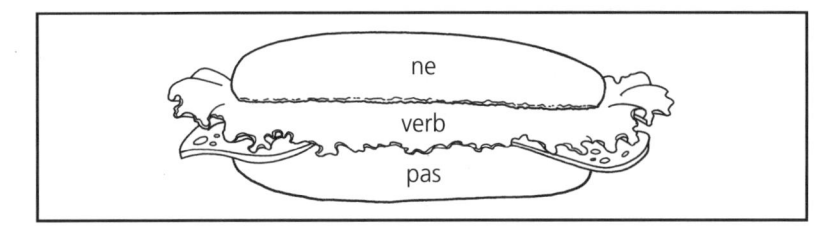

  ne
  verb
  pas

- Some children have problems with auditory sequencing and memory, others with print. If certain sequences and forms of word order can be converted to more graphic symbols, many find them easier to deal with. For example, in dealing with position of adjectives, some before, some after the noun, provide visual clues to guide oral production. The pictures can be labeled at any point and then cards with print and no pictures can be used.

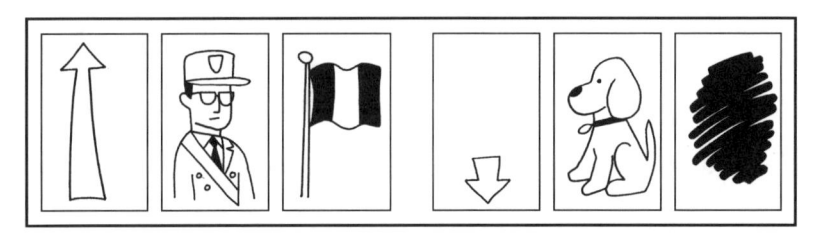

  the tall French policeman   the small black dog

  Even the physical act of arranging the above pictures or symbols provides needed reinforcement for students who need more sensory input in dealing with some of the abstractions of language. Seeing pictures, saying words, and placing the words in sequence gives students the opportunity to program themselves.

- Keep charts in the room that add images to abstract concepts or to agreement problems. Make one chart masculine and one feminine to illustrate contractions:

  le BIJOU   la
  à + le = au   à + la = à la

- Use color coding to emphasize relationships, such as subject and verb endings. Use as many modalities as possible at the same time. Have students spell aloud as they print (not write), print on their desks with their fingers, touch objects or pictures and then say words or sentences, and gesture or model an activity to indicate the meaning of a verb or sentence. Cut sentences apart and have students reassemble them; have cards with subjects, verb stems, and endings accessible for practice.
- Physical activity does not always need to involve whole body movement. In a Gouin series (I get up, I go to the door, I open the door, I go out, I close the door, etc.), while one student acts out the directions, the others can indicate the actions with hand movements.
- Build in a lot of repetition. Review what has been presented, and not only at the beginning of the period. At the end of the lesson, review what is new but also link it to what has been learned. Have several students verbalize what they have learned since entering the classroom.
- Provide palatable repetition in the form of puzzles and games. "Fun and games" and serious language study are not diametrically opposed. They can and should be synonymous.

Alter the method of presentation. When presenting more than one oral exercise or written practice sheet on the same concept, alter their look and form. The focus of the lesson may be the same, the content or topic might be a repetition, but attack it from a different angle, using different visuals, an alternative format, a game, or a contest. For example, to reinforce numbers, use lists of scores from the sports section of the newspaper. Select teams or players by chance and predict their progress, chart the accuracy of the predictions, and so forth.

Use small-increment learning. Present material in small chunks, always linking it to material already learned and reviewing it regularly. Give vocabulary and spelling quizzes with a very short list of words—only five or six. Everything is eventually covered, but not in one exam. Students will thus have more time to study each of the words tested. If there is homework, try to have it take no more than ten to fifteen minutes to complete. Small slices are much more likely to be digested.

Provide immediate reinforcement.
- Devise practice sheets that students can self-correct. A portion of the page folds back to reveal the answers.
- In oral work, have students work in small groups of two or three, so that answers are immediately available.

Use manipulatives. Small cardboard shapes with holes punched around the edges and with words on one side and pictures or words on the other can be used for work in the classroom or can be taken home for practice. Next to each hole (which is just large enough to accommodate the top of a pencil) on the front of the card is a question, a word, or a picture. On the back of the card next to each hole is the corresponding answer to the question, the word in English, or the word in the target language that matches to the picture. The student pushes the pencil through the hole on his or her side of the card and gives the answer or identifies the word or picture. The person on the other side, seeing the tip of the pencil, can determine what the first student is looking at and can also note if the correct response has been given.

Simplify and support.
- Avoid directions that require multiple steps. Always provide a number of examples. Print directions at the top of worksheets but do not read them. Have the students read the directions to themselves and then describe what they are to do. If further direction is required, explain several items, using different vocabulary, if possible. Have several students repeat the directions.
- Give study sheets that point out relationships or the similarities and differences in words.
- Write all of the words that have the same ending sound as a model word, such as "flag." Help students create memory hooks for themselves.
- If exams or quizzes are given, give pretests so that students will be familiar with the form and directions of the actual exam as well as with the content to be covered. No surprises.

Work on organizational skills. Require even younger students to have a folder or notebook exclusively for foreign language in which they keep picture sheets, games, worksheets, and other materials distributed in class. This folder should be kept constantly up to date. For older students, staple a sheet inside the folder on which the students keep a list of materials to be kept in the folder, short- and long-term assignments, and projects with dates of completion.

The teacher should maintain a handout or homework folder in each classroom. A copy of everything that is distributed to students should be included, labeled "file copy." If a game, reference, or homework paper is lost or mangled, a student may make a copy. Sheets for absentees can be kept in the folder. Everyone knows how to keep current and can be held responsible for doing so.

Set Flexible Expectations
- Think in terms of 70 to 80 percent. Everyone needs to get the basic 70 to 80 percent of what is being taught. The remaining 20 to 30 percent is designed for students who need an extra challenge, but it is not critical to understanding the material that will be presented next.
- On quizzes or worksheets, include five items, generally more difficult, for extra credit.
- In games, let students use a clue card, if they wish. The point of games is to practice and learn. If access to the answers helps some students to achieve those goals, why not allow it?
- Utilize exercises and tests of recognition, matching, and so forth. Having to cope with spelling may be one of the most discouraging and defeating elements in foreign language study for students with learning problems, and, in fact, for many students who are average or above. In grading written work, grades for spelling should be separate from those for grammar or accuracy of response. Having the correct ending on a verb is grammar; spelling the word *desk* is not.

Accept student limitations and provide success for everyone at some level. Teachers can create success. Most teachers start a lesson with a few review items, a good technique for all students, but especially beneficial for students with problems. If students are fed items that the teacher knows they can easily answer, they start the day on a positive note, ready to do well.

We all know that one of the greatest motivations to succeed is success itself. Providing opportunities for ALL students to succeed at their own level creates a situation in which everyone wins. As teachers, we are responsible for making it happen.

We Can Teach All Students: **FLES*** Students Rarely Fail!

Gladys C. Lipton
University of Maryland, Baltimore County
Baltimore, Maryland

More frequently than ever, **FLES*** teachers are being asked to include *all* students in their classes. In response to the question "Can they all learn?" most **FLES*** teachers reply *"Mais certainement!"*

This is not to say that it is not challenging to teach and reach all students, but one can readily report that **FLES*** students rarely fail. No matter what their reading scores are, no matter how much difficulty they may be having in mathematics or social studies, no matter if they are at risk or in special education classes, no matter how much they are disaffected with school in general, *FLES* students rarely fail!*

TEACHERS ARE SUCCESSFUL WITH ALL FLES* STUDENTS WHEN THEY PLAN LESSONS AROUND CHILDREN'S INTERESTS AND THEIR NATIVE LANGUAGE KID TALK (N.L.K.T.)

When themes and conversations are about what children usually discuss in their everyday lives, they are more apt to want to try the content in French. Which topics interest them? It varies from year to year, but subjects such as sports and sports figures, films such as *Alladin* and *The Lion King*, television programs such as *The Simpsons* or any of the cartoons readily capture children's attention.

CHILDREN LEARN THROUGH THEIR MUSCLES AS WELL AS THEIR MINDS!

We often forget that children learn many things better when they utilize a number of modalities of learning, such as kinesthetic, physical motion;

the four skills of listening, speaking, reading and writing; and active student involvement. The Total Physical Response (TPR) approach is most helpful in reaching all students in that the physical activity helps to reinforce the cognitive activity. Sometimes, asking students to write a word in the air or on their desks with their finger helps in retention. Holding a puppet is very useful, particularly with shy or reluctant speakers. It does not need to be a very sophisticated puppet . . . it can be a dragon puppet made quickly by folding a sheet of paper in three parts, and then folding in four parts. In the child's mind, it is the puppet speaking in French! Team relay games are also very effective in review and reinforcement of content.

Challenging children's minds is an effective way to reach all students.

Too often, children feel that learning is by rote, that they are not learning how to solve real problems or deal with real situations. Foreign languages can be taught by creating challenging situations or puzzles or riddles that are not difficult to solve. Sometimes it is an information gap, where students must do research in order to solve the puzzle. When they get really good at solutions, they need to be challenged to create some of the puzzles and riddles themselves for other children to solve.

The study of a foreign language at the FLES* level needs to be related to the rest of the curriculum through interdisciplinary activities.

The study of French, for example, is most effective when it is related to other aspects of elementary school learning. This is not to say that teachers of French teach mathematics or science in French (except in Immersion); it means that teachers of French "reach out" to include some aspects of mathematics or science or geography. For example, if children are asked to keep ongoing records of the temperature in Paris and the temperature in their hometown, and are then asked to use arithmetic to compare those temperatures on any given date, it is a meaningful activity in French and it also reinforces some of the content of other curriculum areas. If students are asked to create a dual graph of the temperature fluctuations, that too is an effective learning experience. If students learn about holidays celebrated around the world by French-speaking people and learn some of their songs, that is "reaching out" to music, geography, and social studies. There are many opportunities like this in the elementary school curriculum.

THERE ARE MANY WAYS TO REINFORCE, TO REENTER, AND TO REVIEW; NOTHING IS ASSUMED TO BE LEARNED THE FIRST TIME, WITHOUT COMING BACK FOR EXPANSION AND FOR UTILIZATION IN DIFFERENT CONTEXTS.

It is important in the initial presentation to have many choral repetitions, group repetitions, all girls and then all boys repetitions, children wearing blue repetitions, children having a birthday in March repetitions, and so on. A few days later, there needs to be further repetition with different types of visuals. A few days later, there needs to be reinforcement of weather vocabulary, for example, with clothing and colors and sizes. A few weeks later, weather vocabulary can be combined with shopping and sports events. In this way, there are many opportunities for all children to internalize the concepts.

THERE IS A GROWING BODY OF RESEARCH THAT TELLS US THAT CHILDREN LEARN WELL WHEN THEY ARE WORKING WITH THEIR PEERS.

The cooperative learning phenomenon has grown because researchers have found that while children enjoy studying with their peers, they also learn effectively, especially when the teacher has facilitated the cooperative learning opportunity. The primary requisite is that there be an information gap or problem for the group to solve. Then students of many different abilities work together to achieve a group solution. They are not only working on a problem, but they are also learning how to respect the rights and the abilities of others. Within the group, individual children accomplish different things: Some are greatly challenged and learn very sophisticated concepts; others ask many questions; others learn the vocabulary associated with the concepts; still others learn a very limited amount of vocabulary, but earn acceptance by the group and successfully fulfill their responsibility to the group.

THERE ARE A NUMBER OF SPECIFIC STRATEGIES FOR REACHING ALL STUDENTS.

- Make certain that instructions are clear, understandable, and easy to follow.
- Use a game format for reinforcement of language learning.
- Try to get one response from each and every student during each class session. Be sure to use appropriate praise and encouragement!

- Pay special attention to difficult words. Discuss the configuration of the word; have the children draw boxes for the number of letters in the word, and then have them fill in the boxes with the correct letters.
- Be sure to use paired (or partner) practice to capitalize on pupil-to-pupil help.
- Use the "teacher has a sore throat" technique. You will be surprised at the ways in which students will use the foreign language in their desire to be of assistance.

Mon Parcours: Letting Them Tell Their Story

Lena L. Lucietto
Isidore Newman School
New Orleans, Louisiana

INTRODUCTION

The humanistic literature of the 1960s and 1970s (Combs 1973; Moskowitz 1978; Rogers 1961) offers rationales and strategies that may be helpful to teachers of today who, along with current researchers and educators (Brunschwig 1994; Dornyei 1994; Oxford 1994; Purcell 1993), share renewed concern for questions of classroom motivation and the need to reach students representing a wide variety of learning styles.

Moskowitz, for example, writes in the introduction to her book, *Caring and Sharing in the Foreign Language Classroom* (1978, 2):

> When given the opportunity to talk about themselves in personally relevant ways, students tend to become much more motivated. The result is that they want to be able to express their feelings and ideas more in the target language. They want to communicate. When this happens, growth becomes a reciprocal process: enhancing personal growth enhances growth in the foreign language.

Moskowitz (1978, 15–16) further posits that humanistic education personalizes the foreign language content to a deeper level of exploration:

> It goes far beyond studying a unit dealing with the family or the house and then asking such questions as "How many brothers and sisters do you have?" or "What is the furniture in your bedroom?" Affective questions dealing with these same themes might be: "How does it feel to be the oldest (youngest, middle) child?" "What advantages and disadvantages are there?" "What special object do you display in your room that gives you pleasant memories?" "What does it mean to you?" "What do you think of when you look at it?"

Current writers offer teachers a wide range of activities to motivate their students and to bring about livelier classrooms and more affective as well as effective learning. These activities encourage engagement on the part of students by focusing on the students themselves and by encouraging interaction among them. For example, Brunschwig (1994, 912–913) suggests whole-class activities that promote interpersonal sharing as well as intense oral practice in a relaxed classroom, and Purcell (1993, 912–918) considers a variety of role-play activities to motivate students and to augment verbal skills and self-esteem. Such activities, if processed appropriately, offer deeper and more personalized learning, and, by extension, more enjoyable contact with the target language.

The humanistic activity offered here is inspired by "My Life Line," a self-awareness unit from *Project Charlie* (1983, 109–110). It has been adapted for use in French classes[1] and has been used successfully in a number of French classes of different levels[2] and with students of varying learning styles. In order to benefit from this activity, students need to have some familiarity with expressing themselves in the past. Also, the last point of the *parcours* calls for students to peer into their crystal balls and say what they would like to be doing in the future.

MON PARCOURS

Purpose: The purpose of this humanistic exercise is to develop an appreciation of our uniqueness as individuals. The exercise allows us to explore the significant events of our lives and to see how they have helped to shape the persons we are today.

Method: Set the mood for a look into the past by asking students to close their eyes and put their heads down on their desks. Ask them to imagine that they are traveling all the way back in time, back to when they were just little babies. Ask the following questions, pausing frequently to allow students the time for reflection:

- What is your first memory?
- Travel on to your first day of school. What was it like?
- Can you remember a time when you got into trouble as a child?
- Now travel on into the middle school. Is there something you've done that you are really proud of?
- Is there a person you remember that you really like? Why?
- Is there a time you remember being sad and lonely?
- Up until now, what have been your high and low spots?
- What has been your high point this year?
- What has been your low point?
- Open your eyes and list the events you remembered.
- Would someone care to share some of his or her memories?

Allow the students time to share with each other. This will encourage interesting ideas for the *parcours*.

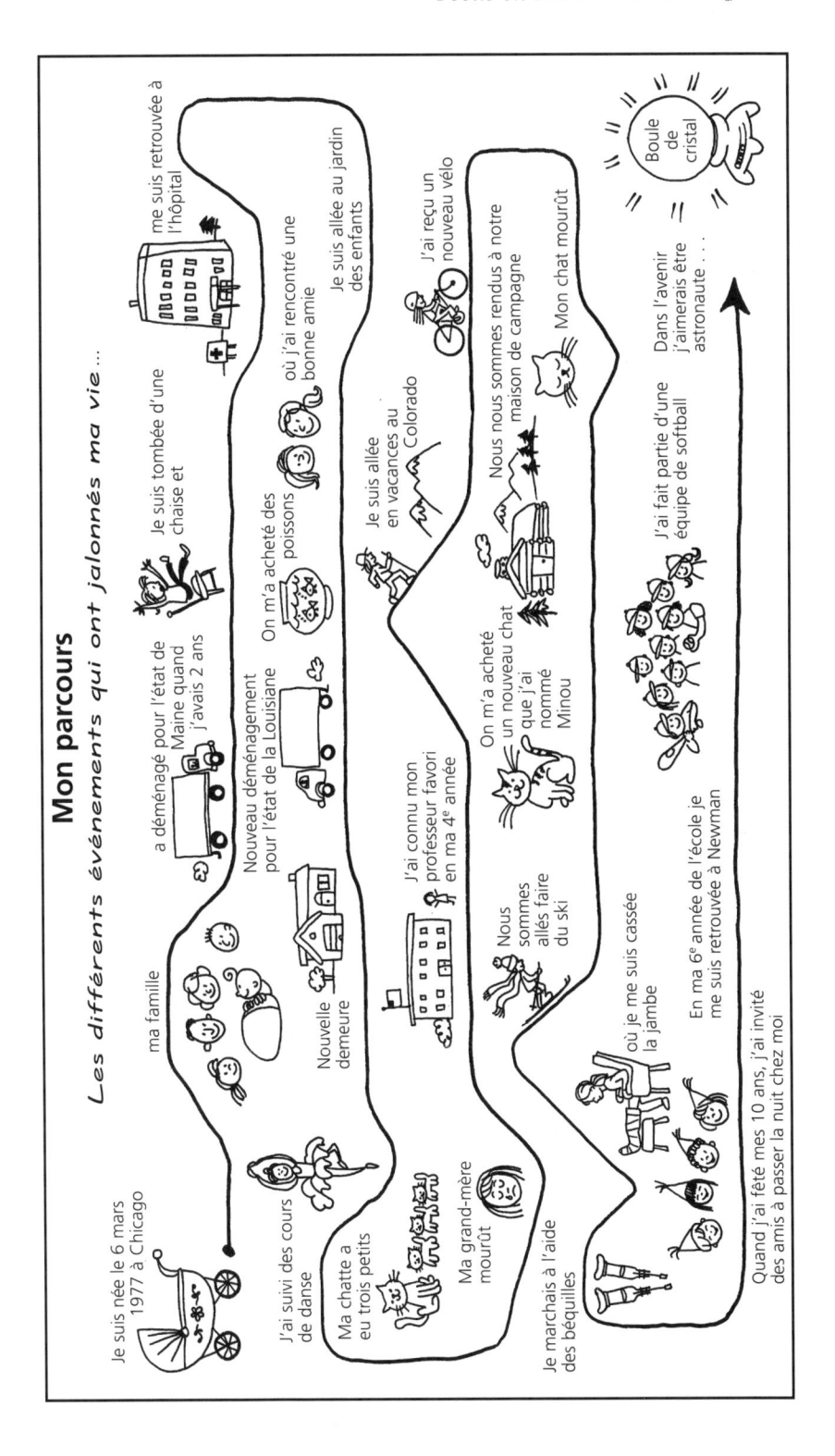

Mon parcours

Les différents événements qui ont jalonnés ma vie...

- Je suis née le 6 mars 1977 à Chicago
- ma famille
- a déménagé pour l'état de Maine quand j'avais 2 ans
- Je suis tombée d'une chaise et me suis retrouvée à l'hôpital
- J'ai suivi des cours de danse
- Nouveau déménagement pour l'état de la Louisiane
- Nouvelle demeure
- On m'a acheté des poissons
- où j'ai rencontré une bonne amie
- Je suis allée au jardin des enfants
- Ma chatte a eu trois petits
- J'ai connu mon professeur favori en ma 4e année
- Je suis allée en vacances au Colorado
- J'ai reçu un nouveau vélo
- Ma grand-mère mourût
- Nous sommes allés faire du ski
- On m'a acheté un nouveau chat que j'ai nommé Minou
- Nous nous sommes rendus à notre maison de campagne
- Mon chat mourût
- Je marchais à l'aide des béquilles
- où je me suis cassée la jambe
- J'ai fait partie d'une équipe de softball
- Dans l'avenir j'aimerais être astronaute...
- Quand j'ai fêté mes 10 ans, j'ai invité des amis à passer la nuit chez moi
- En ma 6e année de l'école je me suis retrouvée à Newman
- Boule de cristal

The *Mon parcours* Activity: Give each student a manila folder[3]. Instruct the students to use markers or crayons to draw the lifeline and, along it, pictures of the important memories they have of their life from birth to the present grade. This will be on a continuous line going back and forth across the inside of the folder. Brainstorm things that they could include: moving, travels, friendships, failures, successes, teams, pets, births, birthdays, deaths, broken bones, favorite toys, and joyful events.

Upon completion, students may divide into small groups and share their Parcours within their group. You may point out similarities or differences. Ask: "Why do we remember certain events in our lives? What did you get out of this activity?"

Follow-up Activity: Have each student draw a crystal ball at the end of his or her parcours. Ask the students to draw a picture in the ball of what they would like to be when they are grown-ups. They might use the construction *J'aimerais être* with the name of a profession.

REFERENCES

Brunschwig, Karen. 1994. "Making Connections with Whole-Class Interaction Activities." *Hispania* 77, 1: 138–140.

Combs, Arthur W. 1973. "The Human Side of Learning." *The National Elementary Principal* 52, 1: 42.

Dornyei, Zoltan. 1994. "Motivation and Motivating in the Foreign Language Classroom." *The Modern Language Journal* 78, 3: 273–284.

———. 1994. "Understanding L2 Motivation: On with the Challenge." *The Modern Language Review* 78, 4: 515–523.

Moskowitz, Gertrude. 1978. *Caring and Sharing in the Foreign Language Class. A Sourcebook on Humanistic Techniques.* Rowley, MA: Newbury House.

Oxford, Rebecca. 1994. "Where Are We Regarding Language Learning Motivation?" *The Modern Language Journal* 78, 4: 512–514.

Project Charlie: Chemical Abuse Resolution Lies in Education. Rev. ed. 1983. Edina, MN: A Program of Storefront/Youth Action.

Purcell, John M. 1993. "Livelier **FLES*** Lessons through Role-Play." *Hispania* 76, 4: 912–918.

Rogers, Carl R. 1961. *On Becoming a Person.* Boston: Houghton Mifflin.

---

[1] A sample of *Mon parcours*, the French adaptation of "My Life Line," may be found on p. 75.
[2] This activity may be adapted to other languages and, with modification, may be used with very young students.
[3] The use of manila folders is suggested because they may be easily filled. However, a poster board or a large piece of construction paper may be substituted for the folder.

Reaching Them All via Multiple Intelligences: Floor Mapping

Patricia R. Duggar
Paul Breaux Middle School
Lafayette, Louisiana

Howard Gardner and other researchers have determined that there are multiple ways of learning. The old "tabula rasa" theory of Descartes is no longer valid. Once we realize that our students learn in different fashions, it behooves us as teachers to present material in different fashions to enhance this learning. Thanks to input from several sources, which I shall note, I have developed activities for active learners.

The first influence was Maureen Regan-Baker from the laboratory school at SUNY-Plattsburgh, who presented activities for cultural learning at the ACTFL meeting in Chicago in 1991. Included in her presentation was a video showing her young students and her classroom, which incorporated a map of Paris on the floor. The second influence was a workbook published by the state of Texas with an article on using a sheet to illustrate a house. My principal would not approve of my painting Paris on the floor of my classroom. However, I had sheets! And I could draw a straight line with a yardstick! I embarked on creating a series of floor maps on sheets. The first was a house.

Dr. Robert Lafayette at Louisiana State University made clear to us in his culture course that illustrations of foreign life needed to be authentic. Therefore, I drew my house as a French house, with an orange roof resembling the tiles used in many parts of France. There is a *cave* (basement) for the storage of wine, a garage, a *grenier* (attic), a kitchen, a dining room, a living room, and two bedrooms. There is also a separate toilet and a bathroom with only a tub and a sink.

My sixth graders learn the rooms of the house and the differences one would find in a French lodging. They learn to ask for the *toilette*, not the bathroom. This is an important cultural difference. The words *restroom* and *bathroom* are our euphemisms for the toilet and will not gain entrance to the desired facility in France. It is permissible to mention the toilet in France. Let's teach students to do so.

The floor map information is presented orally and visually. This helps those who learn in an auditory manner as well as those who learn visually. A list of rooms is also provided on a transparency for everyone to copy. For those who organize with lists, this activity is most helpful. Then we walk around the classroom and the house. The students are asked one by one to point out and name the various rooms of the house. Next they are asked to place labels, which have the correct room names, on the correct rooms. This helps kinesthetic learners to absorb the information required of them. At this point, each student is required to draw my house exactly as it is on the floor map and then to draw their own dream house.

Once the students know the names of the rooms, they are asked to brainstorm items of furniture to put into each room. I create a list on the blackboard and the students copy the list. Then they are asked to cut out or illustrate furnishings or appliances for each room. I provide a list of typical items, such as the toaster, the sink, the bed, and so forth, if these have not come out during the brainstorming. The students are learning many vocabulary items of their choice as they do this part of the house-learning project. In 1989, Wilga Rivers stressed to us in her address at the national meeting of the American Association of Teachers of French in Paris that each person has a set of individual vocabulary items that he or she regularly uses in addition to any required base vocabulary. By allowing each student to build his or her own choice of vocabulary for the house in addition to learning some basic words, we are providing for individual preferences and differences in foreign language learning.

So far in the learning unit on the house, we have visualized the main object, the house and its rooms, and written the words. We then think through which items should be in a typical house and create a word bank from the children's ideas. Next, the students create on paper the objects to match the list. Then for those who only learn well by doing, we place the objects in the rooms. Each child must get up and move, naming the room and the object as he or she is placing it. My sixth-grade students are eager and willing to move around the room and show off their knowledge. It is so simple to place objects on a floor map that this activity lowers the shield of fear that can entrap the foreign language learner at any level. The students are comfortable with this learning activity. They are showing off their drawing skills and their creative talents in choosing furnishings for the house and, at the same time, enjoying French class.

Once students have learned the vocabulary, they take two tests to prove their knowledge. The first is to label the rooms and their contents. Each student is called up to the front of the room. He or she is handed four furniture or room cards at random. The student must then place the cards and call out the name of the room and the items placed on the floor map. Points are assigned for each placement and a grade is determined for each student.

The second test is a written test. To study for this test, the students refer to their individual copies of the floor map. The test consists of a blank drawing of the house with a word bank at the top of the house and lines for writing in each room. The students label the house, filling in the necessary room names and two items of furnishings. No item may be repeated at any point during the activity, so no one can fill in more than one bed or table in the house. This test is worth 100 points and has met with tremendous success. Students may add two items of their choice to make up for any items they are afraid they missed. Scores ranged this year from 85 to 110. Of sixty-five scores, there were only five in the 80s. At least twenty students scored 100 or better. During the presentation of material to be learned, there was a conscious effort on my part to incorporate multiple intelligence learning. I included written, oral, auditory, kinesthetic, and artistic activities in my presentations, practice efforts, and testing. Success was the direct result of these efforts.

I have made floor maps for several other areas of learning. One is a village that I use with the eighth graders learning the verbs conjugated with *être* in the *passé composé*. Another floor map is of Paris. This I use to teach my sixth graders the major monuments in Paris. I have used several testing methods. There is always a kinesthetic test in which each student answers my questions regarding map directions, left bank, right bank, and major monuments. Each must show and state where a specific monument is located on the floor map. The best written test seems to be one that requires students to locate the monuments in the *arrondissements*. This accomplishes the learning of roman numerals as well as the sites of the major monuments in Paris. I provide a word bank of monuments and a map with the monuments whited out. The word bank has proved to be necessary on the test. I found that forcing students to know the spelling of twenty-four monuments and squares as well as their individual locations proved to be too difficult for beginning learners.

As part of the preparation for this learning unit, we look at a video in French, and I narrate my personal slides of Paris. The students each receive a copy of a map of Paris and a metro map. I have carried home many free maps from my trips to Paris and I photocopy the best of them for student use. My test maps are now laminated for yearly use. This is my fourth year of using both the house and the Paris floor maps in my classes.

At the end of the eighth-grade French class, students are required to sit for a credit exam. A passing score will earn them one Carnegie unit in French to be applied toward high school graduation. We teach with the Valette and Valette book. The test involves an OPI worth 10 points, a listening comprehension test on tape worth 25 points, and a written multiple-choice test for the balance of the 100-point total. The students are expected to be conversant regarding house vocabulary, major monuments in Paris, and so forth. During our oral conversational practices last year in class, I discovered that the students whom I had taught in the sixth grade were able to converse in all of these areas. Those whom I had not taught could not create conversation because they knew nothing about the subject being discussed. We backtracked, using my floor maps to teach them what the other students knew, and they caught up without difficulty.

In summary, as we teachers become aware of new research in learning, we need to tailor our presentations to meet the needs of our students. The use of floor maps allows for kinesthetic learning coupled with oral and visual learning. The layering of methods of presentation enables a maximum number of students to benefit from your teaching efforts. Try a floor map!

PART 3

Focus on **FLES*** Methodology

Reading in Second Language Acquisition

Virginia L. Gramer
Hinsdale Elementary Schools
Hinsdale, Illinois

For students, seeing in print what they have been saying and hearing, verbalizing the print, and being able to extract meaning from print, validate, for them, the authenticity of their language experience. Reading, introduced at the appropriate developmental level and at the proper stage of second language development, can reinforce students' oral skills. Those who have had experience in teaching both first and second language reading find that most of the questions that elementary-school foreign language teachers have fall into the following categories.

1. How are first and second language reading skills related?
2. When should reading be introduced?
3. What process should be used to teach reading?

Before examining these topics, it needs to be stated that there are certain givens:

- Reading in the second language in early Immersion classes is equivalent to first language reading.
- In this paper, we are considering students in second language reading who do not have severe reading dysfunction in first language reading.
- Reading is a transferable skill.

First and Second Language Reading

There is such a mass of information on first language reading that it is tempting to transfer those facts and theories to reading in the second language. In fact, in much of the literature on elementary foreign language, reading in the second language is related directly to first language reading. Though it is wise to be very knowledgeable about what is current in first language acquisition, there are some very significant caveats about making comparisons. Acquisition of first and second language reading skills are very different in the:

1. Age and developmental level of the students when reading is introduced
2. Oral language skills possessed by the child when reading is introduced
3. Time on task (exposure to second language is basically within the second language class or within the school setting)
4. Availability of second language print materials outside of the foreign language class
5. Classes outside of the foreign language period that utilize and upgrade the language reading skills (social studies, science, language arts, etc.)

The average five- or six-year-old has a vocabulary of approximately 6,000 words in his or her first language, has mastered all of the tenses, and uses complicated sentence patterns by the time first language reading is formally introduced. Children in elementary foreign language classes are *not* fluent in the foreign language, and are *not* in control of a vast quantity of language. They are neophytes in second language oral skills and yet are at an age (and of a disposition) when reading is very important and very much emphasized in school. They may want to read in the second language, but their listening and speaking abilities do not precede by years and a high degree of skill their need to read. Their second language reading skills are not reinforced constantly outside of the foreign language class as they are in their first language. Students are not surrounded both in school and out by appropriate print materials as they are in their first language. The language environment and the talents of the students are quite different in almost every circumstance from those that are present in first language reading acquisition. We may try some of the techniques used in first language reading, but all of the techniques, rules, and research in first language reading acquisition will not be totally applicable to reading in elementary foreign language classes.

WHEN TO READ

It seems that the optimum age to introduce reading has been a subject of discussion since someone first took rock in hand at Lascaux. Suffice it to say that the vast quantity of research done on reading in first language acquisition revolves around the concept of readiness. If average children have the maturation factors necessary, they will read—do not try to stop them. If they are not ready, they will stop themselves.

First Language Reading Skills

There are several components to the timing of the introduction of reading—the students' listening and speaking experience in the second language and the degree of their reading proficiency in the first language. Exclusive of early Immersion programs, most elementary school foreign language programs do not formally teach reading in the second language before or simultaneously with reading in the first language. However, those who deal with primary students agree that many young elementary foreign language students, without being exposed to formal instruction, naturally relate to the printed version of the content of their listening and speaking vocabularies. From a purely practical standpoint, though, most elementary foreign language teachers would be loathe to teach phonics in a foreign language at the same time that the classroom teacher was working on phonics in English.

Students' Foreign Language Experience

Years ago those who espoused the ALM method proposed a lag of months and sometimes years between the listening/speaking phase of foreign language acquisition and the introduction of reading. In our youthful enthusiasm, many of us who adhered faithfully to those tenets found that we were frustrating young talented readers who longed to transfer their skills to the second language. The criteria for the timing of the introduction of second language reading should be the students' command and understanding of the material to be read and their skills in speaking, *not* some arbitrary length of time.

Surviving in a Hostile World

Prevention is preferable to correction. We all develop techniques that prevent inaccuracies in pronunciation in the prereading phase. It seems that fear of pronunciation deviation is the reason most cited for postponing the introduction of reading. The concern is valid. If unguided, premature reading can lead to gross inaccuracies in pronunciation. This occurs most often in labeling objects before the word is familiar enough aurally. However, postponing reading too long also causes trouble.

Student Needs

Children in the upper primary grades already have a notion of the power of reading. They have developed reading skills that they are anxious to apply, and they have even learned to take notes to shore up aural input. One elementary school French teacher found a dictionary of "bootlegged French," written in an approximation of English phonetics, authored by a small girl:

bowjr—hello

kskusay—what is that

The child wanted to be able to remember what she'd been introduced to in French class so she could teach it to her baby brother. Her teacher had difficulty in identifying some of the words, but when the child was asked to read her semi-Berlitz version, she did so flawlessly. She was obviously ready and anxious to read. Postponing reading, in her case, resulted in negative reinforcement.

The Process of Teaching Reading

Reading: Sound and Meaning

It is possible to learn to read a language without being able to communicate verbally in that language. Doctoral candidates are witness to that process. It is also possible to teach children to read words that they do not command orally. To a degree, this is acceptable because it is a documented means of acquiring vocabulary. Seeding unknown words in sentences that contain familiar vocabulary in order to extract meaning from context encourages a desirable skill. However, for beginning readers who are only building the raw material of that context, precognition and verbalization are advantageous.

Interference from the First Language: Purely Personal Rules

First reading experiences need to be given careful consideration and need to be carefully orchestrated. Do not let students start visualizing the target language using English phonetics. At any grade level, from the beginning, write words on the chalkboard, at least for a few minutes, while modeling them, and, if that is not the time you choose to teach them as reading vocabulary, erase them. Doing this consistently helps students to realize that words in the second language are not going to look like English. This is not the same as labeling objects around the classroom and leaving them for students to look at before they are very familiar with them aurally. Labeling (especially in French) is hazardous, unless the word or phrase has been thoroughly planted in students' listening/speaking vocabulary. Children who read well in English, and even those who do not, tend automatically to slip into using English phonetics unless a word is immediately recognizable.

Reader-Listener, Listener-Reader

Everyone in first language teaching endorses reading aloud to children. Reading aloud to elementary foreign language students, from their initial exposure to the target language, from day one in the foreign language class, is just as valid. To get the maximum benefits, students must be interested and involved. When instruction in reading is to begin, it is logical to read aloud to students, this time, with the script before them. It is very effective to repeat together the songs and rhymes that students already know, now with the printed version in their hands. These first reading experiences will be like those of young children when they "read" aloud the nursery rhymes that they have memorized—success-oriented and with few pronunciation errors.

After students have had some practice with attaching words to nouns or texts that are very familiar aurally, the elementary foreign language teacher may use a commercial or teacher-made "big book" or prepare a very simple text on overhead transparencies with not much print and large pictures. The teacher first reads the story to the students while they look at the print. As the story is read again, the teacher hesitates at some words, which the class reads together. Then whole sentences from the story are cut apart from the overhead or printed separately on paper strips. On a pocket chart or on the overhead, students place the sentences to construct the story. This is more effective if done as a whole-class exercise, with students suggesting the order of the sentences. Students may then copy the story on their papers and reread it a line at a time.

This process fairly well eliminates the danger of students applying English phonetics. The whole procedure may be repeated again with different vocabulary inserted in the now familiar sentences. Obviously the technique needs to be tailored to the age of the students. Pocket charts may generally not be appropriate for the middle school student.

Phonics

Students, even young ones, need to be able to pronounce words on their own without the constant need for a model. They need some word attack skills to figure out both pronunciation and meaning.

As key words, those that will serve as models for phonetic elements, it is effective to start with controlled sight words, those that the students have learned as whole units. Nouns that can be pictured (*douze, vier, señora*, etc.) can be used to illustrate the sound made by the underlined letters. Each student keeps a sheet with those pictures in his or her folder to help identify troublesome phonetic elements. When students have trouble verbalizing a word, they remind themselves of the key word that illustrates the sound.

Reading Aloud

Having students reading aloud has several purposes:

1. To check their ability to verbalize from the printed word
2. To give other students the chance to hear and see the words at the same time with no pressure to perform
3. To motivate

Those who have taught elementary school children know from the sea of hands raised when the opportunity to read aloud is presented that such a social grace is second only to the privilege of taking a note to the office.

The benefits that accrue to the reader are not the same as those the listener enjoys. It is generally accepted that reading aloud by the individual student has little relationship to that student's comprehension of what he or she has read, but it does demonstrate, as little else can, his or her progress or problems in verbalizing print. The audience has the opportunity to listen critically, if the teacher has posed an element that they need to identify, or just to listen as practice before their turn to perform. It has always been accepted that teachers reading to children has multiple benefits, as does students reading to one another.

In Summary

1. Build a passive and an active listening and speaking vocabulary in the target language.
2. Transfer the vocabulary gradually to print.
   - Amass a set of sight words and phrases (learned as whole units).
   - Combine and recombine those words and phrases, using different contexts.
   - Utilize sight words to build basic word attack skills (phonics, words in context, etc.).
   - Weave new words into familiar patterns, attach the unknown to the known, make linkages and associations, contrast, compare, match.

Bridging the Gap in **FLES***: Suggestions for the Transition to the Written Word

Juliette Eastwick

and

Elizabeth Tomlinson
Bryn Mawr School
Baltimore, Maryland

One of the problems facing **FLES*** teachers is at what point in the program to introduce reading and writing and what methods are most effective for bridging the gap between the oral song and game activities of early foreign language classes and the reading and writing activities that are of such interest to many students. In planning a program, we need to take advantage of the unique ways in which an elementary school child learns language. We need to recognize that a foreign language program for this age child must not be a watered-down version of a middle or upper school program.

We believe that a foreign language program should follow as closely as possible the ways in which a child learns his or her native language. If we look at how our own children learn English, a few key points are evident:

- Children learn to speak from adults they love and trust. We often read of children whose poor languages skills are attributed to neglect when they were infants and toddlers.
- Children learn through play and repetition, and these activities are certainly the backbone of the **FLES*** class. Children understand a great deal more than they can say.
- Children make mistakes that are corrected gently. Often, the correction is so subtle that it does not appear to be a correction at all. The child says, "Look what my grandma 'brang' me from New York," and the adult responds, "Your grandma brought you that nice teddy bear?" Adults praise and reward the young child for his or her ability

to communicate rather than for his or her correct grammar. Our genuine joy and excitement in understanding the young child encourages him or her to communicate further.

- There is always a discrepancy between the vocabulary a young child uses and the vocabulary he or she understands. Later this discrepancy will be between the book the beginning reader can read alone and the book he or she enjoys having read to him or her, and between the sentence the child can write and the sentence the child can read.

At the Bryn Mawr Lower School, we have an intensive four-day-a-week French program that begins in kindergarten. Our classes meet for thirty minutes in kindergarten and first and second grade, and for forty minutes in third, fourth, and fifth grade. The early years of our program are strictly oral and rely heavily on toys, games, and songs. We have a large collection of puppets, plastic fruits and vegetables, dolls, and felt board scenes. We want our students to have a strong background in spoken language before they being to tackle the written word.

After the first years of a strictly oral program, we are faced with the problem of introducing a more definite sense of language structure into the classroom. The children often freely use nouns correctly in independent speech, and they may also use some very basic pattern sentences (It's a ball. The cat is grey. I would like . . .), but how does one introduce more variety into the child's working vocabulary?

Our "Magic Word Stories" seem to meet the need to add more complex patterns to the children's speech and, at the same time, provide an entertaining and exciting "shot in the arm" to our program. We introduce these stories at the second-grade level, thus after one or two years of French. This type of story could easily appear earlier in a program dealing with older students. The "Magic Word Story" is presented to the class by the teacher, who illustrates it in cartoon form on the blackboard. No written words are used. A fine arts degree is not required, and the children seem to enjoy our stick figures and somewhat primitive style. Each story is based on the vocabulary unit being taught.

In the fall, our first story always involves a trip to the stationery store for school supplies: *"Je vais à la papeterie. J'achète un crayon, une règle, une gomme. Je paie à la caisse."* (I go to the stationery store. I buy a pencil, a ruler, an eraser. I pay at the check-out counter.) We repeat the story several times, and soon the children are able to recite it easily with the aid of the cartoon prompts. After giving many students the opportunity to present the story, one child is selected to "own" the story. This child is given a magic word, in this case, *crayon*. Every time the teacher says *crayon*, the child may pop up and recite the story. Of course, we accidentally on purpose mention magic words several times, but indeed we also are occasionally caught by surprise when we inadvertently talk about pencils. After several weeks, every student has a magic word, and classes are very lively indeed. Students stop us in the cafeteria to try to trick us into mentioning their magic words, and French spills out onto the playground and into the halls of the school. The stories allow us to cover a wide range of vocabulary from the weather to shopping to foods, furniture, and clothing. We usually try to invent some very simple stories for the more hesitant children in the class and may even allow a very shy child to share a story with a friend. Since the stories take several weeks to distribute, we offer whole-class stories to make every one feel involved and to soothe the feelings of those who must wait to have a magic word.

The stories lend themselves to wonderful games. We play "You Took the Words Right out of My Mouth." This is a popular game in which students try to steal each other's stories. If they can recite someone else's story without an error, they may "own" the story for the duration of a class. It is always important to allow time for the rightful owner to retrieve his or her story before the bell rings! This type of game ensures that the students learn all the stories.

Another popular variation on the "Magic Word Story" is called "Silly Stories." Children may change the stories by substituting words they know from other stories and vocabulary units. Thus a child may suggest, *"Je vais au zoo. J'achète un éléphant, un ours, un tigre. Je paie à la caisse."* (I go to the zoo. I buy an elephant, a bear, a tiger. I pay at the check-out counter.) Of course, a young child may make some grammar mistakes (*à la zoo*, for example), but these are easily and unobtrusively corrected when the teacher repeats the story to the class. This game allows the children some independence in using the vocabulary they have acquired. It also appeals to their sense of fun. One of our stories lends itself to classroom drama. The original story is *"Nous sommes en automne. Les feuilles tombent. Les feuilles sont rouges, jaunes et orange."* (It is autumn. The leaves are falling. The leaves are red, yellow, and orange.) Students love to put themselves in the picture: "Nous sommes en automne. Suzy tombe. Suzy dit, 'Maman! Maman!'" This of course is accompanied by pratfalls and mock tears and lots of giggles.

As a final project for our "Magic Word Stories," we ask each child to design a television set on a piece of construction paper. We then give the children long paper strips on which they illustrate their favorite stories. By cutting a slit on each side of their homemade television sets, they may "play" their stories and tell them to each other and to the teacher. The illustrations help the teacher check comprehension, and the students enjoy "reading" their pictures to their friends and their parents.

"Magic Word Stories" reinforce vocabulary and provide a variety of sentence structures and patterns. By the second semester of third grade, our students are eager to begin to read in French. This seems an appropriate moment to introduce *written* French because the students are beginning to be secure in their English reading skills.

When we introduce reading, we borrow a technique from first-grade teachers and reading specialists. Beginning reading texts do not expect a youngster to read words that are unfamiliar. All the phonics in the world cannot help a child to decode a totally unknown word.

Those not familiar with the term "language experience stories" will certainly recognize the phenomenon. Our own children have brought such stories home, or we have seen them displayed in classrooms and in supermarkets and bakeries: "Our class visited the grocery store. Mary liked the red apples. Mandy bought a box of cookies." Children can read such a story easily because they dictated it to their teacher. They find it interesting because they wrote it about one of their own experiences. When the children dictate the story to the teacher, he or she may correct any grammar and vocabulary mistakes so that the story reads smoothly. (For example, a child may say, "Mandy 'buyed' a box of cookies.") In the foreign language class, this means that the children have an opportunity to use creatively the vocabulary and language patterns they have learned, and the teacher has the opportunity to correct and simultaneously refine that language.

For the language experience technique to work in a foreign language class, the children must have a fairly broad vocabulary, and the focus and scope of the story must be carefully limited. Waiting until the young child has had several years of oral French provides a strong vocabulary base. We believe our "Magic Word Stories" give children a variety of sentence patterns to use.

At Bryn Mawr, our first forays into the written word are based on an activity especially suited to our constituency. We are an all-girls school, and young girls love to play "Dollhouse." Each girl designs and furnishes a dollhouse room in a shoebox. No real dollhouse furniture is allowed, but children find wonderful ways to use egg cartons, bottle tops, toothpicks, and scraps of fabric. Rooms are brought in as they are completed. This ensures a steady stream of "houses beautiful" over a period of three to four weeks. Coeducational schools and all-boys schools could easily adapt this project to suit their students' interests. Dioramas representing a village scene with various shops, weather scenes showing seasonal activities, or farm scenes would all provide the focus for a story.

Before beginning to write the language experience stories, the teacher conducts an intensive vocabulary review. The vocabulary of the house was introduced in kindergarten and first grade and reinforced in second grade. We add some more sophisticated decorator terms (wallpaper, tile, curtains) and review adjectives of color and basic descriptive adjectives. We do not mention the agreement of the adjective, although of course we write the adjective correctly in the story.

By the time the vocabulary is established, the rooms are beginning to arrive in school. Each room is admired profusely and preserved forever in a language experience story that, at least in the beginning, takes a full class to write. The teacher needs to lead the students through the early stories. She may ask leading questions: "What color is the rug? Where is the lamp?" She then writes the student's answer in the story: "The rug is blue. The lamp is on the table." In future stories, the students will be able to formulate these sentences independently.

There will always be students who want to dictate elaborate sentences in English and who ask the teacher to translate for them. We tell our students that they might enjoy writing about their rooms in English and that they may do this at home and show their stories to their classroom teacher. We remind them that *"Ici on parle français"* and quickly ask a simple question in French that allows the child to contribute directly in French to the story. After the first few stories are written, most students settle happily into the routine.

The teacher reviews the story frequently as it is being composed and gives it a final proofreading after it is completed. Stories need to be short because too much written French will overwhelm the beginning reader. The class reads the story along with the teacher. We are always amazed and delighted to hear how well and naturally the children read. The child whose room is being described is appointed secretary for the day and copies the story for the teacher. Just to add a note of authenticity, we use a French *cahier* to record the stories. The teacher types the story and distributes it to the students during the following class.

After reading the story with the class several times, the teacher can identify some problems American children find in reading French. The children themselves are often surprised by the way words are written. They know how to pronounce *les livres* and *le ciel est bleu*, and they immediately notice the silent letters. Without overwhelming them with rules, we usually look for silent letters and shade them lightly with chalk. Some of our students say that we turn them into "ghost letters." This is simply a concrete reminder of an abstract rule for them. After several weeks of stories, they automatically know not to pronounce silent letters such as the *nt* in a third person plural verb and the *s* at the end of a plural noun or adjectives.

Each day brings a new story and a new opportunity to confer some aspect of French phonics. The children know how to pronounce the French word for hat, *chapeau*, but here again, the spelling is a surprise. When a *chapeau* appears in a story, we use that as a chance to explain the different vowel combinations that make the [o] sound.

Occasionally, observant children will ask why the French word for green or blue is spelled differently in different sentences. We explain in simple terms that in French the adjective agrees with the noun, but we tell them that this is something they will learn in the fourth grade and that for now, they might just enjoy noticing the different spellings. Most are satisfied with this answer.

These language experience stories are wonderful vehicles for developing reading skills and listening skills. After several choral readings of a story, the teacher may ask individual students to read sentences. The students stumble a bit with the first stories, but soon they are reading with some ease. We have developed a game that helps them focus on reading correctly and listening carefully. This game was born after one of us had an overdose of watching the skiing events in the Olympics several years ago, but it does seem to be fun even in a non-Olympic year. We pretend the story is a giant slalom course. We put little chalk flags over the difficult pronunciation points (silent letters, elisions, vowel combinations, etc.). A student "skier" comes to the board and makes a brief statement to the audience. We often ask her, in French, her name, her country, and her favorite food or color. All of the other students are pole judges and raise their hands whenever they hear a pronunciation error. The teacher of course remains the chief judge.

The student begins her "run" by reading her story and continues until she makes a mistake. We always congratulate her on her fine effort and, if necessary, console her by explaining that the course was quite icy, particularly the spot where she slipped. We also assure her that she will have other chances to ski and show her true Olympic quality. In the early stages of our Olympics, students "fall" frequently, but after two weeks of training, we have many who finish the course without a hitch. The students themselves are excited about this and realize how much progress they have made. This activity keeps everyone interested and allows the teacher to focus on phonics in the context of a game.

The cloze method can also be applied successfully to language experience stories. The children know this as the "Hungry Mouse Game." We erase key words from the story on the board and announce to the class, *"Hélas!* A hungry mouse has turned our beautiful story into a *vrai fromage de gruyère* (Swiss cheese)." As the children supply the missing words, they must analyze the meaning of the sentence and the correct placement of words.

The language experience method of introducing reading helps the children to feel confident in dealing with French texts. At the same time, they refine their own patterns of speech and begin to develop a sense of the structure of the French language.

Our school's commitment to foreign language goes back to its founding at the end of the nineteenth century. Our challenge has been to keep foreign language instruction current and viable at the elementary school level. We have developed and refined the teaching methods described above to keep our young students enthusiastic about learning French and to offer them a broad foundation for pursuing their individual interests and learning styles. Our students move on to the middle school French program with an extensive oral vocabulary base, a positive and confident approach to reading French, and a sense of the structure and rhythm of the language.

A Kaleidoscope of Discovery: The Sequential FLES Program in Rutherford, New Jersey

Harriet Saxon
Pierrepont School
Rutherford, New Jersey

The success and survival of a foreign language program in the elementary school depends greatly on several factors:

- The support and enthusiasm of the entire school community
- The interest, cooperation, and financial support of the local town or city government and population
- The involvement and the interest of the student community
- The vitality, creativity, and language ability of the foreign language teacher
- The integration of second language study as an interdisciplinary subject in the elementary school classroom

The integration of the French language elementary school program in the curriculum of the Rutherford School District has, during the past fourteen years, provided a rich, multifaceted second language learning experience to young people. The program has successfully combined the above five factors to ensure an experience in second language acquisition for students in grades 5 through 8 that involves every learning experience in the classroom and combines the skills, knowledge, cooperation, and creativity of the subject teacher with those of the foreign language teacher. The foreign language classroom becomes a living experience that introduces the basic skills required to *begin* the mastery of a second language and provides a cultural, artistic, and intellectual environment for learning, accepting, and enjoying the second language. The **FLES*** teacher attempts to bring a world of adventure, beauty, and discovery to the young language student.

This article focuses on one of the factors for a successful and vital French language program in the elementary school classroom: the integration and implementation of the French language into an interdisciplinary program that creates an exciting challenge to be explored and shared by the students and by the language and subject teachers.

INTEGRATION

The integration of an interdisciplinary foreign language program makes the classroom extend beyond its own culture and environment! The entire school—its students and staff—becomes involved as part of the language experience. The themes of *discover, challenge, explore,* and *share* should be discussed with the subject teachers to develop the themes and lessons that involve the target language. During the past years, the administration and the teachers in the Rutherford District have provided the interest, cooperation, and time to integrate French with their lessons and school functions. As Mary Cleary, a teacher of mathematics, stated: "A French class is a marvelous sojourn into the world of the arts, science, and history. It successfully integrates all the arts into a lasting knowledge of the French language."

Goals should be established for special units, and criteria for special projects should be carefully listed and explained to students. The language and classroom curriculum should be integrated with topics such as "Québec: The French in North America," or with school and community activities such as those for National Education Week. For such an event, students might make posters for a display in the public library and on corridor bulletin boards in the school with the theme of "The Importance of Knowing a Second Language."

The language, people, history, and cultures of French-speaking people throughout the world *(les pays francophones)* are integrated with the following subjects and their curricula:

- Social studies units may include discussions of the French explorers in the New World, the French in Québec, the French and the American Revolution, France and the United States as allies in the two world wars, the Statue of Liberty as a gift from the French, the United States and the bicentennial of the French Revolution, and celebrations of the anniversary of D-Day in France and in the United States.

- Mathematics units may be integrated with the French program through units on French terminology for geometric vocabulary, discussions about the metric system, conversion from Fahrenheit to Celsius, and mathematical computer programs. The review of mathematics calculations and numbers may become an integral part of the foreign language classroom, as well as research about René Descartes and Blaise Pascal—important French mathematicians.

- Science units may be integrated with language classes that discuss French scientists and the impact of their discoveries on the world in which we live: discussions and research about Lavoisier, Pasteur, Marie and Pierre Curie, Braille, the Brothers Lumière, Pascal, the Brothers Montgolfier, and important French engineers such as Gustave Eiffel.
- Physical education classes are easily integrated with language classes through lessons on the games of the *Olympiques* (its modern-day history, events, and heroes in France) and current important contests in the world of sports, such as tennis, soccer, running marathons in Paris and the United States, ice skating competitions, and skiing events that involve French and American athletes. Discussions may also touch on baseball and hockey competitions between the Americans and the Québécois. The unit may also include the French terminology used in sporting events and important current events in the world of sports in French-speaking countries.
- Music units present a vital picture of France—its people and personality. The music and French teachers are able to coordinate units about French composers and their influence on the history of music, French opera, operettas, and ballets and about popular music, singers, and composers from French-speaking lands such as Québec, nations of Africa, Guadeloupe, Martinique, and Haiti.
- English language and literature and drama classes are directly involved and integrated with the French curriculum. After a lecture and performance of *Les Misérables,* Tony Bucco, a teacher of reading and drama classes, observed: "What better way to teach children about a country's literature!" When one of that country's most classic works is made into a world-famous musical, it affords students the opportunity to see and be swept along and surrounded by the culture and scenery of *Les Misérables.* The English language teacher and French language teacher both discuss the derivation of words and the development of grammatical structures. Literary texts such as *A Tale of Two Cities,* may be introduced for discussion. Michael Yacono, a sixth-grade reading teacher, says: "The characters become alive as students act the roles in *A Tale of Two Cities* and enjoy *The Phantom of the Opera!*" The students read and discuss *Le Petit Prince* and memorize short selections of poems by Hugo, Verlaine, and Prévert.
- The art curriculum and the French language classroom directly involve the teachers and each student in exploring and discovering French art and its history and influence throughout the centuries. This coordinated curriculum also permits each student to create and appreciate the impact of French art on humans and society. It

also allows for sharing, activity, individuality, free expression, and diversification in the language classroom. Integrating art and the French class allows units on vocabulary, culture, geography, history, holidays, and topics such as time, foods, travel, and weather to come alive with fun and creativity. Diana Hecking, a teacher of art and the creative arts, notes: "The influence and interaction of the world of the artist and the arts fit perfectly into the foreign language curriculum. It provides an appreciation of the beauty of the artists' world of that nation and its impact on the students' own world, and it extends the language curriculum and stimulates the imagination and creativity." The language classroom thrives on action, activity, and expression, and the integration of art and French allows all students to go beyond themselves to discover the world of French art and its impact on life and society. It presents a picture of France, its people, and its personality!

Other school subjects may also be integrated into the French program with the cooperation and imagination of the teachers. For example, units about French foods can be coordinated with the home economics teacher. Units on geography, industrial arts, architecture, theater, dance, choral music, business, and almost every phase of the school curriculum can be coordinated and planned with the subject teachers. It is very important to integrate the subjects easily into the classroom sessions. The coordinating teachers should:

- Plan at the beginning of the year or even start planning the previous year for topics that will be integrated.
- Establish the criteria for the integration of the subjects.
- Plan to evaluate the impact, importance, and interest that the interdisciplinary approach will provide to the language students and teachers.
- Plan to evaluate the impact, importance, and relevance to students in a non-second language learning experience.
- Plan the materials that will be required, such as films, supplies, texts, maps, slide programs, and bulletin board displays. Decide which special projects will be completed and the criteria and goals of the projects.
- Schedule guest speakers who can present relevant and interesting presentations to supplement the integrated subjects.
- Plan field trips to historical sights, museums, exhibits, and lectures.
- Plan an in-class trip to the province of Québec to integrate all the units of art, music, history, literature, geography, culture, economics, sports, and the study and use of the French language.

Implementation

Below is a list of ideas and projects that subject and language teachers may use to supplement the different units of study. The suggested activities reinforce subject matter, develop ideas and originality, and share with the school and community the importance of language learning and all its components in the world of today.

1. Students trace patterns and create life-size paper figures of important historical characters, such as Samuel de Champlain, Jacques Cartier, Anne de Bretagne, Napoléon, Jeanne d'Arc, and Lafayette. When the figures are glued to cardboard, they can stand freely in displays or be used in history or French classes.

2. A guest artist is invited to the school to sing French arias and songs based on French poetry. Selected classes are invited to attend the performance. The students first learn the poems and lyrics that will be sung. The music teacher and French teacher are important resource people to work together on this project. Students who play instruments such as the flute, piano, and violin may be asked to accompany the group or to present musical selections by French composers.

3. The students create a large wall mural that depicts life in a city, such as life in Québec during *le Carnaval* and then at the time of the French in-class trip to that city in the spring. This provides a study of Québec, its people, geography, important streets, monuments, buildings, culture, architecture, and seasons. (The wall mural that our students completed was presented as a gift to the children of Québec and is currently on exhibit at Le Centre Communautaire Lucien Borne in Québec.)

4. Students study the story and staging of the Broadway play *"Les Misérables,* with the drama teacher as a resource person. He or she presents an explanation of the various facets of the making of the musical, which is accompanied by selections from the video of the *Stage by Stage* of *Les Misérables*. The students then create their own posters or playbills to advertise the French version of *Les Mis*. The art teacher will also be a resource person to complete the project.

5. The social studies teacher discusses with the class the role of the French in North America and presents a unit about Québec and the French and Indian Wars as part of the social studies curriculum.

6. Students and the French teacher interact directly with the art teacher, who is a vital resource person for the integration of French in the elementary school curriculum.

7. The art teacher creates projects and initiates ideas to help vitalize the language classroom and the study of the history of French art and artists and extends the world of French to the school. Each unit of study is supplemented with a special project that includes a goal, a method, and an evaluation.

The following project accompanied a unit on Paris:

Goal: To know and recognize *le quartier de la tour Eiffel* and its sights and monuments.

Methods: Students will create in three dimensions the area of *la tour Eiffel*. They will complete research on the places of interest in the area and will include reproductions of *les Invalides; l'Ecole militaire; le palais de Chaillot* and its fountains; the bridges, gardens, and parks of Paris; and a three-foot replica in wood of *la tour Eiffel* that will include the restaurant Jules Verne. Students will create Parisians, tourists, and other interesting Parisian sights, such as the flower vendor, the souvenir cart, the cafés, the cars, the signs for *le métro*, and streets. Students will study a map of Paris and plan the area according to the location of *la Seine* and boulevards, avenues, and streets.

Evaluation: The display was used as a supplement to the French class for the study of Paris. The project was on display in the school and was admired by students, faculty, and visitors. The students, with the guidance of the art teacher, exhibited their creation at the Bergen County Educational Association exhibit. Then it was on display in the window of a local bank and in the Rutherford Public Library.

A foreign language as an interdisciplinary subject provides students with an enriching experience in the study of the humanities and creative arts. Students develop pride in their accomplishments in their language classes and enjoy sharing their new language and activities with the school community. They become enthusiastic and inquisitive concerning multinational cultural diversity. Dr. Luke A. Sarsfield, superintendent of schools of the Rutherford School District stated: "The study of French allows students to develop a sense of discipline and to understand a nation so closely allied during the past centuries to their own." This knowledge equips them to become better leaders and citizens of the twenty-first century.

In conclusion, when developing a second language as an interdisciplinary subject, it is vital to plan, research, establish rationales, develop, and evaluate. The cooperation, dedication, and talents of an entire school staff interplay with the foreign language program and attest to its strengths, enjoyment, and success.[1] The discipline of second language learning is multifaceted and enables young students to discover new worlds, seen through the adventures of speaking a new language and "making it their own." Anna Amorelli, an educator and the former principal of Pierrepont School, who helped pilot the foreign language program, summed up the interdisciplinary approach by stating: "The nature of the program encompasses a universal attitude towards education, and a multilingual society is a mark of global success."

---

[1] The enthusiastic support of Dr. Luke A. Sarsfield, the superintendent of schools of the Rutherford School District, the school administrators, and the board of education has permitted the activities and goals of the program to succeed immeasurably to continually provide foreign language education to the young people in our elementary school.

Reading the World: **FLES*** and Global Education

Katherine C. Kurk

and

Hilary W. Landwehr
Northern Kentucky University
Highland Heights, Kentucky

All of **FLES*** is part and parcel of global education, teaching that emphasizes different countries of the world and their national cultures. And global education links to multiculturalism, an appreciation of diversity: ethnicity, religion, class, identity groups, and language distinctions. Multicultural education leads students to move from a focus on the self to a recognition of plurality within their own country and, further, to a great awareness of global people, issues, and problems. We, as **FLES*** teachers, know that foreign language education, at any level, teaches an appreciation of the other. In elementary settings, it is often the foreign language teacher who can, and should, be the catalyst for the promotion of multicultural and global education, who can encourage colleagues to integrate diversity into the curriculum and into their everyday classroom practices.

Marcia H. Rosenbusch argues persuasively that "research suggests that the elementary school years may be the most appropriate time to begin global studies because children's attitudes toward people different from them appear to develop early and may become permanent with time" (1992, 131). She discusses three global units developed by the Ankeny, Iowa, community schools in conjunction with Iowa State University: *French West Africa* (grades 1–3), which focuses on family and rural culture in comparison and contrast to their American counterparts; *Federal Republic of Germany* (grades 4–6), a comparative study of environment and land use; and *Mexico* (grades 1–3), which examines issues such as hunger, housing, and community in Iowa and Acapulco (132–133). The pilot program implementation of these units was very successful and indicates just how crucial a **FLES*** program can be in the promotion of students' global understanding. However, Rosenbusch concludes that there is much to be done in the areas of preparation and dissemination of materials and of building bridges with teachers in other subject areas—quite simply, in spreading the wor(l)d. This brief note is but an introduction to possible avenues of communication between **FLES*** teachers and their non-target-language colleagues, and it is followed by lists of current materials to be shared with students, parents, librarians, and educators alike.

Students who take a foreign language, who participate in foreign language fairs or festivals, who take part in introductory after-school programs or full-scale Immersion weekends, who find a Web page on another country, or who hear a song from another culture often wish to extend those initiations, to explore their acquaintance further. They go to school libraries or computer rooms and ask for help. How disappointing it can be not to find new, well-illustrated, culturally accurate, and engaging materials! Without input from **FLES*** teachers, resource persons may not know what to order or may not be aware of the interest level that exists. At parent-teacher conferences, parents often confess that they know nothing (or remember little) about the language their children have been studying. Sometimes they express the desire to explore their own cultural heritage with their children and ask where to obtain information that will allow them to do so. Foreign language teachers can prepare a one-sheet guide with suggested books, videos, and area resources for their own use or to give to the homeroom teacher to share. And many times teachers and administrators may be willing to incorporate more global education into the curriculum but do not know enough about materials that are age- or cost-appropriate. Unless **FLES*** teachers take the lead by encouraging their colleagues to explore and read the world via books, magazines, and videos, both in the target language and in English, we are missing valuable opportunities. We must build a community vision, not the sole property of a foreign language class, one weekend, one week, one period in the day, but one that is clearly articulated throughout the disciplines and is both immediate and accessible.

FLES* teachers who are in pull-out programs, who are not in Immersion settings, can increase global awareness by suggesting appropriate materials for learning centers in history, language arts, math, or science. They can provide dates of multicultural significance to the classroom calendar, hang a flurry of world country flags on the walls, or propose target language presentations for holiday festivities. **FLES*** teachers can also prepare community resource guides: listings of speakers, events, and sites that correspond to and expand the curriculum. In their own classes they can explore the heritage of each child and together make a construction paper "quilt," with each color square telling the background of one child and his or her family. Countries of origin can be examined in geography lessons, and the quilt squares themselves can be used to practice colors or counting in the target language. The quilt would reinforce both the unique qualities of the individual learner and all that a cultural past contributes to the whole. And the quilt would provide an opportunity to discuss events in the past that have shaped peoples and cause prejudices. To have works such as *Joshua's Masai Mask, Escape or Die! True Stories of Young People Who Survived the Holocaust,* and *Talking Walls* in the classroom helps students to realize the strengths of their own identities and those of others.

It is essential that we encourage children "to read the world" and to celebrate April 2, International Children's Book Day. There are many ways that we can focus on the global aspects that make stories even more meaningful. And when our colleagues are presenting works that feature the world, we should offer enrichment for their experience. For example, if students are reading Tomie de Paola stories in third grade, the **FLES*** teacher can suggest books about the countries where the tales take place or can help with the foreign phrases. Such commonly used works as the Petunia goose tales by Roger Duvoisin, the Pippi Longstocking stories of Astrid Lindgren, or even Esphyr Slobodkina's *Caps for Sale* offer opportunities to "visit" Switzerland, Sweden, and Russia respectively. We can also encourage students to consider global issues such as war and peace via works such as the Babar stories by Jean and Laurent de Brunhoff. The little elephant Babar's mother is killed and his "youth" is destroyed by war. It affects the way that he, in turn, rules his kingdom peacefully.

Only when *all* teachers have knowledge of multicultural resources and materials can they change their own classrooms and curricula. Only when *all* libraries have holdings that document the world can children explore and develop a global vision of their own. Foreign language teachers, especially **FLES*** instructors, should be in the vanguard providing opportunities for their colleagues and classes alike "to read the world."

References

Brunhoff, Jean de. 1981. *Babar's Anniversary Album: Six Favorite Stories.* New York: Random House.

Duvoisin, Roger. 1991. *Petunia Takes a Trip.* New York: Knopf.

Friedman, Ina R. 1982. *Escape or Die! True Stories of Young People Who Survived the Holocaust.* Reading, MA: Addison-Wesley.

Hru, Dakari. 1993. *Joshua's Masai Mask.* New York: Lee & Low.

Knight, Margy Burns. 1992. *Talking Walls.* Gardiner, ME: Tilbury House.

Lindgren, Astrid. 1978. *Pippi Longstocking.* New York: Puffin.

Rosenbusch, Marcia H. 1992. "Is Knowledge of Cultural Diversity Enough? Global Education in the Elementary School Foreign Language Program." *Foreign Language Annals* 25, 2 (April): 129–136.

Slobodkina, Esphyr. 1947. *Caps for Sale.* New York: Harper.

Materials to Share

Global Education: Selected Books for Children in Levels K–6 (some appropriate for older levels)

GENERAL

Alles, Hemesh, and A. J. Wood. 1992. *Errata: A Book of Historical Errors*. New York: Green Tiger Press.

Bernhard, Emery and Durga Bernhard. 1996. *Ride on Mother's Back: A Day of Baby Carrying Around the World*. San Diego, CA: Harcourt Brace.

Birdseye, Debbie Holsclaw, and Tom Birdseye. 1996. *What I Believe*. New York: Holiday.

Bursik, Rose. 1992. *Amelia's Fantastic Flight*. Cambridge, MA: Holt.

DeSpain, Pleasant. 1993. *Thirty-Three Multicultural Tales to Tell*. Little Rock, AR: August House.

———. 1996. *Eleven Nature Tales: A Multicultural Journey*. Little Rock, AR: August House.

Dorros, Arthur. 1992. *This Is My House*. New York: Scholastic.

Ege, Christine. 1992. *Words for the World*. Houston, TX: Comprehensive Language Communications.

Gackenbach, Dick. 1989. *With Love from Gran*. Boston, MA: Clarion.

Jeness, Aylette. 1993. *Come Home with Me: A Multicultural Treasure Hunt*. New York: New Press.

Kindersley, Barnabas and Anabel. 1995. *Children Just Like Me*. In association with UNICEF. New York: Dorling Kindersley.

Knight, Margy Burns. 1996. *Talking Walls*. Gardiner, ME: Tilbury House.

———. 1996. *Talking Walls: The Stories Continue*. Gardiner, ME: Tilbury House

———. 1993. *Who Belongs Here?* Gardiner, ME: Tilbury House.

Livingston, Myra Cohn. 1996. *Festivals*. New York: Holiday House.

Medlicott, Mary. 1926. *Tales for Telling from Around the World*. New York: Kingfisher.

Pop-Up Book of European Cities. 1991. Nashville, TN: Ideals.

Rosen, M., ed. 1992. *The Oxfam Book of Children's Stories: South & North & East & West*. Cambridge, MA: Candlewick.

Sanders, Marilyn. 1995. *What's Your Name? From Ariel to Zoe*. New York: Holiday House.

Yolen, Jane. 1992. *Street Rhymes Around the World*. New York: St. Martin's.

AFRICA (GENERAL)

Anderson-Sankofa, David A. 1991. *The Origin of Life on Earth: An African Creation Myth*. Mount Airy, MD: Sights Productions (Coretta Scott King Award).

Onyefulu, Ifeome. 1996. *Ogbo: Sharing Life in an African Village*. San Diego, CA: Harcourt, Brace.

AUSTRALIA
Fox, Mem. 1990. *Possum Magic.* San Diego, CA: Harcourt, Brace & Jovanovich.

Oodgeroo. 1994. *Dreamtime: Aboriginal Stories.* New York: Lothrop.

CARIBBEAN
Burgie, Irving. 1992. *Caribbean Carnival: Songs of the West Indies.* New York: Tambourine.

Keller, Holly. 1992. *Island Baby.* New York: Greenwillow.

CENTRAL/LATIN AMERICA
Ada, Alma Flor. 1992. *The Gold Coin.* New York: Atheneum

Delacre, Lulu. 1996. *Golden Tales, Myths, Legends and Folktales from Latin America.* New York: Scholastic.

CHINA
Armstrong, Jennifer. 1993. *Chin Yu Min and the Ginger Cat.* New York: Crown.

Goldstein, Peggy. 1991. *Long Is a Dragon.* San Francisco, CA: Pacific View.

Reddix, Valerie. 1991. *Dragon Kite of the Autumn Moon.* New York: Lothrop.

Tan, Amy. 1992. *Moon Lady.* New York: Macmillan.

Young, Ed. 1989. *Lon Po Po: Chinese Red Riding Hood.* New York: Putnam.

EGYPT
Lattimore, Deborah Nourse. 1992. *The Winged Cat: A Tale of Ancient Egypt.* New York: HarperCollins.

FRANCE
Hutchins, Pat. 1981. *The Mona Lisa Mystery.* New York: Greenwillow.

McClintock, Barbara. 1989. *Heartaches of a French Cat.* Boston, MA: Godine.

McCully, Emily Arnold. 1992. *Mirette on the High Wire.* New York: G. P. Putnam's.

Milton, Nancy. 1992. *The Giraffe That Walked to Paris.* New York: Crown.

Munro, Roxie. 1992. *The Inside-Outside Book of Paris.* New York: Dutton.

GHANA
Chocolate, Deborah M. Newton. 1993. *Talk Talk: An Ashanti Legend.* Mahwah, NJ: Troll.

IMMIGRANTS TO THE UNITED STATES
Bartone, Elisa. 1996. *American Too.* New York: Lothrop.

Bunting, Eve. 1996. *Going Home.* New York: HarperCollins.

Hippley, Hilary Herder. 1996. *A Song for Lena.* New York: Simon & Schuster.

Joosse, Barbara. 1995. *The Morning Chair.* Boston, MA: Clarion.

Kroll, Steven. 1995. *Ellis Island: Doorway to Freedom.* New York: Holiday House.

Maestro, Betsy. 1996. *Coming to America: The Story of Immigration.* New York: Scholastic.

Pryor, Bonnie. 1996. *The Dream Jar.* New York: Morrow.

INDIA

Rodanas, Kristina. 1988. *The Story of Wali Dad.* New York: Lothrop.

Gilsmore, Rachna. 1995. *Lights for Gita.* Gardiner, ME: Tilbury House.

Wolf, Gita. 1996. *The Very Hungry Lion.* Buffalo, NY: Annick.

INDONESIA

Myers, Christopher A., and Lynn Born Myers. 1994. *Forest of the Clouded Leopard.* Boston, MA: Houghton Mifflin.

ISRAEL

Edwards, Michelle. 1992. *Alef-bet: A Hebrew Alphabet.* New York: Lothrop.

JAPAN

Kalman, Maira. 1989. *Sayonara, Mrs. Kackleman.* New York: Viking.

Miyazawa, Kenji. 1996. *Milky Way Railroad.* Berkeley, CA: Stone Bridge.

KENYA

Mollel, Tololwa M. 1993. *The Princess Who Lost Her Hair: An Akamba Legend.* Mahwah, NJ: Troll.

KOREA

McMahon, Patricia. 1993. *Chi-Hoon: A Korean Girl.* Stonesdale, PA: Boyds Mill.

NIGERIA

Gerson, Mary-Joan. 1992. *Why the Sky Is Far Away: A Nigerian Folktale.* New York: Little, Brown.

PERU

Charles, Donald. 1992. *Chancey and the Secret of Fire: A Peruvian Folktale.* New York: Putnam.

PHILIPPINES

San Souci, Robert. 1996. *Pedro and the Monkey.* New York: Morrow.

ROMANIA

Matthews, Wendy. 1995. *The Gift of a Traveler.* Mahwah, NJ: Bridgewater (Troll).

RUSSIA

Langton, Jane. 1992. *Salt: A Russian Folktale.* New York: Hyperion.

Mayers, Florence Cassen. 1992. *A Russian ABC Featuring Masterpieces from the Hermitage.* New York: Abrams.

Trivas, Irene. 1992. *Annie Anya: A Month in Moscow.* New York: Orchard.

VIETNAM

Gilson, Jamie. 1985. *Hello, My Name Is Scrambled Eggs.* New York: Lothrop.

Vuong, Lynette Dyer. 1993. *The Golden Carp and Other Tales from Vietnam.* New York: Lothrop.

WEST AFRICA

Alexander, Lloyd. 1992. *Fortune-Tellers.* New York: Dutton.

Chocolate, Deborah M. Newton, 1993. *Spider and the Sky God: An Akam Legend.* Mahwah, NJ: Troll.

Series

"Count Your Way Through the World" (Arab World, China, French Canada, India, etc.). Minneapolis, MN: First Avenue Editions.

"Fifth World Tales" (ex., Tran-Khanh-Tuyet, *Little Weaver of Thai-Yen Village).* San Francisco, CA: Childrens' Book Press. Bilingual editions.

India, The Land, People, Culture. (Japan, China, etc.) New York: Crabtree.

"Legends of the World." Mahwah, NJ: Troll. *See* Mollel, Chocolate (authors).

"Let's Go Traveling" (France, England, Egypt, China, Mexico, Peru). New York: Morrow Junior.

"New True Book" (on individual countries [ex., *Bolivia*]). San Francisco, CA: Children's Book Press.

"People Around the World" (ex., *Bread, Bread; House and Homes; Tools*). New York: Lothrop.

This Place Is _____ (Cold, Crowded, etc. [ex., Cobb, Vicki. *This Place Is Crowded: Japan.*]). New York: Walker Press.

Tintin's Travel Diaries (China, Tibet, India, etc.). Hauppauge, NY: Barron's.

Toto in Spain (France, Italy). Lincolnwood, IL: Passport Books.

"Vanishing Cultures" (ex., *Himalaya, Down Under, Amazon Basin, Mongolia*). San Diego, CA: Harcourt, Brace.

Global Education and Multiculturalism: Selected Articles, Books, and Program Information

Carlson, Laurie. 1994. *More than Moccasins: A Kid's Activity Guide to Traditional North American Indian Life.* Chicago: Review Press.

Cech, Maureen. 1991. *Global Child: Multicultural Resources for Young Children.* Boston: Addison Wesley.

Cook, Deanna. 1995. *Kids' Multicultural Cookbook: Food and Fun Around the World.* Charlotte, VT: Williamson.

Day, Frances Ann. 1994. *Multicultural Voices in Contemporary Literature: A Resource for Teachers.* Portsmouth, NH: Heinemann.

DeBuhr, Astrid M. 1991. "From Sukiyaki to Croissants: Global Education at Work in the Elementary Schools." In *Implementing FLES* Programs*, ed. Gladys C. Lipton, pp. 38–44. Champaign, IL: AATF.

Global SchoolNet Foundation. www.gsn.org.

Grossman, Herbert. 1995. *Teaching in a Diverse Society.* Boston: Allyn & Bacon.

Helbig, Althea K., and Agnes Regan Perkins. 1994. *This Is Our Land: A Guide to Multicultural Literature for Children and Young Adults.* Westport, CT: Greenwood.

Knight, Margy Burns, and Thomas V. Chan. 1992. *Talking Walls Activity Guide.* Gardiner, ME: Tilbury House.

Knowlton, Jack. 1988. *Geography from A to Z.* New York: Crowell.

Ladybug. Spider. Cricket. The Cricket Magazine Group, P.O. Box 11319, Des Moines, IA 50350.

Lieberman, Tanya. 1995. *Storybooks Teach About World Cultures.* Palo Alto, CA: Monday Morning.

Many Voices: A Multicultural Literature Program. 1993. New York: Scholastic.

Mellgren, Millie Park. 1989. "Global Education in the Language Classroom: The African Connection." In *Defining the Essentials for the Foreign Language Classroom.* ed. Dave McAlpine. Lincolnwood, IL: NTC.

Miller, Lynda, Theresa Steinlage, and Mike Printz. 1994. *Cultural Cobblestones: Teaching Cultural Diversity.* Metuchen, NJ: Scarecrow Press.

Miller-Lachman, Lyn. 1992. *Our Family, Our Friends, Our World.* New Providence, RI: Bowker.

O'Hare, Jeff. 1992. *Best Board Games from Around the World.* New York: Highlights.

Orlando. Louise. 1993. *The Multicultural Game Book.* New York: Scholastic.

Rief, Linda, 1992. *Seeking Diversity: Language Arts with Adolescents.* Portsmouth, NH: Heinemann.

Rosen, Lauren, and Roy Bowers. *Language Learning Activities for the World Wide Web.* http://www.wfi.fr/est/activity.html

Rothstein, Gloria Lesser. 1994. *From Soup to Nuts: Multicultural Activities and Recipes.* New York: Scholastic.

Seelye, H. Ned. 1993. *Teaching Culture: Strategies for Intercultural Communication.* Lincolnwood, IL: National Textbook Co.

Sernett, Liza. 1992. *Un poco de todo.* Minneapolis, MN: Denison.

Sesame Street Magazine, P.O. Box 52000, Boulder, CO 80321-2000.

Sevaly, Karen. 1993. *International Children.* Riverside, CA: Teacher's Friend.

Siccone, Frank. 1995. *Celebrating Diversity: Building Self-Esteem in Today's Multicultural Classrooms.* Boston, MA: Allyn & Bacon.

Sierra, Judy. 1991. *Multicultural Folktales: Stories to Tell Young Children.* Phoenix, AZ: Oryx Press.

Terzian, Alexandra M. 1993. *The Kids' Multicultural Art Book.* Charlotte, VT: Williamson.

Tiedt, Pamela L., and Iris M. Tiedt. 1990. *Multicultural Teaching: A Handbook of Activities, Information and Resources.* 3rd ed. Boston: Allyn & Bacon.

Vieth, Janice, and Anne Weber. 1995. *Crafts from World Cultures.* Palo Alto, CA: Monday Morning.

Walter, Virginia A. 1993. *War and Peace. Literature for Children and Young Adults.* Phoenix, AZ: Oryx Press.

Selected Addresses for Books and Materials in Target Languages or English

Annick Press
Division of Firefly Books
P.O. Box 1325
Ellicott Station, NY 14205
800-387-5085

Asia for Kids
P.O. Box 9096
Cincinnati, OH 45209-0096
800-888-9681

Barron's Educational Series
P.O. Box 8040
250 Wireless Boulevard
Hauppauge, NY 11788
800-645-3476

Dover Publications
180 Varrick Street
New York, NY 10014
800-223-3130

Harrap's
222 West Fifth Avenue
Collegeville, PA 19426
215-489-3451

Highsmith Multicultural Bookstore
W5527 Highway 106
P.O. Box 800
Fort Atkinson, WI 53538-0800
800-558-3899

Holiday House
18 East 53rd Street
New York, NY 10022

Knopf, Alfred A., Inc.
(Borzoi Sprinters, Bullseye, Dragonfly)
201 East 50th Street
New York, NY 10022

Lothrop, Lee & Shepard Books
Division of William Morrow & Co.
1350 Avenue of the Americas
New York, NY 10019
800-843-9389

Passport Books
National Textbook Company, a division of NTC/Contemporary Publishing Group
4255 West Touhy Avenue
Lincolnwood, IL 60646-1975
800-323-4900

Putnam Publishing
(Playland, Sandcastle, Tuffy, etc.)
200 Madison Avenue
New York, NY 1016
800-631-8571

Random House, Inc.
201 East 50th Strett, 31st Floor
New York, NY 10022
800-733-3000

Scholastic, Inc.
Subsidiary of SI Holdings, Inc.
730 Broadway
New York, NY 10003
800-392-2179

Usborne
Division of Educational Development Corp.
10302 East 55th Place
Tulsa, OK 74146
800-331-4418

Also of note:

Lafayette, Robert C. "French and Francophone Children's Literature." Louisiana State University French Education Project, Baton Rouge, LA 70803 (for an extensive selected bibliography in French). Available from the author.

Schon, Isabel. 1992. "Outstanding Children's Books in Spanish." *Hispania* 75 (May): 413–416 (an excellent, well-annotated list).

Is There Life after *"Simon Dit"*?: Expanding Your **FLES*** Classroom through the Use of Learning Centers

Astrid M. DeBuhr
Clayton High School
St. Louis, Missouri

If, indeed, we are in the business of expanding our students' horizons, increasing their cultural sensitivity, and providing them with yet another effective tool for communication, then it behooves us to do whatever we can as **FLES*** teachers to make sure this happens. Furthermore, if we can reinforce the learning going on in our students' regular classrooms, our efforts will be received even more favorably in the learning community within which we work.

Learning centers can be very effective tools for enlarging the focus of the **FLES*** classroom because they support the concept of, provide for, and depend upon a multioptional environment. Including learning centers in the **FLES*** classroom repertoire benefits all members of the second language learning community. The payoff for teachers is obvious. Teachers are freed to work with individuals or small groups or simply to observe more closely as students manipulate concepts and vocabulary in the target language.

Learning centers also allow for the continuous introduction of new materials, and since such centers are fundamentally self-instructional, teachers spend less time explaining materials, and students spend more time on task. Through the use of such centers, students' learning is no longer completely teacher-dependent.

Your students will gain numerous other benefits from the introduction of learning centers into your classroom. Because they are curious by nature, exposure to learning centers will allow them to discover new things *on their own* or *in very small groups*. Learning centers can be a very effective method for introducing a variety of materials not otherwise available in the curriculum, and they readily accommodate many different learning styles.

The skills your students develop through the use of learning centers can have a powerful effect on their learning in other areas of the curriculum. Most learning centers can be set up to be self-instructional, so your students will learn to work both independently and in small groups without much teacher direction or intervention. Students learn to cooperate with one another while learning new or reinforcing previously learned material. Not only will your students gain skills in working independently, but they will also transfer those skills to new settings and situations.

If we believe that the best second (or third) language learning occurs in an atmosphere where students feel safe taking risks, then learning centers should most certainly be part of that ambience. If you include multisensory activities in your centers, you will find that your students eagerly look forward to working with them. The self-instructional and self-checking activities in your centers will be among your students' favorites. The warm working atmosphere that learning centers can help to create will also develop your students' cognitive and affective skills.

Can learning centers actually be integrated into your existing curriculum? If they help you save time so you can maximize contact with individual students or with small groups of students, then they should become an important part of the learning environment you create in your classroom. Each center, for example, should offer several activities, allowing for a wide range of individual student choice. Within the parameters of the activities you assign to a particular center, your students will be able to design and direct their own learning. Your role as teacher, then, becomes that of lead learner or facilitator in the classroom.

How do you go about the business of setting up learning centers for the **FLES*** classroom? How do you go beyond the confines of picture flash cards and playing *"Simon Dit,"* for example, when working with the parts of the body and all their aches and pains? When focusing on the parts of the body, I simply chose a line from Matt Maxwell's song *"Bonjour Monsieur"*—*"J'ai mal partout"*—as the title for the center. The children know this song well, and the title serves as a descriptive rubric for all of the activities the center contains.

The *"J'ai mal partout"* learning center activity board is set up on an easel on a table in the classroom. Several envelopes attached to the laminated activity board are used to store task cards and nonbulky materials used for various activities. Larger items, such as audiotapes, a cassette player, bingo games, self-correcting vocabulary activity books, and shape cards, are placed in baskets near the activity board.

Perhaps the most important element of the activity board is the set of task cards contained in one of its pockets. Each card should clearly describe a different activity for the students to complete. New activities are regularly added to the learning center, so that students' choices are constantly changing. A change simply requires the addition of a new task card to the collection already located in the activity board pocket and the addition of appropriate materials. Completed activities are recorded on a special log page in each student's notebook.

The following is a partial list of the activities included in the *"J'ai mal partout"* learning center:

1. Listen to *"Bonjour Monsieur"* on the Matt Maxwell cassette and sing along with the tape. Read the words in the *"Bonjour Monsieur"* storybook as you listen and sing. (This song will help you review the names for many parts of the body.)

2. With a partner, take a set of vocabulary picture cards from the basket on the table next to the activity board. Use the cards to quiz your partner on the names for the parts of the body. Your partner will then quiz you. (If you and your partner get stuck on one of the pictures, you can find the answer on the back of the card.)

3. With your partner, use the same set of vocabulary picture cards to play *"La Course au Sommet."* (This game includes a game board showing a large drawing or photo of *la Tour Eiffel*. Numbered points are marked along each side of the tower. The object of the game is to be the first player to reach the *sommet*. The cards are stacked face up in front of the players, who take turns identifying the pictures. A correct answer allows the player to move his or her marker forward one space. An incorrect answer requires the marker to be moved backward one space.)

4. With a partner, take two matching sets of vocabulary picture cards and mix them together. Now you can play two different games. The first game is like "Concentration." Lay all the cards face down on the table or the floor and try to find matching pairs. As you turn up each card, you must say the name of the body part pictured. The second game is played like "Old Maid." Remember, when you ask your partner for a particular card, you must ask in French. (For these activities, choose only cards that have no names written on the back.)

5. On your own or with a partner, take one of the vocabulary flip books and see how many of the pictures you can identify correctly. This activity is self-correcting. The vocabulary flip book contains two stacks of index cards held together with jointed rings. One stack of cards contains pictures with the correct names written on the back. The other stack, in a different order, of course, contains just the names. The student selects a picture from the first stack to identify and then flips through the second stack until he finds what he or she thinks is the correct name. (Answers can be checked by turning over the picture card and looking at the name on the back.)

6. With a partner, take one of the shape cards showing a kiosk, the Eiffel Tower, or the Arc de Triomphe to practice identifying parts of the body. One side of the shape card has pictures pasted on it. Each picture is numbered and has a hole punched next to it. The correct term for each picture is written on the back of the card next to the appropriate hole. One partner holds the card with the answers facing him or her. The other partner looks at the pictures on the front of the card and pokes a dull-ended chopstick through the hole next to the picture he or she is identifying. Based on where the chopstick is, the partner holding the card can tell whether the identification is correct. After the first student has tried to identify all the pictures, the partners switch roles.

7. With three other classmates, choose one of the body parts bingo games to play. One of you should be the caller while the other three play. The caller must call out the names of the various body parts pictured on the bingo cards. If you win, call out *"J'ai gagné"* to your group. Then verify that you have marked the correct pictures by repeating their names in French. A different person should be the caller for each game.

8. Take the *"Bonjour Monsieur"* body parts picture cards and mix them up well. Choose three and use them to make up sentences telling where you hurt. You may want to listen to the Matt Maxwell cassette again to review how to talk about your aches and pains. When you feel that you can say your sentences well enough, use the tape recorder to record yourself saying them. You will enjoy listening to yourself speak French. Next, show your teacher the three cards you chose. Your teacher will ask, *"Comment ça va?"* Answer with the sentences you have been practicing. If you are lucky, your teacher will give you some "medicine" to make your aches and pains to away. (Lifesaver Holes work well for this.) You can also practice this activity with a friend.

9. Make a poster about the parts of the body. Cut out pictures from one of the magazines on the shelf in the classroom and glue them on one of the big sheets of white paper. Your poster may be a collage or a picture of just one person. Be sure to label the body parts you have pictured on your poster. Have fun! This is a chance for you to do something colorful and creative.

10. Stories, stories, stories. This is a chance for you to write your own book in French. Take one of the blank story books from the pocket on the story board and write and illustrate your own book. You may want to make a simple picture book showing the parts of the body and their names, or you may decide to tell a story about aches and pains.

Beyond the obvious enrichment that learning centers can provide your students, how do they further contribute to your life as a classroom teacher? Learning centers can be a godsend when a substitute teacher must take over your class. As long as you provide a learning center the students have worked with before, your substitute will thank you profusely for all your careful preparation. Learning centers can also come in handy when you have laryngitis but must come to school anyway because you have already used up all your sick leave and personal days. At other times, learning centers can provide just the right change of pace.

The possibilities are endless. Just about any activity can be included in a learning center, and the more variety you have, the more appealing the center will be. If you pique your students' interest, they will want to go back to the learning center again and again. Your students will be "hooked," and from then on, they will take greater responsibility for the "recycling" or review component of their learning. Empowering our students to become the next generation of world citizens is important. Why not make it more fun and productive for everyone concerned?

Let the Theme Draw Them In

Suzanne Cane
Lincoln School
Providence, Rhode Island

It's a trick to reach everyone in a class of students with differing abilities, interests, learning styles, maturity levels, and cultural assumptions. We want them all to feel positive about the foreign language and about our particular course so that they all will feel they can achieve some success. We want to encourage the ones who are less involved at the same time that we challenge the ones who are enthusiastically engaged. One solution is to use a variety of teaching techniques in every class period and to capitalize on students' individual strengths.

Frequent changes of pace help the teacher reach almost everyone for at least part of each class period and keep most of the class engaged for the whole time. It's a good idea to move back and forth among oral, physical, and written activities. Although we may emphasize oral proficiency, some students learn well through the written word. Presenting material in several different ways and supplying several different forms of practice help students solidify their new knowledge.

The thematic approach provides children with a reliable framework while allowing the teacher flexibility to pursue content areas of her own choice or to tap into the children's interests and strengths. A thematic unit can be coordinated with a classroom theme, such as the rain forest or space; it can follow a cultural theme, such as Puerto Rico; or it can be based on a book. I presented a variety of activities in a thematic unit based on "The Princess and the Pea."

Use a picture book version of the story, which you can find in a bookstore or library. Even if you have a copy of the story in your target language, you may want to simplify the vocabulary and structure for young students. If you translate or rewrite the text, a good idea is to use words, phrases, and sentences you want your students to learn. Then paste your words over the English words. (If you're using a library book, you might cover the English text with Post-its, or use the copyright-free script in French included at the end of this article.)

The story begins: "There was once a royal family. There was a king, a queen, and a prince." This is the time to introduce a unit on the family, including all the family words and relationships you choose, not just the ones in the story. Here are a few ideas to vary your reinforcement activities.

Because some children can be reached through role-play and movement, try playing "Family Introductions." If you make up names for your games in the target language, children will use the target language to refer to the games and will recognize which rules to follow, which will save the time you would otherwise have to spend on giving directions. Divide the class into several "families" of three or four members each: the Red Family, the Blue Family, the Orange Family, the Yellow Family. (If possible, choose colors that sound the same in the masculine and feminine.)

There are many fun ways to divide children into groups. Surprise holds their interest! For this game, you might use the Magic-Mystery Box suggested by Helena Curtain and Carol Ann Pesola in their book *Languages and Children: Making the Match* (1994 Scott Foresman–Addison Wesley 304–305). The Magic-Mystery Box is a large oatmeal box topped by a heavy sock. The teacher puts paper or objects in the box for the children to pull out. In this case, you would put in pieces of papers in the different family colors, with each piece of paper saying in the target language "mother," "father," "son," or "daughter." As each student pulls out a piece of paper he or she discovers which part he or she is to play and sees the word correctly spelled. Children then select construction paper of the appropriate color and make themselves headbands on which they write which family member they are. The Red Father, for instance, will wear a red headband on which is written "Father," so it will be obvious to everyone who the Red Father is. The teacher warms up the class with conversations such as the following:

Teacher *(speaking to Red Father):* Who are you?
Red Father: I am the Red Father.
Teacher: Yes, you are the Red Father.

Teacher *(pointing to Blue Mother):* Who is she?
Student: She is the Blue Mother.
Teacher: Yes, she is the Blue Mother.

After everyone has warmed up, the students move about the room with a partner who is a member of their family, introducing themselves and their family member to the other pairs. You can include a lesson in culture by having students shake hands or kiss each other on both cheeks as they are introduced.

Another game that involves writing, reading, speaking, and listening to family words is "Who Is It?" The teacher displays on the blackboard all the family words that have been taught. The children each choose five or six family words and write each word on a separate index card. Four students stand at the front of the class, each holding one word card turned so the class cannot see it. The other students guess who they are:

First guesser: Mary, are you the brother?
Mary: No.
Second guesser: Donald, are you the father?
Donald *(showing his card):* Yes, I am the father.

Since the second guesser is correct, he or she takes Donald's place and Donald sits down. Because the students have several cards, they can have several turns.

Some children can be reached through their abilities in art. "The Princess and the Pea" continues with these words: "The prince went looking for a real princess. The girls were too short, too tall, too fat, too thin, too happy, too angry, or too sad. The prince was disappointed. The prince was sad." Time to teach a unit on physical characteristics and feelings! Include the word for "surprised," because it will figure later in the story. "Same or Different" is a listening, speaking, reading, and writing pair activity that can be used with any set of vocabulary words to engage children who like to draw. To reinforce understanding of the words for different physical characteristics and emotions, have the children draw pictures of figures or expressive faces and label them appropriately. The children must draw their pictures a particular size, which the teacher regulates by having them fold their paper into six or eight squares and draw one picture to a square. The teacher then selects some of the children's drawings to create the game. Two children will work together, each holding a different page on which the teacher has pasted four rows of three pictures each. Partner A reads (or speaks) her first row, for example: "He is happy. She is angry. He is fat." Partner B listens and checks whether or not his first row has pictures representing the same characteristics. If it does, he answers "The same," and they both write an S at the end of the row. If Partner B's first row is different, he says "Different," and they both write a D at the end of the row. The teacher will have created the game so that some of the rows are the same and some are different. At row 2, they change roles, with Partner B reading (speaking) and Partner A listening. Children feel validated and included when their pictures are used by the whole class. The game itself can be created by the students working in pairs rather than by the teacher.

Graphs are a good way to bring math into the foreign language classroom. On the blackboard or on a large piece of paper, draw a graph with a column for each of the emotions and physical characteristics you want to reinforce. Head each column with the written word and with a picture, if you feel your students need that extra help. Have children each copy two words of their choice on separate index cards or slips of paper. Put all the papers in the Magic Box and have each child pull out two papers. As you ask questions, the students come forward to write their names under the appropriate column. Each student will write his or her name two times.

Teacher: Who is sad today?
Student: I am sad. *(She writes her name under the "sad" column.)*

After all the students have written their names under the appropriate columns, analyze the graph with such questions as: How many of us are sad? Who is angry? Is Jeremy tall?

Most people can be reached through song. Most of us can easily sing many songs we learned in childhood, even if they were in incomprehensible foreign languages or consisted of nonsense syllables. Singing is an entertaining way to set words and phrases in impressionable minds. A good French song for learning "to look for," which figures in "The Princess and the Pea" when the prince looks for a princess, is *"Où est Mimi?"* on the audiocassette *Sing, Dance, Laugh, and Eat Quiche 2* by Barbara MacArthur (Applause Learning Resources, Madison, WI). This song also introduces prepositions and is a lead-in to playing hide-and-seek and learning how to say "to find" as well as "to look for." A good idea is to tape-record or videotape the class singing because children love to listen and see themselves, and will sing along with the tape. You can record each new song sequentially on a single tape, so that by the end of the year you will have a collection of all the songs the class has learned. Some children will want a copy of the tape so they can sing along with it at home or in the car. You can send the tape on with the class from year to year.

Science experiments in the **FLES*** classroom are a way of reaching children whose interests are scientific and help connect foreign language activities to content being studied in other classes. In connection with "The Princess and the Pea," the "Smart Pea" experiment teaches a logical sequence of actions, described in Curtain and Pesola as a Gouin series (111–114). In this experiment, children discover that a seed can tell the difference between up and down: The stem always grows up and the roots always grow down. You will need a plastic jar for each student, paper towels, water, some whole dried peas (available in supermarkets), and a bowl in which to soak the peas. Start by teaching the opposites "up/down" and "dry/wet." A wonderful picture book is Bruce McMillan's *Dry or Wet?* (1988.) Cover the English text with Post-its bearing words in your target language.

This is the sequence the children learn (see box for the French equivalent of this presentation):

- Soak the peas one night.
- Wet some paper towels.
- Place the wet paper towels in a jar.
- Place two peas against the side of the jar.
- Wait three days.

Result: After three or four days, roots grow down. A stem grows up.

- Cover the jar.
- Turn the jar over.
- Wait three days.

Result: After three or four days, the roots and stem change direction.

Besides the words connected with plants and growing, children learn the words "to soak" and "wet," which will figure in the story "The Princess and the Pea." This is the procedure to follow over several days:

DAY 1
- "Today we are going to grow peas in a jar." On the blackboard or on a large piece of paper, draw a seed, a stem, a root, and a pea and teach the corresponding words.
- "Here is a bowl, some water, paper towels, a jar, and its cover." Let the children handle the objects. Do some TPR, asking the students to give the objects to other students, place the objects in different parts of the classroom, and hold the objects up or down.
- "Here is some water. I pour the water in the bowl. The water is wet. My finger is dry. I put my finger in the water. My finger is wet." Have the students wet their fingers and talk about wet and dry.
- "Put two peas in the water." Have each student drop two peas into the bowl. Talk about the peas being wet.
- "Soak the peas one night."

Un Petit Pois Intelligent	***A Smart Pea***
Aujourd'hui nous allons faire pousser des petits pois dans un bocal.	*Today we are going to grow peas in a jar.*
Voici une cuvette, de l'eau, des serviettes en papier et un bocal avec son couvercle.	*Here is a bowl, some water, paper towels, a jar, and its cover.*
Je verse de l'eau dans la cuvette. L'eau est mouillée. Mon doigt est sec. Je mets mon doigt dans l'eau. Mon doigt est mouillé.	*I pour the water into the bowl. The water is wet. My finger is dry. I put my finger in the water. My finger is wet.*
Les graines de petits pois sont dans la cuvette. Ils sont mouillées.	*The peas are in the bowl. They are wet.*
Fais tremper les graines de petits pois une nuit.	*Soak the peas one night.*
Mouille des serviettes en papier.	*Wet some paper towels.*
Place les serviettes mouillées dans le bocal.	*Place the wet paper towels in the jar.*
Glisse deux graines de petits pois contre la paroi.	*Place two peas against the side of the jar.*
Attends trois jours.	*Wait three days.*
Le petit pois pousse. C'est la racine. C'est la tige. Les racines poussent vers le bas. La tige pousse vers le haut.	*The peas are growing. This is the root. This is the stem. The roots grow down. The stem grows up.*
Ferme le bocal avec le couvercle.	*Cover the jar.*
Renverse le bocal.	*Turn the jar over.*
Maintenant, les racines et la tige changent de sens.	*Now the roots and stem change direction.*

DAY 2
- Using your drawing, review the words for "seed," "stem," "root," "pea," and teach the word "to grow." Draw and teach "The roots grow down" and "The stem grows up."
- "We soaked the peas one night."
- "Here are some paper towels."
- "Wet some paper towels." Demonstate.
- "Place the wet paper towels in a jar." Demonstrate.

- "Place two peas against the side of the jar." Demonstrate. Repeat this demonstration with the students miming the steps with you. When the students are ready, they carry out the actions themselves. It's a good idea for the teacher to prepare at least one extra jar in case some peas don't germinate.
- "Wait three days." Make sure the paper towels stay wet during this time. Do not cover the jars.

DAYS 3 AND 4
Children check the peas every day at the beginning of class, repeat the Gouin series orally, and read and repeat the sentences and pertinent vocabulary. When the roots and stem sprout, encourage them to say "The roots grow down" and "The stem grows up." You can add the word for "leaves."

DAY 5
- "Cover the jar." Demonstrate.
- "Turn the jar over." Demonstrate. Students practice and carry out these instructions.
- "Wait three days."

DAYS 6 AND 7
Let the children manipulate the sentences physically. You can use sentence strips in a pocket chart or have children, each holding a different sentence strip, line themselves up in order. You can write the sentences in random order on a piece of paper, make and distribute copies, and have the children cut apart the sentences and resequence them. Then students can create their own set of mixed-up sentences and exchange with another student for proper sequencing. One of these exercises can be used to evaluate reading ability.

DAY 8
By this time the children can be talking about the desired result: "After three or four days, the roots and stem change direction." To wrap up the experiment, the children can review the whole process with the actual materials (bowl, peas, water, paper towels, jars), write the Gouin series by copying it, and then read and record their own writing on a tape.

The next part of "The Princess and the Pea"— "One night it was raining. There was a storm with lightning and thunder"—provides an effective springboard to either an introductory or a more advanced unit on weather, which may be expanded to include seasons, months, and days of the week. Many of the weather expressions are memorized exchanges (What's the weather today? It's fine. It's raining, etc.), so the teacher can capitalize on the students' interest in playing teacher by having everyone make weather wheels. Then one child stands in front of the class with his or her weather wheel pointing to whatever weather he or she chooses and asks, "What's the weather today?" Many kids adore the chance to call on their classmates, and, in this case, the role is low-risk because the child with the weather wheel repeats the same question several times without having to think of an answer.

A good song in French that teaches weather and seasons and the appropriate prepositions is *"Chantez quelque soit le temps"* on *Sing, Dance, Laugh, and Eat Quiche 2* (MacArthur, 1995). "The Days of the Week" is another French song that incorporates rhythm and movement in the form of hand gestures. Sing it to the tune of "Twinkle, Twinkle, Little Star":

lundi	*(Pat thighs twice.)*
mardi	*(Clap hands twice.)*
merceredi	*(Roll hands around each other.)*
jeudi	*(Snap fingers of right hand.)*
vendredi	*(Snap fingers of left hand.)*
samedi	*(Make horizontal motion with both hands in front of you, right on top of left.)*
dimanche, dimanche	*(Make a circle by raising both arms overhead and joining fingertips. [It's the sun.] Sway to left and right.)*

Later in the story, the children will encounter the expression "the next day." To teach this expression and reinforce the sequence of the days of the week, children can create and play the game "The Next Day." This activity practices reading, writing, speaking, and listening. Each child needs seven index cards. He or she writes one day of the week on each card. In groups of four or five, children mix their cards and deal them all out. The first player lays down a card and announces it: "It's Tuesday." The second player looks through her cards for the next day. If she has it, she puts it down and announces, "The next day is Wednesday." If she doesn't have it, she says "Pass" and play continues with the third player, who must lay down the next day of the week, saying: "It's Thursday." The winner is the first player to lay down all his or her cards.

Total Physical Response reaches children who learn well through body movement, and has figured in many of the activities already described. "Line-Up" is a TPR activity that requires reading, writing, and speaking. Seven children, each holding a word card for a different day of the week, organize themselves into a line in correct order in front of the class. Then, while the seated children close their eyes, the teacher taps one child in the line-up on the shoulder and turns his or her card around so it cannot be read. The class open their eyes and a volunteer identifies the day that is missing. To make the game harder, two, three, or even four children can hide their cards. "Line-Up" can be used for any set of vocabulary words that need to be sequenced—alphabet, numbers, months, seasons, etc.

You can use TPR to teach the next lines of the story, "Someone knocked at the door. The king opened the door." Since the princess now enters the castle, you can move into a unit on house and furniture. Although there are many activities for reinforcing this vocabulary, "Tick-Tack-Toe" and "Concentration" are two that can be adapted to any thematic group of nouns. For "Tick-Tack-Toe," lay nine picture or word cards (the rooms of a house, furniture, or the exterior architectural features of a house) on the floor in a "Tick-Tack-Toe" grid and divide the class into two teams. In a large class, organize two simultaneous games so each child has the opportunity to play more often. The first student on Team X touches a card and identifies it. ("This is the bedroom.") If he is correct, the teacher collects the card and the student puts down a card marked X. Now the first student on Team O touches and identifies a card of her choice. If she is wrong, she does not put down a card marked O and play returns to Team X. When one team wins with three Xs or three Os in a line, instead of earning a single point, they can roll a die and earn the number of points shown. This method not only reinforces numbers, but also allows a losing team to stay in the competition. For "Concentration," you can use two copies of the same pictures or words (that is, match two pictures of a kitchen or two cards that say "the kitchen"), or you can have the children match a picture to a word or match a singular word to a plural word ("kitchen" and "kitchens"). It is important in this game that the children identify aloud the card they turn up; for example, "This is the dining room." Other ideas for reinforcing rooms and furniture include drawing maps, making dioramas, and describing locations with appropriate prepositions.

The class will understand most of the next part of the story, which they learned with the units on family and emotions and the "Smart Pea" experiment: "It was a young girl. She was damp. Her clothes were soaked. She said, 'I am a real princess.' The prince was happy." The next line, "The queen said, 'We'll see about that,'" needs to be demonstrated by the teacher.

Some children respond to competition. The next lines of the story—"The queen put a pea under the mattress. She put twenty mattresses on the bed"—afford a chance to reinforce numbers. Use a real pea and twenty pieces of foam, felt, or other fabrics to represent the mattresses. After reviewing the numbers while manipulating the mattress, children can play the competitive "Around the World." This extremely popular game can be used to reinforce any content area using picture cues, numbers, or word cards, depending on whether or not you want the children to practice reading. The children arrange themselves in a semicircle with the teacher (or a student playing the teacher's role) facing them. The first player moves to stand behind the person to her left. The teacher then shows these two players a picture or word card, and the first one to call out the correct word wins. For example, if the teacher shows 9 (or 8+1=), the first person in the pair to call out "Nine!" wins. If the winner is the player standing behind, she moves to stand behind the next person in the semicircle, and the game continues. The goal is to beat everyone in the circle—to go "around the world"—and to make it back to your own seat. In reality, this almost never happens. If the seated player wins, he moves to stand behind the player to his left, and the defeated player sits in the empty seat. Often, the two players call out the word at the same time ("It's a tie"), in which case they get another chance. This game offers the opportunity to engage a child who usually does not participate by asking him or her to be the "teacher." The "teacher" does not have to speak, yet he or she bears the responsibility for moving the game forward.

The interest of many girls and some boys can be captured through dolls. Using Barbie and Ken dolls, children can act out the next part of the story: "The princess undressed, took a bath, washed herself, dried herself, put on her pajamas, brushed her hair, brushed her teeth, and went to bed. Good night!" Use the dolls as well as real objects (toothbrush, hairbrush, soap, and towel) to demonstrate. Then have the children manipulate the dolls or role-play in a game of charades with the rest of the class. For reading and writing practice, students can each draw and label four different activities, mix their four pictures with those of a partner, sequence the activities in the order in which they personally perform them at night or in the morning, and then read the sentences aloud to each other, to the teacher, or into a tape recorder. A good idea is to teach an authentic lullaby. In French, the song *"Fais dodo 'Colas mon p'tit frère"* also reinforces the words for "up" and "down," which children learned in the "Smart Pea" experiment.

The story continues with the expression "the next day," which the children have already learned: "The next day the queen said, 'Did you sleep well?' The princess said, 'No, terribly. My back hurts. I have black and blue marks all over.' " Time for a unit on body parts! You can start with the well-known song "Head, shoulders, knees, and toes," with appropriate motions, and move on to the game "Simon Says." Instead of saying "Simon Says" you can reinforce words from the story by saying "My ____ hurt(s)." Work into the game gradually. In the first round, the teacher says "My head hurts" and touches his or her head; the students repeat the words and imitate the gesture. In the second round, the teacher touches his or head without naming it; the students touch their heads and say "My head hurts." In the third round, the teacher says "My head hurts" but doesn't touch anything; the students touch their heads and repeat the words. In the fourth round, the teacher fools the students by touching the wrong part. He or she says, "My head hurts" while touching his or her knees. The students imitate the words and touch the right body part, their heads. Finally, different students play the role of teacher.

There are several good songs for learning body parts in French, including *"Bonjour, Monsieur!"* by Matt Maxwell, in the book and tape collection *Let's Sing and Learn French* (1992), and *"Mal à la tête,"* on the tape *Sing, Dance, Laugh, and Eat Quiche 1*. If children have trouble remembering the order in which the body parts are mentioned in these songs, you can post picture cues in the correct order. After all, the point is for students to identify the body parts, not to learn their sequence in a particular song. If you have a separate microphone for your tape recorder, have the children sing "karaoke." Each student sings part of the song individually into the mike before handing it to the next student. The sound quality is better—making evaluation easier for you—and the children love hearing themselves.

An effective way for children to practice writing words for body parts is for them to trace their own bodies on large sheets of butcher paper and then to label the parts. They can make their own "Bingo" game cards by writing words of their own choice in a grid that you hand out—no duplicates allowed! If children take turns acting as callers, they get speaking as well as listening and reading practice.

Another popular game that requires writing, reading, speaking, and listening is "Change Chairs!" All of the children but one write a word assigned by the teacher on a Post-it note that they attach to their desktop. The desks are arranged in a circle, and the extra child stands in the center. That child then calls out two words, such as "shoulders and back." The students sitting at the desks labeled with "shoulders" and "back" have to switch places while the extra child tries to take one of their seats. If the extra child succeeds, the child with no seat will be the new caller. Since children are always changing seats, they must read, understand, and sometimes say several different words. This game can be adapted to any group of vocabulary words, and the name of the game can be altered to fit the game. For example, to practice words for body parts, the game can be called "Hospital" and the caller can be the "doctor"; to practice vegetables or fruits, the game can be "Salad" or "Fruit Salad" and the caller can be the "cook."

"The Princess and the Pea" ends with the words, "The queen was surprised. She said, 'You are a real princess!' The prince was happy. The king was delighted. The prince and the princess got married."

Because some children can be reached through drama, a good way to wrap up this unit is with a play that can be presented live and/or videotaped. Some teachers avoid producing plays because children can become preoccupied with costumes and who will play which part. You can lessen the competition over roles by requiring everyone to learn the whole play and by not actually assigning roles until two or three days before the presentation, and you can relieve the stress over wardrobe by requiring children to be totally responsible for their own costumes.

An alternative wrap-up is to make an illustrated class book of the story, which is likely to reach artistic students. This project could provide a link with art classes if the art teacher can incorporate it into his or her lessons.

Because children vary in the length of time they can focus, frequent changes of activity in every lesson help to keep all students engaged. Teachers are also more likely to reach all students by using different approaches, such as song and rhythm, movement, reading, drawing, crafts, drama, writing, and conversation in pairs and small groups. It is a good idea to capitalize on the narcissistic tendencies of young children by recording them on audio- and videotape, and by arranging small informal performances for other children or for parents.

La Princesse et le petit pois

Il était une fois une famille royale. Il y avait le prince, le roi et la reine.
Le prince cherche une vraie princesse. Les filles étaient trop petites, trop grandes, trop grosses, trop minces, trop gaies, trop fâchées ou trop tristes. Le prince est déçu. Le prince est triste.
Une nuit il pleut. Il y a une tempête avec des éclairs et du tonnerre.
On frappe à la porte. Le roi ouvre la porte.
C'est une jeune fille. Elle est mouillée. Ses vêtements sont trempés.
Elle dit, "Je suis une vraie princesse." Le prince est content. La reine dit, "On va voir."
La reine a mis un petit pois sous le matelas. Elle a placé 20 matelas sur le lit.
La princesse se déshabille. Elle se baigne. Elle se lave. Elle se sèche. Elle s'habille en pyjama. Elle se brosse les cheveux. Elle se brosse les dents. Elle se couche. Bonne nuit!
Le lendemain matin (Le jour suivant) la reine dit, "Avez-vous bien dormi?"
La princesse dit, "Non, horriblement mal. J'ai mal au dos. J'ai des bleus partout."
Le reine est étonnée. Elle dit, "Vous êtes une vraie princesse!"
Le prince est content. Le roi est gai. Le prince et la princesse se marient.

Linking Language and Context: An Example of an Interdisciplinary Approach

Lena L. Lucietto
Isidore Newman School
New Orleans, Louisiana

INTRODUCTION

It has been recognized that children learn a foreign language best and retain their learning longer when they are given the opportunity to connect language with something else, such as art, dramatization, geography, music, or dance (Brooks 1960; Hirsch 1954). Focusing the child's attention on the activity rather than on the language heightens motivation and encourages learning and retention (French Education Project 1989; Early 1991,32; Pottier and Communeau 1990).

By conjoining the foreign language with other disciplines, the teacher enriches the foreign language classroom and helps to reveal the differences between the native and the target cultures. By exploring related fields, even at a young age, students become aware of important cultural features. As early as the 1960s, Lucietto and Milanesi (1964,5) suggested to teachers that they correlate foreign language topics with those of other curriculum areas:

> Important cultural values may be found in areas of learning related to that of foreign language. Such areas of learning are history, science, music, art, geography, and literature. Exploration of these related fields will make the student aware of the depth and complexity of the culture and civilization of the country whose language he is studying.

Wilga Rivers (1983,28) encourages foreign language teachers to cooperate with teachers of social studies and other subject areas to develop in their students the flexibility required to live in a world in need of solving problems of planetary concern.

The purpose of this article is to report a high-interest interdisciplinary activity (Lucietto 1993) that has been used successfully with students of French and whose methodology has the potential to be adapted for use with other languages.

A unit on the *santons* of Provence was rich in cultural and creative potential for young students. It offered students the opportunity to work with teachers from another discipline and to use authentic materials—original *santons* from towns in Provence. The project also allowed the students to learn about an interesting area of France, rich in tradition. Creating their own *santons* gave the students the opportunity to express their own imagination and personality.

A number of textbooks, travel books, books on French customs and traditions, and children's books (Buther 1965; Canta, Lorge, and Rensonnet 1991; François 1953; Sacré and Backes 1992) were consulted to organize a background presentation to students. Then, with the help of both the French teacher and the art teacher, students received an introduction to Provence, its landscape, its historical, cultural, and artistic features, and its products. As preparation for making their own *santons*, students learned about the origins of the *crèche* and the *santon* tradition and how that tradition continues in Provence today (de Sales 1986,16; Foley 1959; Guieu 1990; Ross 1991, 58–63).

The *Santon* Tradition

In Provence, Christmas traditions have always been very strong (Guieu 1989,3). During the seventeenth and eighteenth centuries, the story of the nativity was presented in live performances or pastorales, in puppet shows, and in figurine displays, or *crèches*. Jean-Louis Lagnel, who was born in Marseille in 1764, is credited with creating the first clay *santon* in 1803 (Sacré et Backes 1992,10). Others attribute the introduction of the *santons* to Italian peddlers who, it is said, were the first to bring the small, simply crafted, brightly colored clay figurines to Marseille (Foley 1959, 78). Eventually, local artisans began to make them in the dress of the period (Ross 1991, 60). The Provençal figurines came to be known as *santons*, or "little saints." Today, the little figurines are still made of raw clay and then fired and hand painted with watercolors or acrylics. Their gentle appeal continues to be as strong today as it was 200 years ago.

Since the *santon* tradition emerged at the time of the French Revolution, the figurines include, in addition to the biblical personages and animals, about 150 characters portraying humble folk, not the monarchy and the bourgeoisie. They include the peasants and tradespeople of the typical Provençal village. The highest placed *santon* is the mayor, with his tricolor sash. He is represented because of his important position in the local community.

Farmyard animals—horses, sheep, lambs, goats, geese, ducks, chicks, pigs, hens, cats, and the shepherd's dogs—are a significant and lively element of the *crèche*. Their presence has inspired the imagination of people through the ages (Foley 1959, 105–108), and a number of Provençal folktales owe their origin to this presence. One of the best-known legends is that of the golden goat, a mythical creature who wanders in the moonlight and is the protector of ancient monuments and ruins. There is also the belief that cats receive the power of speech on Christmas eve, but alas, they speak only in Provençal.

Each *santon* tells his or her own story by the modest gift that he or she brings to the Newborn Child (Dufrenne, Potier, and Carbonel 1986; Foley 1959; Guieu 1990). For example, the shepherd Gervais brings a wheel of cheese. The drummer brings music, which he plays on the drum and the flute. A woman offers a cradle so that the child may be more comfortable. The mayor carries no gift in his hands, but instead offers a speech. The animals keep the baby comfortable with their warm breath. Students certainly have a wide selection from which to choose!

Some *Santons* and Their Gifts	
Baker	Carries a basket of bread, *pompes,* and *fougasses,* the favorite cakes of the Provençal Christmas season.
Chimney Sweep	Carries his brushes and his *marmotte* (woodchuck).
Fishwife	Carries baskets of fish, shiny scales fastened at her waist.
Mayor	A portly gentleman, the mayor sometimes carries a lantern and an umbrella. He wears a blue, white, and red sash.
A Peasant Woman	Carries a half-litre can. The metric system has been used in France since 1801.
Ravi	Village simpleton, with arms raised in wonder, and his female counterpart, *la Ravido.*
Shepherd	Portrayed in both upright and kneeling positions, often with a sheep or lamb. The old shepherd has a white beard and leans on a long staff. The younger shepherd carries a sheep on his shoulders.
Washerwoman	Carries Marseille soap.

Woman with a Brass Foot Warmer	Her bright red umbrella is a sign of status and wealth.
Woman from Arles	*L'Arlésienne* wears a traditional, but chic costume. As depicted in the Bizet/Daudet drama, women from Arles have a reputation as heartbreakers.

The making of *santons* continues as a cottage industry, and entire families are often involved in their production. Many well-known *santonniers*, or *santon*-makers, are active today in Aubagne, Aix, and Marseille. They use their imagination in creating the costumes, coloring, and postures of the *santons*. Every December, *santon* fairs are held in Marseille, Aix, and other cities in Provence. Many people start or complete their *crèches* with purchases from these fairs. Visitors to Provence may view collections of *santons* in shops and museums in Marseille and nearby towns.

SUGGESTIONS FOR CLASSROOM ADAPTATION

The following suggestions for *santon*-making projects may be adapted for use in kindergarten, primary, and middle schools.

Singing Songs and Writing Short Poems about the *Santons*. Younger children may delight in singing songs about the *santons*. The charming book, *The Saintons go to Bethlehem* (Hill and Maxwell 1935), presents accompaniments for twenty different songs of the *santons*. They are adaptations of old Provençal folk songs, each one featuring a different *santon*.

Dramatic Presentations. In some kindergartens or primary schools, it may be possible to follow the old Provençal custom of presenting a Christmas play of the *crèche* (a *pastorale* or *crèche vivante*) some time during the week before Christmas. The roles of the *santons* are taken by the children, who may also wish to stage a mini-parade, or "Christmas March to the Star," in their costumes before the play begins (Butler 1965). Hill and Maxwell (1935) include several full-page pictures that suggest simple ideas for the staging of the scenes. Arranged in appropriate order, the whole book of songs may form a Christmas play or *pastorale*.

Another option for dramatization might be a playlet that demonstrates how the making of *santons* could involve the whole family (de Sales 1987, 65–68). Children may take the roles of parents or children in telling the steps involved in making the *santons:* clay, color, and love.

Making *Santons* from Red Clay. True *santons* are molded from the red clay in Provence. The red-colored terra cotta clay available to schools here provides students with an opportunity to create an "authentic" *santon*. After studying the individual characteristics of a number of *santons*, each student selects a personage and an animal whose story and gift appeal in a personal way. Under the direction of the art and French teachers, students fashion their two figurines. They allow the figurines to dry slowly, and after the figurines are fired, the students paint them with acrylics. Students should be encouraged to use their creativity in making and painting their *santons*.

An Alternative to Working with Clay. An enjoyable alternative to creating with clay is to use the overhead projector to project large pictures of *santons* onto poster board or construction paper. The pictures are colored with felt tip pens and may be laminated, or simply used as they are, to create an interesting classroom display.

Oral Presentations and Evaluation of the Completed Projects. Upon completion of the *santons*, each student gives a brief oral presentation in French about his or her *santons* and about the gifts offered by the *santons*. Depending upon the level of the student, this could be simply an identification of the *santon* with a statement such as *"Elle offre un petit lit pour l'enfant."* Students are evaluated on how well they have followed instructions in making their *santons*. Consideration also is given to creativity and accuracy in depicting the personage or animal.

A Santon Social. A party or tea just prior to the Christmas vacation provides a joyful send-off and an opportunity for the youngsters to display their *santons* and share the various aspects of their *santon*-making experience with other students and teachers. Administrators and parents could be invited as well. Such a social function affords an effective way for other members of the school community to recognize the accomplishments of the students and the excellence of the French program.

A Field Trip. *Santons* are fascinating to collect, and displays of *santons* may be found not only in museums, but anywhere someone has developed a love for them. A field trip may be organized to view a *santon* display. It is useful for students to see a wide array of the figurines before embarking on their own project. The field trip would give them a context for their work.

Applications to Other Languages. The approach and procedures described in this paper are appropriate not only for different stages of learning, but also for teaching other languages and cultures. Teachers of other languages may wish to develop an interdisciplinary project that would bring students into direct contact with salient cultural features of the language they teach.

I am grateful to Marcel Carbonel, world-renowned *santonnier*, Ateliers Marcel Carbonel, Marseille, France, author of *Petit dictionnaire des Santons de Provence*. I also thank Suzanne González, School of Art and Design, University of Illinois, Urbana, Illinois. The Cultural Services of the French Embassy in New York have long made available to teachers *santon* drawings by André Filippi.

REFERENCES

Brooks, Nelson. 1960. *Language and Language Learning: Theory and Practice.* New York: Harcourt, Brace & World.

Butler, Suzanne. 1965. *Starlight in Tourrone.* Boston: Little, Brown & Company.

Canta, Lillo, Cathy Lorge, and Paul Rensonnet. 1991. *Un Noël en Provence.* Belgique: Editions Presse Européenne Averbode. Edition Spéciale: Tremplin Noël.

de Sales, R. de Roussy. 1987. *Noël: Christmas in France.* Lincolnwood, IL: National Textbook Company.

Dufrenne, Pascale, Georges Potier, and Marcel Carbonel. 1986. *Petit Dictionnaire des Santons de Provence.* Marseille, France: Ateliers Marcel Carbonel.

Early, Margaret. 1992. "Key Visuals: Links between Language and the Context in Which It Occurs." *Language Teaching* 25(1):32.

Foley, Daniel J. 1959. *Little Saints of Christmas: The Santons of Provence.* Boston: Dresser, Chapman and Grimes.

French Education Project. 1989. *Kit ou Double.* Baton Rouge: Louisiana State University.

Françoise. *Noël for Jeanne-Marie.* 1953. New York: Charles Scribner's Sons.

Guieu, Jean-Max. 1989. "Christmas in Provence." *Jerome Quarterly* 5(1):3–4.

———. 1990. "Noël en Provence." Videotape and videoscript. Washington, DC: Laboratory Center, School of Languages and Linguistics, Georgetown University.

Hill, Helen, and Violet Maxwell. 1935. *The Saintons Go to Bethlehem.* New York: Macmillan.

Hirsch, Ruth. 1954. *Audio-Visual Aids in Language Teaching.* Washington, D.C.: Georgetown University Press.

Lucietto, Lena L. 1993. "*Les Santons de Provence:* Inspiration for an Interdisciplinary Project." *Mid-Atlantic Journal of Foreign Language Pedagogy: Practical Applications to Theoretical Concerns* 1(1): 77–90.

———. and Albert Milanesi. 1964. *Curriculum Guide for French, Grades 7–12.* Chicago: Chicago Board of Education.

Naughton, Helen T. 1978. *"Contact et Créativité:* Team Teaching in a French C.E.S." *The French Review* 52(2): 261–266.

Pottier, Patricia, and Pascal Communeau. 1990. *"Des objets pour agir et pour parler* (Objects for Action and for Speaking)." *Le Français dans le monde* 232(4): 51–53.

Rivers, Wilga. 1983. *Speaking in Many Tongues.* 3rd ed. New York: Cambridge University Press.

Ross, Corinne Madden. 1991. *Christmas in France.* Lincolnwood, IL: Passport Books.

Sacré, Marie-José, and Jacqueline Backes. 1992. *Arthur et les santons.* Belgique: Editions Presse Européenne Averbode. Edition Spéciale: Dorémi Noël.

PART 4

Expanding the Focus of **FLES***

A "French-ship" with the Community

Harriet Saxon
Pierrepont School
Rutherford, New Jersey

A foreign language program in the elementary school must be totally integrated within the school curriculum. The success of the second-language acquisition program depends on the support of the administration, the faculty, the students, and the parents. The **FLES*** program must be coordinated on all levels with the district's senior high school foreign language program and should include successful transitions and advancement on all levels.

The foreign language program in the elementary school must be an interdisciplinary subject that combines the efforts and the creative talents of the entire school staff. This may include the integration of the science departments, the art and music curriculums, the social studies departments, the English and reading curriculums, the home economics and industrial arts departments, and all other components of the elementary school curriculums and staff.

Success of the foreign language program must also depend on the support of the community of the school district. This support is both financial and educational and is vital for the continuation and success of the second-language acquisition program in the elementary school. The French language program in the Rutherford, New Jersey, School District has successfully, since its adoption in 1979, maintained an interest and working relationship with local businesses and the citizens of the community. The French students, teachers, parents, and friends actively participate each year to create new projects and activities that will interest the Rutherford community and show the relevance and necessity of teaching second languages at an early age.

The following is a description of successful projects and activities in the elementary school French language classroom that have involved the entire community—its administration and citizens of the district. The program at all times has received the cooperation and encouragement of the business community and local citizens' organizations. The ideas and special activities may be adapted to other cities, towns, and districts according to the individual foreign language programs in their elementary schools.

NATIONAL FOREIGN LANGUAGE WEEK, NATIONAL FLES* DAY

Each year, the students in the French language classes present a program to the mayor and the members of the borough council. They are joined by students in the foreign languages at Rutherford High School. The students in the second-language acquisition classes in the elementary school dress in French costumes, prepare posters about language study, and present a program about the importance of language study in today's world. Each year, the eighth-grade French students visit Québec and are welcomed at a reception at the *hôtel de ville*, the city hall. The students then present gifts to the mayor of Rutherford and the council members from the mayor of Québec and the city of Québec. This program is presented at a meeting of the mayor, the council, and the citizens of Rutherford. The mayor proclaims the week as *National Foreign Language Week* and declares a specific day (March 1st) as *National Foreign Language in the Elementary Schools (FLES*) Day.*

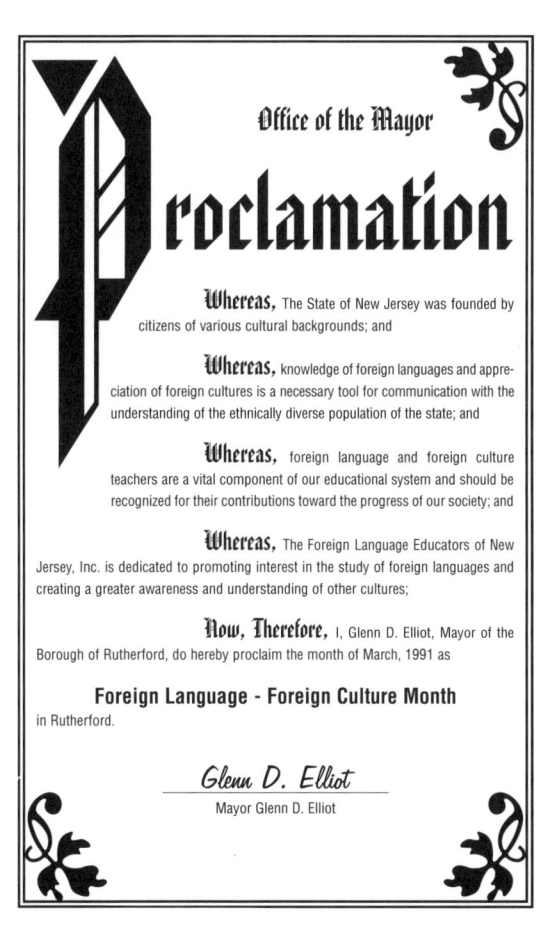

Office of the Mayor

Proclamation

Whereas, The State of New Jersey was founded by citizens of various cultural backgrounds; and

Whereas, knowledge of foreign languages and appreciation of foreign cultures is a necessary tool for communication with the understanding of the ethnically diverse population of the state; and

Whereas, foreign language and foreign culture teachers are a vital component of our educational system and should be recognized for their contributions toward the progress of our society; and

Whereas, The Foreign Language Educators of New Jersey, Inc. is dedicated to promoting interest in the study of foreign languages and creating a greater awareness and understanding of other cultures;

Now, Therefore, I, Glenn D. Elliot, Mayor of the Borough of Rutherford, do hereby proclaim the month of March, 1991 as

Foreign Language - Foreign Culture Month
in Rutherford.

Glenn D. Elliot
Mayor Glenn D. Elliot

During this time, the foreign language classes also decorate the windows of the public library and prepare exhibits of posters and projects at the library. The projects have included the following:

- A giant mural of the city of Paris that was completed with the assistance of the art teacher
- A three-dimensional display of the area of the *Tour Eiffel* that featured a large wooden Eiffel Tower decorated with white lights and surrounded by the parks, gardens, cafés, monuments, and people of Paris
- Large posters with various themes, such as

    "Shake Hands with the World, Learn a Second Language!"

- Three-dimensional Mardi Gras "chars," or floats, with French themes, such as French foods (a Perrier or Orangina float), French gardens and parks, Paris, Parisian and Québécois monuments, a French classroom, and French sports, and French and American themes, such as *Les Misérables* and *Le Fantôme de l'Opéra*.

During National Foreign Language Week, the French students, with the assistance of the art teacher and the French teacher, also present a display at the Bergen County Education Association's "Excellence in Education" display at the Bergen shopping mall in Paramus, New Jersey. Thus, the French classroom extends beyond the immediate community and reaches the entire county and its school districts.

The French teacher must be aware of important events in the community and nearby districts and try, whenever possible and practical, to incorporate class projects and community activities. For example, as part of the Rutherford community's recent bicentennial celebration, the students presented an outdoor French poster and painting exhibit in one of the borough's parks.

Bienvenue à Québec (In Class)

Each year, the eighth-grade students who have successfully completed the four-year French language program in the elementary school spend a four-day in-class experience in French Canada. Members of the local board of education are invited to join the class. People in the Rutherford community are also invited to join the class and may assist with various aspects of their trip. For example, the owner of the local art shop assisted with her knowledge of art and architecture. The owner of a local specialty food shop discussed the special foods and cheeses of Québec. A local opera singer assisted with singing French and Québécois songs. Recently, the French teacher and several students presented a program about Québec to the senior citizen groups of Rutherford.

The program was enthusiastically received and thereby earned wonderful support from the senior citizens of the community, who have volunteered to assist students and love the opportunity to speak French. Many had already visited Québec and several have visited Québec since the presentation. *Bravo, Québec et les Québécois!*

LE MARCHÉ AUX PUCES

The eighth-grade French class each year sponsors a French flea market, *Le Marché aux Puces*. This is a total school and community project that involves students, parents, faculty, and the contributions, assistance, and participation of the entire Rutherford community. The day is filled with fun, food, and activities for all and has become a French-Québécois social and cultural event.

> You are invited for lunch at the
> *Marché aux Puces*
> Pierrepont School
> 70 E. Pierrepont Avenue
> Rutherford, NJ 07070
>
> Saturday, March 22
> 9:00 A.M. – 4:00 P.M.

Le Marché aux Puces is a fund raiser for the students who will travel to Québec in May. Local businesses graciously contribute items for *le tombola* (raffle and door prizes) and are invited to be guests at the Café Pierrepont for a French luncheon. This includes *la soupe à l'oignon gratinée, quiche, crêpe, salade verte,* and special French desserts from *La Pâtisserie Québec*. Parents and students prepare the luncheon, and students from all the classes help serve and host the Café-Restaurant and assist with arts and crafts and sales. The mayor and members of the borough council, the board of education, and local service associations are invited to be guests at the *Marché*. Local politicians and members of Congress are also invited, as are friends from the local French hotel, Le Novotel. Advertisements and publicity are essential for the success of the day, and shops and businesses allow signs and posters to be placed in their windows. Local radio and cable stations make announcements of the *Marché* and the newspapers publicize the event with pictures and news articles. A guignol puppet show (*Le Théâtre du Guignol*) welcomes young children from the entire community and neighboring towns. Local florists help provide flowers, plants, and balloons for the French flower markets and gifts. *Le Marché aux Puces* is a wonderful way to combine the delights of learning a second language with a true friendship with the community!

Let's Join a Parade! Rutherford Celebrates the Bicentennial of the French Revolution

Students plant the *arbre de liberté!* The French students of Rutherford, with the assistance of the Shade Tree Commission of the borough, planted a linden tree (*un arbre de liberté*) at the same time that children in France celebrated the bicentennial by planting linden trees throughout their country. The entire school community attended the planting of the tree, including the mayor, parents, and friends. The ceremony, which took place in front of the Union School, included songs, poems, and the singing of *La Marseillaise*. French students were dressed in special costumes that copied the styles of the French Revolution. The French classes also prepared a special *bicentenaire* window during July at the Rutherford Public Library and asked the local and school libraries to display books about the French Revolution. School display cases showed posters, books, and souvenirs of the Revolution.

The final event of the commemoration of the French Revolution in Rutherford was the students' participation in the Rutherford Memorial Day Parade. The students prepared felt banners and garlands of blue, white, and red paper flowers and designed pictures and posters. The students were dressed in Revolutionary costumes and carried large American and French flags. The entire community applauded and, once again, supported and enjoyed the activities of the elementary school French program.

Nos Amis au Novotel

The students in the French program have become *les amis* of the staff of Le Novotel Hotel in Lyndhurst, New Jersey. The students have been invited to decorate the hotel for the December holidays and they have created life-size paper figurines of French book characters such as Bécassine, Madeline, Babar, and Linnea in Monet's garden. The students also created holiday figurines, such as Père Noël, Cendrillon, Anges, and French can-can dancers. The art projects, with the assistance of the art teacher, Diana Hecking, also included representations of the Phantom of the Opera and the dolphin of the Novotel Hotel. In addition, the students decorated Christmas trees at the Novotel Hotel in Lyndhurst and the one in New York City. The students were welcomed at a reception at the hotel and then honored at a special *Fête des Chandeleurs*. The students were thanked by the staff for designing the hotel's Christmas card, which was then duplicated and sent to Novotel affiliates throughout the world.

The students also recently spent an entire day with the Novotel staff to experience a "working day" at a French hotel. The students were taught how to make reservations, set tables, and fold napkins in Le Café Nicole, arrange the guest rooms, and prepare special children's beverages at Le Bar. The students learned how to complete passports and welcome guests at the hotel. They then entered a contest sponsored by the hotel, and the winning posters and compositions were submitted for publication in the Novotel Hotel international newspaper. The winning entries were later framed and mounted on the wall at the entrance to the hotel restaurant, Le Café Nicole. These projects and the friendship with the hotel have brought a bit of Paris to the students and friends in the Rutherford school district. Often, members of the community are invited to join the students and enjoy experiencing the culture of the foreign language being taught. The projects with Novotel have also provided wonderful publicity for the Rutherford French Program and incentives for the students and the community.

Other projects that involve the businesses and citizens of the community may include the following:

- Contact local restaurants that serve French or Cajun food and plan a visit to the restaurant.
- Invite a local chef to school to discuss French cooking.
- Locate a French *pâtisserie* to visit with the class. Ask senior citizens to help chaperone the group.
- Publicize all events and projects in school publications, including calendars and newspapers.
- Ask local newspapers and community bulletins to publicize **FLES*** events.
- Seek out local service organizations that would be interested in funding scholarships for study or travel to Québec. The Kiwanis Club International recently awarded a scholarship to a handicapped student that enabled him to travel to Québec.

FLES* students and teachers *must* be involved in the community because the funding for budgets and special programs is often voted on by the citizens of the community. **FLES*** programs must continue to expand to include *all* students on all grade levels so that our young people will be prepared to meet the challenges of the twenty-first century and become the peacemakers of tomorrow's world! Create, communicate, and celebrate so that the community will welcome its young citizens and their contributions. Then, you and your students will maintain and enjoy a true French-ship with the community.

Of Tapestries, Tortillas, and Mulberry Bushes

Lena L. Lucietto
Isidore Newman School
New Orleans, Louisiana

Each year, for one afternoon in late January or February, depending upon the timing of the Mardi Gras break, sixth-grade foreign language students at the Isidore Newman School in New Orleans enter an international world as they participate in the annual Sixth-Grade International Festival. The event dates back to 1989, the year in which sixth-grade French and Spanish classes joined the existing sixth-grade Latin class as the beginning point of our foreign language offerings. Since that initial year, the international festival has continued to capture the attention of key decision makers in our school.

The festival, in which the sixth-grade students perform for each other, their teachers, other teachers, and administrators, features three important components:

- Researching and writing skits
- Staging and presenting the skits
- Sharing an International Foods Table featuring dishes prepared by the parents

A middle school foreign language teacher coordinates the event each year. The coordinator begins to organize the details of the festival and to meet with other teachers in mid-November or early December. The children receive information about the festival and begin to plan their skits. A letter is sent to parents explaining the festival and inviting them to prepare a food that is representative of the culture whose language their child is studying. Depending upon the number of classes presenting skits (usually eight or nine), each group is given from eight to ten minutes for its presentation. The principal of the middle school opens the event with a brief presentation during which, through skillful questioning, he draws the children into a discussion about the value of the foreign language study and the interconnections between English and the foreign language they are studying. A thirty-minute intermission midway into the presentations allows the students to enjoy the various international dishes.

The festival generates many positive results. In addition to calling attention to an outstanding Sequential FLES program, it:

- Energizes the students
- Calls upon student and teacher creativity
- Encourages parental participation
- Provides young students with a memory of a positive early foreign language experience
- Allows teachers to show their excellent organizational skills
- Captures the attention of school administrators and parents.

The event also enables students to demonstrate their creativity and talent before classmates, teachers, and administrators.

SELECTION OF THEMES AND PREPARATION OF SKITS

The heart of the program remains the creation and presentation of the class skits. Under the guidance of the teacher, children brainstorm and participate in all aspects of the skit's creation—discussing the ideas, developing the story, researching information in the library and on the Internet, writing the script, preparing the props and costumes, and anticipating the event, where they will be the focus of attention for the duration of their presentation. Since the skit is presented in the foreign language the students are actually studying, its development can serve as the springboard for some homework assignments. Teachers prepare cassettes for take-home practice and reserve some class time for rehearsals. The week before the festival, the mini-theater, where the festival will take place, is reserved for rehearsals by the various language classes. The drama teachers add to the students' confidence by serving as consultants during the staging of the skits.

The material for the skits has been as varied as the talents and inspiration of the individual classes. In addition to acting, the skits have included singing, dancing, and the playing of musical instruments. In larger classes, so that everyone could have a speaking role, students have prepared humorous commercials for presentation between skits. Portable backdrops representing appropriate cultural settings have been painted by teachers and students, and are recycled and refurbished from year to year. The themes of the skits presented over the years have included:
- The reenactment of the Battle of Hastings and the French conquest of England, as told in the Bayeux tapestry (students wore "armor" made of colorful paper, painted with black markers to simulate the mail worn by soldiers of that time)

- Baseball in Santo Domingo, with "speaking trees" serving as narrators
- The Annual International Cooking Contest (inspired by a television program seen on Univision)
- Presentations based on the fables of La Fontaine
- A pageant featuring the dances, music, and flags of the Hispanic countries (children entered by twos, carrying the flag of a particular country as a song was sung in that country's honor)
- Presentations based on tales of Greek and Roman mythology—for example, the story of the star-crossed lovers Pyramus and Thisbe, or "How the Mulberry Bush Got Red Berries," or "Androcles and the Lion," the story of the Christian who was saved for his kindness toward a lion
- A television commercial for selling bulls

Great attention is given to the costumes worn in the presentations. While some costumes may be as simple as dark pants and a white shirt, when a particular role calls for it, students and parents often use their creativity to prepare more elaborate outfits. The making of the props gives students with artistic talent the opportunity to share their gifts.

The International Food Table

An initial letter explaining the international festival is sent to parents early on. Then, two weeks before the festival, each teacher sends home with her students a letter specific to the International Food Table. The letter explains that a thirty-minute block of time will be set aside for everyone to taste foods typical of the various countries. To avoid waste and to have each child contribute to the refreshments, parents are asked to provide enough food (or juice, soda, small cups, paper plates, napkins, or utensils) for the needs of their child's class group. To ascertain that all needs are provided for, the parents are asked to indicate ahead of time the food or item that they plan to provide. Examples of typical foods included on the food table are French cheeses, croissants, flan, tropical fruits, guacamole, Spanish tortillas, salsa and chips, tacos, corn bread, éclairs, and piña colada smoothies. The food table is also used as an opportunity to share with students simple, but authentic international recipes.

Parents may prepare a favorite recipe or something special, if they wish. Once students select a food or item that they wish to bring, the letter to parents, which specifies the food or item selected, is sent home with the child. The "stub" at the bottom of the letter is signed by the parent and returned with the student. Students are asked to identify the food they bring by affixing a label containing the name of the dish written in the foreign language. They are also asked to affix a label showing their name and the name of their foreign language teacher, so that any plates or containers may be appropriately returned to the parents. On festival day, during the half-hour preceding the opening of school, the students bring their food to the food-gathering location next to the Mini-Theater, which is staffed by room mothers and parent volunteers.

The students are given a second opportunity to sample the foods after all the skits have been presented. (The children have been advised to eat a very light lunch on that day!) The remaining food is shared with members of the school staff, with those who have helped to set up the event receiving first call.

Clean-Up

Students are required to help their teachers break the sets, restore order to the staging area, and return the props and costumes to their classrooms. A teacher serves at a final checkpoint to verify that the students have completed all of their obligations and that they may, therefore, be dismissed.

A Giant Step Forward for FLES*

"When you have a good product, it is important to let people know about it" (Lipton 1998, 273). By showcasing our very effective **FLES*** teachers and students via this internal program we are reaching a number of our publics: younger students, who truly look forward to their year to participate in this event; older students, who are put back in touch with the memory of their own festival experience; teachers of foreign language at other levels; other teachers; librarians; the headmaster; the principal; other administrators; staff members; and parents. It gives us the chance to explain our program, publicize its goals and activities, and demonstrate what the children have accomplished in their foreign language study. It provides an opportunity to show that our children can actually use their foreign language. By giving our students this opportunity to use the language actively, we help them to become more confident and successful in their use of the language. We also demonstrate to our decision makers what successful students can do with their foreign language skills. As our students demonstrate that they enjoy learning foreign languages, they convince others that it is important to work hard and to do well in foreign language classes (Brown 1997, 8). Perhaps what the Sixth-Grade International Festival means to our students may best be summed up by the words of a sixth grader to his teacher right after the festival—"Merci, madame!" Is there a better way to teach future decision makers the value of learning a foreign language?

Endnote

Participation in the International Festival is considered such an important part of our Sequential FLES students' learning experience that new sixth and seventh graders who have been placed in our special X classes (French 7X, Latin 7X, and Spanish 7X) also participate in the festival. Students who enter Newman School after fifth grade, where our Sequential FLES program now begins, and who have had no previous foreign language study, are placed in X classes for one year, where they are prepared to enter seventh-grade foreign language the following year.

References

Brown, Christine. 1997. "A Case for Foreign Languages: The Glastonbury Language Program." *Learning Languages* 2(2): 3–8.

Lipton, Gladys C. 1998. *Practical Handbook to Elementary Foreign Language Programs.* 3rd ed. Lincolnwood, IL: NTC/Contemporary Publishing Company.

From Sukiyaki to Croissants: Global Education at Work in the Elementary School

Astrid M. DeBuhr
*Clayton High School
St. Louis, Missouri*

After being asked for the umpteenth time by parents and students alike why a trip to France was not planned for the students at St. Paul's Episcopal Day School, a Japanese colleague and I decided to address the problem. We had both been campaigning to add Japanese to the curriculum for a long time, so when we were offered the opportunity to team teach a class in St. Paul's summer program, we jumped at it. Of course, it was impossible to take a group of students that might range in age from six to ten years out of the country, so we decided to do the next best thing: spend an Immersion week right at home.

At the outset, Japanese and French seemed an unlikely pairing. However, as planning for the week-long class progressed, the wisdom of our choice became increasingly apparent. A mandate to integrate global studies into St. Paul's schoolwide curriculum gave credibility to the study of two cultures as diverse as those of France and Japan. We wanted to show the various school constituencies how such a program would work. Hence, our class, "From Sukiyaki to Croissants," was born.

We certainly did more than just eat, although that was what the title of the class might imply. Language lessons, culture, singing, dancing, children's games, crafts, folktales, and visits to the local art museum were also vital elements of the week's activities. The class has become so popular, in fact, that for the past two years we have had to turn applicants away.

Two weeks before the beginning of the class, students who had registered received a letter instructing them to bring a passport photo with them the first day. As students arrived they were issued special passports, which they had to sign and fill out with pertinent biographical information, just like a real passport. These passports, complete with copies of Japanese and French visas, became a vital link between our two worlds. Each time the students went from one country to another, they went through customs and received, of course, special stamps in their passports.

Before passing through customs on the first day of class, the children were divided into two mixed-age groups. One group spent the morning in "Japan" and the other spent the morning in "France." After lunch, the groups went through customs again and switched countries, which, in the case of our class, meant going from one side of the hallway to the other.

The two classrooms that we used were lavishly decorated to represent their respective cultures, and from the first moment the students entered one of the rooms, they had the feeling of actually being in France or Japan. Of course, posters, maps, flags, and other realia were de rigeur. Students saw slides and videos about the countries they were visiting, and at the end of the first day wrote postcards home to their parents. The children even posed in costume for souvenir photos, which we gave to them as gifts at the end of the week.

We in fact created two artificial worlds solidly based in reality. To that end, we structured our program so that the children spending the morning in "France" learned not only about that particular culture, but also about the culture and people of Japan as children in France might do. The reverse was also true. The daily visits to each country always began with language and geography lessons. Whenever possible, the geography lessons were also conducted in the target language. We had target language maps not only of the world, but also of France and Japan in each of the classrooms. Children in "France," for example, learned that Japan is called *le Japon*, that the people who live there are called *les Japonais*, and that the language people speak there is called *le japonais*.

Food, landmarks, famous monuments, songs, folk- and fairy tales, dances, art history, and important historical events were among the many topics we explored with the children. On the day the children discussed the French Revolution, for example, they all made patriotic *cocardes* out of red, white, and blue crepe paper to wear home. Every subject we addressed was accompanied by a hands-on activity of some sort. When geographical features were being discussed, the children in "Japan" built a papier-mâché model of Mount Fuji; and when the children in "France" studied the monuments of Paris, they built models of the *Tour Eiffel* and the *Arc de Triomphe*. Each completed activity earned the students another visa stamp in their passports.

We brought the cultures of France and Japan to life for our students in many ways. Some of the most fruitful such activities involved numbers and related math activities. When our students visited "Japan," all math and number activities were done with an abacus. By the end of the week, our travelers were all very adept at using this tool to perform math operations. Math and number activities in "France" were more closely tied to working with French money, which was available in great abundance. Students made daily trips to our *marché* to buy ingredients for our cooking activities. They also used the French money to buy their postcards on the first day of class.

Music and art added another dimension to the reality of the worlds we were creating for our students. Japanese and French music was always playing in the background, and singing became the students' favorite way to regroup after their morning and afternoon visits to both countries. My Japanese colleague made up a wonderful counting song that I translated into French. We also made up songs about colors and the days of the week that the children could sing in both languages. A group bilingual songfest was held each morning as we waited for the children to arrive. This activity really seemed to set the tone for the day before the children "went through customs" for the first time.

Many other activities continued our interweaving of language and culture into the fabric of the two countries we studied with the children. Calligraphy and origami became daily activities in "Japan." Every student not only learned the characters for his or her own name, but also learned how to write numbers from one to twenty. After the second day of our "trip," regular matches of *boules* or *pétanque* (lawn bowling) in "France" were often accompanied by cries of *"Bravo, bien joué"* or *"Dommage, c'est raté."*

Visits to local Japanese and French restaurants and to the Nelson Art Gallery in Kansas City provided some of the richest opportunities for integration during our week-long excursion. The children were able to speak briefly with the owner of the Japanese restaurant as he seated them at their tables. They were also able to identify, in the target language, many of the food items placed before them. Our visit to a nearby French bakery/restaurant proved just as fruitful. The children were able to order their own filled croissants and Orangina in French.

The culminating activity, on the last day of our "trip," was a visit to the art gallery. The children were not only able to talk about the symbolism of the Kabuki masks and painted silk screens of the gallery's Oriental Collection, but also thrilled at their ability to recognize the works of various impressionist painters. Imagine the amazement of a museum guard when a kindergartner walked up to a panel of Monet's "Water Lilies" and identified it correctly.

The success of our "Sukiyaki to Croissants" summer school adventure at St. Paul's was important for several reasons. First, it extended the impact of our French **FLES*** program beyond the confines of the school year. Children involved in the class had the additional benefit of continued exposure to the spoken language, and in most cases showed improved retention at the beginning of the next school year. Second, the children's enthusiasm for the study of Japanese made both parents and administrators aware of the need to expand the offerings of our **FLES*** program. Third, the children were given much more thorough exposure to the cultures of Japan and France than would ever have been possible in the context of St. Paul's existing foreign language program.

The children's enthusiasm for our program became one of our best public relations tools. The students' excitement at learning to process other cultures and solve problems in another language was contagious. Many parents asked when we were going to begin offering language classes for adults. Such parental support has been a valuable tool in the continuing development of our **FLES*** program. When the rest of our constituents begin to see the fruits of exposing their students and children to other languages and thus expanding their world view, they will begin to understand what we as **FLES*** educators have known all along.

The Jewel in Our Crown

Alan S. Wax, Lydia Hurst,
Kathleen Durkin, and Diane Merenda
School District 123
Oak Lawn-Homewood, Illinois

The use of traveling is to regulate imagination by reality, and instead of thinking how things may be, to see them as they are.

Samuel Johnson

For the past twelve years, the Oak Lawn-Homewood School District has been on the move both domestically and internationally. Eighth-grade members of Douglas McGugan Junior High School's French Club culminate their intermediate and junior high school language experiences with the opportunity to travel within the francophone world.

Students who choose to become members of our French Club participate in a wide variety of activities, the most ambitious being our travel-related component. Once the students are aware of their destination, the fun begins! Preparations begin in the spring of the seventh-grade year with the formation of a Parent Booster Club, which is the fundraising arm of the French Club. A parents' meeting is conducted by the previous year's chairperson, who explains some of the fundraising efforts of the past, along with successes, difficulties, advice, and suggestions for new ideas. A new chairperson takes over, discussion follows, and committees are formed to take charge of fundraising to cover some of the expenses of the upcoming trip. Parents have sponsored candlelight bowling parties, hosted benefit nights at local fast-food eateries, sold coupon books, promoted shopping days at local grocery stores, and held raffles by offering goods and services donated by local businesses. Students have sold candy, assisted with benefit nights, staffed French Club booths selling various items, and made and sold Eiffel Tower cookies and lollipops.

In the fall of the eighth grade, at least twice a month after school, meetings are scheduled to introduce students to the intricacies of travel, including:

- Passport photographs: taken at school by a professional
- Passport applications: discussed at a club meeting and taken to the local post office for completion
- Travel tips: packing
- Money exchange
- Metric system/conversion
- Useful expressions/travel-related vocabulary
- Guidelines for student behavior
- Medical forms/legal and waiver forms
- Parents' telephone and fax tree
- Anti-jet lag diet/menu translator
- Diary/log/journal
- Correspondence with pen pals
- Culture shock: anticipating and dealing with it
- Final itinerary: rooming, meeting points, etc.

We always have a high ratio of chaperones to students, and there is a waiting list, even though chaperones must be with students at all times and pay full price. This is our way of curtailing the final cost for the students, which allows as many as possible to participate.

For our North American trips, we usually plan long weekends, departing Wednesday night and returning Sunday. Such destinations have included Concordia Language Villages in Bemidji, Minnesota; Disney University, located at EPCOT Center; Montréal; Québec; and New Orleans and Lafayette, Louisiana.

Our international trips usually last seven or eight days, generally over our spring recess. We have toured Switzerland, Monaco, and France, focusing on Paris/Versailles, *la Côte d'Azur, Bretagne, Normandie*, and many other points between. To support what students have learned in other curricular areas, we have also ventured to Italy and England.

Among the most attractive aspects of our trips have been the unique opportunities we have enjoyed that are unavailable to the individual traveler: lunching with a countess while touring her château, enjoying a treasure hunt while on an island, and dining at an intimate restaurant that closed to cater to our group. Likewise, we have been among the very daring indeed to visit places at the height of popularity: attending the opening week of Disneyland Paris, kicking off the International Parade at Lafayette, and experiencing the thrill of the Eurostar train as it speeds to link England with France. Another highlight is a French homestay during Easter Sunday and Monday, when all get to meet the pen pals with whom they have long been corresponding. What unforgettable happiness and memories!

We owe the unique itinerary for each of our trips to the extraordinary efforts of our travel specialist. Because he understands so well the psyche of the typical thirteen- to fourteen-year-old, he provides the perfect blend of educational, athletic, cultural, and linguistic activities. We are prepared for a metamorphosis, as unseasoned travelers become *bon vivants*, filled with a new sense of cultural awareness, independence, responsibility, and maturity!

We are confident that the travel component of our Sequential FLES program has added a dimension that cannot be overemphasized, for it challenges all of us to reach for higher goals, enlivens our lessons, bolsters our self-esteem, and has become the talk of the town . . . indeed, the jewel in our crown!

Summer Language Immersion Day Camps

Evelyne Cella Armstrong
Charles Wright Academy
Tacoma, Washington

In recent years, the renewed interest in preparing students to function as global citizens has identified the need to begin language instruction at the elementary school level. Parental and student enthusiasm for foreign language education at an early age is prompting interest in many schools and communities. They are actively engaged in researching the instructional alternatives available and the process for establishing strong programs. As a viable option, summer programs can provide both an alternative to the incorporation of **FLES*** in the curriculum or an extension to established **FLES*** programs. This paper will focus on the planning of summer language Immersion day camps.

A summer setting for language instruction naturally allows young people, who have unique advantages when it comes to learning languages, the opportunity to move through a series of experiential, interactive, language-rich activities. Children learn language with ease, naturalness, and lack of self-consciousness when they are engaged. The summer Immersion day camps provide many opportunities for young campers to move through learning centers and group activities that engage them as active learners and respondents carrying out tasks that reinforce language functions. The summer camp setting can also provide the unique opportunity to include a valuable experiential teacher-training program.

THE PLANNING PROCESS

To be successful, a foreign language program for young learners requires detailed planning and forethought. Many factors need to be carefully analyzed as the program is organized and the curriculum is defined. The goals of the summer language program should support the goals of the regular curriculum. A summer setting lends itself to further flexibility and innovation uniquely characteristic to that time period, when enrichment and fun become primary. The program generates a rich integration of themes, culture, indoor and outdoor activities, and multi-age collaboration, all presented in a natural environment. The staff may be as diverse as the activities themselves. Furthermore, because amount of time spent on language instruction is directly related to student proficiency, day camp programs can provide the concentrated instruction time that enables learners to intensify their progress.

Planning Considerations

Choice of Language

Children receive paramount benefit not so much from the particular language chosen for instruction, but from the experience and process of learning a language. This experience develops the intellectual flexibility necessary for subsequent language acquisition. Summer Immersion camps may provide opportunities to offer languages that are not regularly taught in the school curriculum. Many factors need to be carefully considered before actually planning a foreign language program: community interest, availability of teachers, obtainable materials, and articulation with the language programs available during the academic year.

Sample Schedule

8:30–8:45 A.M.	Greetings, warm-up games
8:50–9:10 A.M.	Cooking, games, writing/computers
9:15–9:35 A.M.	Cooking, games, writing/computers
9:40–10:00 A.M.	Cooking, games, writing/computers
10:05–10:25 A.M.	Relays—organized recess
10:30–10:45 A.M.	Marionettes
10:50–11:10 A.M.	Art, visual to word connections, skit
11:15–11:35 A.M.	Art, visual to word connections, skit
11:40–12:00 P.M.	Art, visual to word connections, skit
12:05–12:15 P.M.	Small-group activities
12:20–12:30 P.M.	Large group, good-bye
12:30–1:30 P.M.	Lunch, recess
1:30–3:30 P.M.	Afternoon sports

Scheduling

The scheduling of an elementary school foreign language summer camp depends to a large extent on the program's goals. Programs differ in the intensity of their activities and the amount of time spent learning the target language. Charles Wright Academy, a private, college preparatory school in Tacoma, Washington, offers its summer Immersion language camp in two-week blocks. During that period, on the ten weekdays, learners meet four hours per morning to rotate through a series of centers and activities. The campers may continue their day by playing sports using the target language for two additional hours after lunch. Although the intensity of instruction is greater in the morning than in the afternoon, the sports activities allow learners to apply the target language while physically engaged. Several two-week camps may be offered in succession throughout the summer to provide campers options for additional advancement.

Age Grouping

Issues of age grouping need to be addressed in the instructional goals, especially if the camp invites all ages to participate. Ideally, the campers should be placed in groups of no more than twelve students. These groups may contain a variety of ages and levels, or may be organized by specific age or ability. The method of grouping will depend on the ages of all enrolled and the goals of instruction. Interlevel grouping will allow for multi-age activities where the interaction between children of varying abilities will provide instruction naturally. Same-age grouping may require additional staff, particularly for the younger age groups.

Staffing

The ideal staffing ratio is six campers to one leader. It is beneficial to have one master teacher and one camp counselor or assistant for every block of twelve students. Master teachers may be native speakers, teachers, and university students trained in appropriate methodology. Teachers take an active role in the development of the camp as they meet in the spring to define its curriculum, themes, and special events. Camp counselors or assistants are high school and university students interested in developing their communicative language skills. They must show an interest in working with young learners and have camp leadership skills as well as some language proficiency. Granting community service credit for the involvement of counselors is one way to attract high school students to the program. Summer also lends itself to the use of exchange students from universities in the target country or countries. Their participation can greatly enrich the cultural environment.

Training of Staff

Appropriate training of staff is extremely important. Three to five days need to be dedicated to staff development and program implementation. Discussions of methodology include the development of target language activities, age-appropriate behavior, techniques for presenting new and review language, and the management of students in their language-learning process. Activities that will take place in each area of the program are reviewed and practiced. The staff members are given the opportunity to develop teaching strategies and procedures and to practice their role as leaders. Strong emphasis is given to the organization of materials and the presentation of new concepts. Teachers are also trained to incorporate innovative thinking skills that invite learners to apply acquired language to new concepts.

DAILY ACTIVITIES

The camp day features a variety of activities that motivate camper involvement and actively use interconnected vocabulary. Every day, the campers participate in many activities, such as singing, dancing, skits, cooking, art projects, word games, interactive vocabulary building, writing, reading, computer-based instruction, communication games, and active games. Teachers and counselors lead these activities to promote language learning, provide repetition in entertaining ways, and maximize use of the target vocabulary. Special care is taken to encourage the campers to use the target language among themselves, especially when working on art or cooking projects or during competitive sports.

Small-Group Activities

Most of the activities are carried out in small groups. After the opening greetings, remarks, and short games, which may take place in either small groups or a large group, the small groups are ready to move through a series of activities presented at centers. For instance, for a period of sixty minutes, three small groups may take turns spending twenty minutes each at centers for cooking, games, and skits. The skit may connect to the cooking activity by having students act out a restaurant scene. The third center may emphasize the same food-related vocabulary through the playing of games. The master teachers lead each of the activity centers.

Counselors are each assigned to lead a specific small group and move through the centers with their group throughout the day. Each group chooses a name relating to the theme. To boost enthusiasm, the groups are periodically given time to work together as a group. They develop their own identity and prepare presentations, such as creating a group cheer or their own rendition of a song.

Large-Group Activities

Activities that bring the large group together promote the richness of the language, culture, and country or countries. The marionette show introduces the skit for the day to the large group. The full group may periodically join together at other times during the day, such as for relay races at recess. Large-group meetings provide opportunities to introduce staff, especially those who may be visiting from the target country, and to recognize exceptional campers. Song and dance activities in large groups are a lot of fun. Songs with movement are an effective way to signal all campers to gather together. The first campers to respond when the music starts form a circle and begin an action-filled song; the others join in as they arrive. Including the same songs in daily opening and closing activities can lend structure and continuity to the Immersion day camp.

CURRICULUM AND CONTENT

The national foreign language standards form the basis of the program goals. The areas of communication, cultures, connections, comparisons, and communities, both at home and around the world, are addressed in the summer Immersion camp setting. The program is developed to focus on content from different curricular areas, such as geography, social studies, mathematics, science, art, music, and physical education. As themes and target vocabulary are chosen, the concepts are integrated into the typical culture and content areas of the regular curriculum. Thus, general themes are carefully chosen and the language used in activity centers is carefully interconnected to integrate the content of the curriculum. Each day progressively builds upon the previous day, a practice that is of paramount importance in language acquisition.

Expanding the Focus of FLES* • 159

Sample Thematic Progression	Possible Skits and Song Connections
Day 1 Greetings Names, countries, numbers	Greetings and Presentations
Day 2 Presentations, you and me Going on a trip, flags, colors	Going on a Trip On the Plane or At the Train Station
Day 3 How are you? Action verbs Body parts	At the Restaurant
Day 4 Where are you going? Places to visit, geography	Visiting Landmarks of Target Country
Day 5 Time, schedules Modes of transportation and use in country, i.e., trains	**Culture Connections** Greetings and Presentations
Day 6 I'm hungry, Restaurant and foods Full lunch preparation, special lunch Entertainment, authentic music and art	Country(ies) Flag(s) Landmarks Geography Transportation
Day 7 Outing Places to go, i.e., to market	Foods and Eating Habits Restaurants, Markets
Day 8 Use planning for celebration as review	Music Art
Day 9 Practice celebration	Celebrations
Day 10 Celebration—parents invited	

Methodology

In a specific situation, natural language always occurs in context. Thus, the activities chosen and materials prepared for the summer Immersion day camps are designed to resemble real language in use. The components that make up the activity centers not only present meaningful authentic situations, but also build continuity for the progressive development of the theme. Having small groups of learners move through centers of activities allows for students to be engaged at their level of interest and maturity. A multitude of authentic language-use situations help achieve communicative competence and an awareness of language use. Natural kinds of activities enable the target language to grow and develop within the learner. Moreover, the types of activities are chosen to encourage personal expression and early creative language use. Music provides a natural repetitive process vital to second-language acquisition. As such, song, dance, and music-related play are important to include in programs for early language learning.

Materials

A variety of materials, such as visuals, props, and realia, need to be prepared for the various activity centers and large-group presentations. To create a camp atmosphere, additional materials may be prepared, such as a logo designed to match the theme and the country or countries, tee-shirts, a notebook of word games and activities, audiocassettes, marionettes, posters, wall hangings, and name badges. In addition, information pamphlets and letters to parents are valuable tools that will help communicate the goals and plans of the program to the school community and to the community at large.

Conclusion

If a **FLES*** program is to experience continued interest, growth, and success, its backers need to consider a variety of program models. The summer Immersion day camp setting attracts students into language learning. Through a variety of fun-filled, learner-centered activities, the camp provides experiential, active, and interactive involvement for participants of all ages. Summer Immersion day camps lend themselves well to the content-based approach, with valuable integration into the regular curriculum. Such programs call for thorough advance planning, and their implementation requires a dedicated, energetic staff. Well-defined goals, schedules, group assignments, thematic units, and engaging activities need to be developed with care. The ultimate result will be an enriching summer that is extremely rewarding for all involved.

All the World's a Stage (You and Your Students the Actors)

Elizabeth Miller
Crystal Springs Uplands School
Hillsborough, California

I just can't fit it into the schedule!
It was wasting valuable teaching time!
I'm not creative!
It's so much work!
Who wants to go to all that fuss when most of us are part-time teachers?
It creates such chaos in my classroom!
I have to put all learning on hold while we rehearse!
The plays are too hard!
The whole thing is too hard!

How many times have we heard these reactions at workshops on activities for **FLES*** students? Doing a play is threatening to **FLES*** teachers in so many respects. But it really is easy, and dialogues, skits, plays, and even advertisements can and should be integral parts of a **FLES*** program (and of middle school and high school language classes). Learning does not stop during such activities, and, moreover, there are strong academic, linguistic, and psychological justifications for weaving them into whatever method the teacher is using.

Foreign language teachers are under a great deal of pressure to prove their worth in school systems all over the country. Languages are among the first programs to be cut as school funds diminish—along with other "unnecessaries," such as music, art, team sports, and drama. Many administrators do not look at foreign languages (especially in the elementary school) as essential elements of an American education. After all, the rest of the world has learned to speak English, *n'est-ce pas?* Therefore, it can be frightening to pursue an activity that might appear frivolous (such as a skit or a play) when it is so important to prove that every minute of our class time is devoted to serious academic pursuits. Few of us have the luxury of teaching our students every day. The majority of

FLES* programs meet only three times a week—which gives the language teacher even more excuse to avoid the uncertainty of a play.

One very valid reason for mounting a real performance is the publicity it will bring to the **FLES*** program. The more public exposure we can gain for the success of our classes, the better. Inviting the parents to come to a performance may seem threatening, but parents *love* to see their children do anything! It doesn't have to be polished, with scenery and the works. It does *not* have to be ready for Hollywood! Through their performances, your students themselves can ensure the existence of **FLES*** in your school for at least another year. For further publicity, take photographs and include them in press releases, brochures, the yearbook, and other publications. The event will enable students to feel the satisfaction of having completed a group project, and of having learned a sufficient amount to create a whole play, no matter how short.

You Are Doing It Already

Language teaching by its very nature is theater. You are creating small plays every day if you are really trying to create a communications-based program. We all try to reproduce realistic communication by creating and facilitating dialogue. We have graduated beyond the days when **FLES*** meant having children recite colors in order, count to fifty, name all the rooms of the house, and point to the parts of the body in a resounding game of *"Simon* (or *Pierre) Dit."* We are now trying in each class to reproduce realistic communication. It still starts with listening, repetition, then response—and ultimately, directed response or directed dialogue: *Demande à Jacques comment il va. Jacques, comment vas-tu? Je vais bien, et toi?* You have just created a little theater piece. You see, you are doing it already. A play is just an extension of the directed dialogue.

Motivation!

There is nothing more enjoyable than putting on something, even if it is as short as a five-line dialogue. It is not a book exercise. It is not a paper-and-pencil activity. It is moving around. It is sharing with classmates (in one's own class or outside). It creates variety in the foreign language program, which contributes to students' eagerness to participate. It is astonishing what one small prop or wig or ugly dress can do to the number of volunteers who would like to "act," even though they might be reluctant if they thought it was "reciting"! The performance of the dialogue or skit also gives students the opportunity to prepare and present their French in a safe environment. There is a stable setting with stable lines. Thus, it is the perfect format for children who have difficulty with the unknown of classroom interactions, because they know in advance just exactly what is going to happen when. The stage also provides students with characters to hide behind while practicing correct pronunciation and intonation—something they might not agree to with such enthusiasm at their desks.

Different Learning Styles

One of the burning questions in schools that do include a **FLES*** program is whether or not to include the whole class. In some schools, a language aptitude test is given to children to determine if they should pursue a foreign language. In my own school, students with special academic problems are given support tutoring during the foreign language period. It is an issue I fight every year. My program is rigorous, but there are ways of including children with all language capacities in a foreign language program, if for nothing else than to expose them to the cultural tolerance that is inherent in the language-learning process. Some language teachers themselves contribute to this discrimination because they prefer to work with only the most academically motivated. But everyone is able to learn his or her own language, so learning a second language is not an impossibility.

Skits, plays, and dialogues give a real chance to shine to many academically more restricted students who may not easily grasp some grammatical concepts. These are the forgotten students who can go entirely unnoticed if we don't provide a place for them. Students who seem to be totally lost in the formal section of the language program can bring their own special contributions to a play. They have the security of specific lines to learn. They often blossom in the dramatic potential of the event and steal the show! Give them a chance. We don't really want languages to be considered an exclusive academic area. If our programs aren't reaching everyone, they can be too easily cut. *Every* child needs to speak a second language, and *every* child needs to absorb the global sensitivities that accompany language learning. It is up to us as teachers to create opportunities for all students to reach their particular potential with a foreign language.

Wasted Time?

There is nothing more valuable than the time spent on a dialogue or skit or play, no matter how simple or how short. It does, however, take a little preparation time from the teacher to make sure that the dramatic "event" includes usable linguistic structures. Gone are the dialogues of ALM (Audio-Lingual Method), which fell into disrepute when the memorizing of dialogues took precedent over realistically usable language. Even a two-line dialogue in question-answer format between two students approaches communication more closely than does a restrictive class where only the teacher asks the questions and only the students do the answering. Longer dialogues have their place later when directed dialogue "graduates" to standing on its own. Try to create a situation in which the dialogue would be appropriate (a grocery store, a train station, a parent in the kitchen) by using a prop or two (a box of cereal, some play money, an apron), or use puppets. The students are more willing to tolerate repetition when it has been transformed into a mini-play. In addition, placing a verbal exchange in context transfers the linguistic goal from the structure itself to what the student can actually *do* with the language.

Active!

Language is behavior. This is one of those almost religious statements made by foreign language teachers! But on the stage, every statement is translated into movement—and for some students, it isn't until the visual or the kinesthetic accompanies the spoken word that learning takes hold. This is the ultimate TPR (Total Physical Response) activity! On stage it is essential to exaggerate the mime of every statement, for in most situations the skit, if performed to an audience, will be to people (moms and dads and Aunt Louise, or non-French-speaking fellow students) who don't know French. While exaggerated movement helps the audience, it also confirms the meaning of the sounds — and slowly eliminates the need to translate directly from one language to the other. Instead, the student transfers the visual cue or the movement directly to the utterance, and real language learning is in progress. There is nothing more valuable than this process! This is language in context—with all the gesture and activity of a normal language experience (as opposed to responding to a page in a book). Even though the language is artificially fabricated for the scene, the students are using it as it would be used in a real-world situation. Language is behavior and needs to be *used*, not just dissected and labeled.

How?

I agree that the plays and skits available to **FLES*** teachers are not adequate for our students. Plays written for native speakers are too difficult and filled with extraneous linguistic structures. Or, if the plays are at the level of our students' language acquisition, the content is painfully infantile. Translating straight from an English play is also filled with pitfalls. The trick is to "borrow" an existing idea—from a camp skit, nursery rhyme, fairy tale, or current TV show. Pinpoint three or four relevant structures that you want to reinforce. Then do some writing to fit your level. The key is to use as much repetition as possible (just as the oral storytellers do to help themselves remember the story line). Including a narrator or two helps to keep the story moving and provides a safe role for students who don't have the confidence to memorize. Costumes are essential—and a trip to the Salvation Army will provide you with all you need. It helps to add a twist or an anachronistic gem for humor (Monsieur Magnifique saves Goldilocks, or the Three Little Pigs build condominiums). If you've never done it before, do what other successful **FLES*** teachers have been doing for years: borrow! Call colleagues who have already adapted pieces for their classrooms. Copy and adapt material to your own level. Sometimes the addition of one little detail that relates to your own school is just what the play needs to bring the house down! In the adaptation process, provide for students who are timid on stage. Create a few characters who speak only a few lines or who read (narrators) and add the repetition in the play. Simplicity and repetition are the key factors. Once you've done adaptations a few times, you'll be ready to make your own creations.

Commercials provide a natural format for language learning because they already contain the essential features of a successful language exercise: short, simple, visual, exaggerated, repetitive, and usually humorous! Commercials can be used simply as classroom activities, or in addition to other language plays, or as comic relief before a classroom play that is being performed in English. To be effective, they should be current, and your students are the best source of material here, because they tend to be more faithful TV viewers than their teachers! Once you have the essential idea, you can work in a linguistic structure you want well established. I can guarantee that the main line of your commercial will be remembered by every student in the class! Some of the tried-and-true commercials we've performed include ones for Folger's Coffee, McDonald's, Energizer Batteries, American Express Checks, Perrier, Pepsi, and Parkay margarine.

You Can Do It!

All successful foreign language teachers are really actors at heart—*des acteurs manqués*. Everything we do in the classroom to ensure that we are understood carries an element of theater. A skit or dialogue or play is just an extension of what you have been doing all along, and it is worth the effort. Children are natural hams and adept at mimicry. It's easier for them than for adults. The benefits are endless—especially for those students who find a text-oriented class relies on vocabulary recall, spelling, and grammar that are outside the realm of their learning style. The stage also provides the visual and kinesthetic cues to aid retention of structure and vocabulary. Teachers need to incorporate as many teaching styles as possible to discover how many learning styles are represented in their classrooms. One system will not work for everyone, and we cannot be satisfied with educating only those students who respond to one limited teaching method.

Culture Note

Don't forget to *frapper les trois coups!* Choose a student to sound three knocks on the stage floor with a large stick as they do in French theaters to signal both actors and audience that the curtain is about to rise. All the world's a stage . . .

PART 5

Evaluating **FLES*** Programs

Using Class Quizzes to Promote the Linguistic Accuracy of Younger Learners

Rebecca M. Valette
Boston College
Boston, Massachusetts

In developing goals for foreign language instruction in the United States, the Student Standards Task Force of the National Standards in Foreign Language Education Project stressed the importance of a well-articulated K–12 sequence of instruction. The first and, in many ways, primary goal was that of communication, followed by cultures, connections, comparisons, and communities. The authors of the report write: "While the focus [in Goal 1] is on the use of language and the development of communicative competence, students will need experience in the other goal areas in order to have content worth communicating. Knowledge of the linguistic system, its grammar, emerging vocabulary, phonology, pragmatic and discourse features, undergirds the accuracy of communication (National Standards 1996, 38).

The challenge facing the elementary school teacher of French is how to keep to the focus of the class on interpersonal communication (Goal 1), while at the same time teaching students to express themselves accurately and guiding them toward a rudimentary and age-appropriate appreciation of how the French language differs from English (Goal 4). Class quizzes, especially when introduced in a game-style format, can help teachers meet these Standards.

THE NEED FOR DEVELOPING THE LINGUISTIC ACCURACY OF BEGINNING LEARNERS

One of the main reasons for introducing French at the elementary school level is that younger students have a definite facility for imitating a new language and acquiring good pronunciation (Lipton 1992, 35). However, just like teenage and adult learners, American children have difficulty internalizing features of French that do not have a counterpart in English (Wesche 1992). For example, it has been the experience of most immersion programs that children do not *automatically* acquire the gender of nouns and make the necessary gender distinctions because in English such distinctions are not made. In English, a singular determiner, such as *the, my, this,* has one form, whereas in French a singular determiner has two or three forms, the choice of which depends on the gender of the noun it introduces and whether that noun begins with a vowel sound.

Research has also shown that children who do not acquire basic grammatical distinctions early in their instruction tend to make the same mistakes year after year. These errors do not automatically correct themselves. On the contrary, they run the danger of fossilization (Hammerly 1992, ch. 1).

Already many years ago, teachers in Canadian Immersion programs became aware of the problem elementary school children were experiencing with linguistic interference. André Obadia (1984) published a guide entitled *Analyse des fautes orales des élèves en immersion et techniques de correction.* His position was that teachers should use creative ways to focus student attention on grammatical accuracy and precision. In his publication he suggested a variety of correction techniques adapted to the student's age and level of instruction.

Fortunately, building accuracy is much more rewarding (and less frustrating!) than repeated (and often futile) attempts at error correction. Teachers can heighten the children's awareness of specific linguistic features by incorporating frequent quizzes or quiz-games into the lesson. In fact, since poor listening habits are so very difficult to eradicate, these linguistic quiz-games should be introduced very early in instruction so that children are encouraged to develop effective listening skills. Such activities can be an effective complement to the communication-based lessons of the elementary school French curriculum.

SAMPLE QUIZ AND QUIZ-GAME FORMATS

Linguistic-awareness builders can be introduced as full-class activities and friendly intragroup competitions (quiz-games), or they can be used as informal tests (quizzes). The main objectives are to stimulate students to become aware of the grammatical distinctions characteristic of the French language and to bring all students to the level where they can make these distinctions naturally in speech and writing. The activity must focus on acquisition rather than formal learning (Krashen 1982) and should engage a variety of learning modes.

As an example, let us look at the challenge of awakening the students' awareness of gender. The gender of a noun is important in

French not only because it determines the form of corresponding articles, adjectives, and related pronouns, but also because gender-related errors are very irritating to native French speakers (Ensz 1982). The notion of gender can be introduced on the first day of class.

When assigning students their French names, write the boys' names on blue cards (or in blue marker) and write the girls' names on red cards (or in red marker). Or put blue balloons next to the boys' names and red balloons next to the girls' names. Rather than mention the color coding, simply let the notion of blue and red enter the children's subconscious awareness. Whenever new nouns are introduced, include the same color code. For example, with magazine pictures of food, put the masculine nouns on blue construction paper and the feminine nouns on red construction paper. When articles and determiners are presented, maintain the same system, writing *un* on the board with blue chalk, and *une* with red chalk.

Such color coding should be continued and reinforced throughout the entire language sequence. When students begin writing French, they should be encouraged to color-code new nouns in their workbooks and in their written activities. If older students make their own vocabulary flash cards, have them write masculine nouns on blue cards and feminine nouns on red cards.

STEP ONE: Getting the Students to Hear the Gender Markers

The first step in building awareness of gender is to encourage students to distinguish among gender markers (especially articles and demonstrative and possessive adjectives) and to see the relationship between the basic masculine forms (*le, un, ce, mon*) and feminine forms (*la, une, cette, ma*). In French, particular emphasis must be placed on hearing these distinctions and pronouncing them clearly.

1. Listening Quiz-Game

FORMAT: Identifying gender with blue and red cards

COMMUNICATION THEME: Shopping for clothes

Divide the class into several teams. Give each team a blue and a red index card. The first player of each team goes forward and stands facing the class, holding a blue card in the right hand and a red one in the left hand. The teacher reads three sentences about what different people are buying. If the students hear *un*, they are to raise the blue card. If they hear *une*, they are to raise the red one. The first one to raise the correct card wins a point for his or her team.

Je vais acheter une cravate.	[red]
Paul va acheter un pantalon.	[blue]
Sophie va acheter une robe.	[red]

2. Listening Quiz-Game

FORMAT: Identifying gender with self-adhesive note paper

COMMUNICATION THEME: Describing parts of the body

After students have played "Simon Says," gender awareness can be reinforced in a game format using a cardboard Halloween skeleton. Have available small pink and blue self-adhesive note pads. In TPR style, call on individual students to point out various parts of the skeleton. Each student must sticker the correct body part with appropriately colored note paper: blue for masculine, pink for feminine.

Vous connaissez Clovis, n'est-ce pas?	(Clovis is the skeleton.)
Pierre, montre-moi sa tête.	[places pink note on the head]
Marie, montre-moi son bras droit.	[places blue note on the right arm]

3. Listening Quiz

FORMAT: Understanding new cognates and listening for gender markers

COMMUNICATION THEME: (a) Leisure activities in the city: going to the zoo; (b) ordering at a café

For a gender-listening quiz, describe a series of pictures using words that are unfamiliar to the student but are easily recognizable as cognates.

Example a: Animals (on transparency)

Prepare a transparency of zoo animals, writing a number next to each one. As you point out the animals, ask the students to listen for the gender of each noun and to circle the article they hear on their answer sheets. As you point to each picture, identify it in a brief sentence.

> Numéro un. Voici un lion.
>
> Numéro deux. Voilà une girafe.

Student answer sheet:

1. (un)　　une
2. un　　(une)

Example b: Menu (on individual test sheets)

Give each student a quiz sheet with a copy of a simple French menu. As you read the menu to the students, have the students write *un* or *une* next to each item, as appropriate.

> Un croissant coûte six francs.
>
> Une pizza coûte onze francs.

Student test sheet:

```
        CAFÉ DE LA GARE
   ____ croissant      6 francs
   ____ pizza         11 francs
```

4. Listening-Speaking Quiz-Game

FORMAT: Understanding the correspondence between gender markers

COMMUNICATION THEME: Leisure activities: sports

Divide the class into two teams and send two scorekeepers to the board. Call on students one after the other, alternating between the teams. Each time a student gives the correct answer, the scorekeeper for his or her team marks a point. The teacher names a piece of sports equipment, and the student claims it, using *mon* or *ma* as appropriate. (The teacher can use real objects, flash cards, composite pictures, transparencies, posters, etc.)

Teacher	**Student**
Voici un ballon.	[C'est mon ballon.]
Voici une raquette	[C'est ma raquette.]

STEP TWO: Checking Whether Students Know the Genders of Familiar Nouns

Once students are sensitized to gender markers and have been working with a given thematic vocabulary grouping, it is important to assess whether they have internalized the genders of the nouns.

5. Paper/Pencil Quiz

FORMAT: Identifying gender by using colored pencils or crayons

COMMUNICATION THEME: The home

Use a vocabulary transparency or workbook illustration of a young person's room to prepare quiz sheets for the students. Number all of the things in the picture that the students have learned to identify. Tell the students to look at the picture of various items in Marc's room and think of the corresponding French words. Some are *un*-words and some are *une*-words. If the picture represents an *un*-word, draw a blue circle around it. If the picture represents an *une*-word, draw a red circle around it.

Sample pictures:
1. chair   2. table   3. lamp

6. Paper/Pencil Quiz

FORMAT: Matching nouns and articles

COMMUNICATION THEME: Transportation

Have the students write the words from the box in the appropriate columns, classifying them as *le*-words or *la*-words.

| camion | moto | scooter | vélo | voiture |

le _____ la _____

le _____ la _____

le _____ la _____

These are just a few suggestions for using brief class quizzes and quiz-games as changes of pace to heighten the elementary students' awareness of gender and common gender markers. A similar approach can be used to focus the students' attention on other basic grammatical points, such as subject-verb agreement and singular-plural distinctions. Although one should not lose sight of the fact that French should be taught as a means of interpersonal communication, it is important to help students become sensitized to how French differs from English and to encourage them to express themselves accurately.

REFERENCES

Ensz, K. 1982. "French Attitudes Toward Speech Errors." *Modern Language Journal* 66:133–93.

Hammerly, H. 1992. *Fluency and Accuracy: Toward Balance in Language Teaching and Learning.* Clevedon, England: Multilingual Matters Ltd.

Krashen, S. D. 1982. *Principles and Practice in Second Language Acquisition.* Oxford (England): Pergamon Press.

Lipton, G. 1998. *Elementary Foreign Language Programs (FLES*): An Administrator's Handbook.* 3rd ed. Lincolnwood, IL: National Textbook Co.

National Standards in Foreign Language Education Project. 1996. *Standards for Foreign Language Learning: Preparing for the 21st Century.* Lawrence, KS: Allen Press.

Obadia, André. 1984. *Analyse des fautes orales des élèves en immersion et techniques de correction.* Burnaby, BC: Simon Fraser University, School of Education.

Wesche, M. 1992. French Immersion Graduates at University and Beyond: What Difference Has It Made? *Georgetown University Round Table on Languages and Linguistics 1992.* Washington, DC: Georgetown University Press.

Portfolio Assessment of Second Languages in the Elementary Classroom

Philip Korfe
Jane Addams Elementary School
Sioux Falls, South Dakota

The purpose of this article is to describe assessment of student growth in an elementary **FLES*** program. But first, why assessment? It is important to examine the purposes of assessment and how the results of the assessment will be used. Does the assessment process offer opportunities for the students to grow and succeed in their study of a second language? Does the assessment process identify the strengths and weaknesses of the students? Also, does the assessment process provide information that can be used to enhance instruction and therefore help the students to become better learners?

The emphasis in assessment should be on teacher observation. In whole language, this is called "kidwatching," a term coined by Yetta Goodman. Teacher observation of student second-language behaviors over a period of time has been documented as being the best and most valid form of overall assessment. Because learning a second language is not just a matter of sequential skills development, tests over isolated skills can provide only a limited view of the students' second-language development. A truer picture of development comes by using alternative types of assessment with or without tests. Assessment for individual students should be based on assessment forms that document the students' use of the skills and material taught, growth and change over time, and attitudes.

A portfolio approach to assessment is an effective assessment of student progress in a second language. Portfolios are concrete records that provide physical evidence of academic growth. The portfolio is a valuable tool to show teachers, students, parents, and administrators that learning has taken place. Anecdotal records of teacher observations, checklists, attitude surveys, work samples, writing samples, video- and audiotapes, oral and/or written tests, and other samples of student work can be included in the student portfolio.

Anecdotal Records

Anecdotal records are written observations of students in action. They can be done in a variety of ways: individual student sheets in a three-ring binder, index cards in a file box, class roster sheets on a clipboard, and Post-it notes later placed in individual portfolios. The key is that the teacher actively observe students daily even though the teacher may only average a written observation on each student once every week or two. Teachers observe individual and group behavior in the areas of language use, classroom activities, work habits, and the like. Teacher-student interaction, student-student interaction, small group interaction, and tape recordings of oral work are all ways teachers can observe and rate student performance.

Checklists

A checklist is a list of activities, skills, steps, or learner outcomes that the teacher records when monitoring student performance. Checklists may focus on a single topic for a particular activity (such as comprehensibility or fluency), or they may be more global in nature to show a student's achievement for one assessment period.

Attitude Surveys

Attitude surveys reflect student attitudes toward a particular language, the target culture(s), and reasons for or against studying the language. Attitude surveys can be given at the beginning, in the middle, and at the conclusion of the language study to determine shifts and trends in student attitudes.

Work Samples

Work samples represent students' efforts on projects other than written activities. They include language-based and culture-based hands-on activities that involve cutting, gluing, matching, coloring, and other art skills. The teacher and student may collaborate on selecting the work samples for the portfolio.

WRITING SAMPLES

Writing samples are activity sheets and other written work that the students do in the second-language class. Since it is impossible to include every piece of written work in a student's portfolio, only a representative sampling of the work is necessary. Again, the teacher and student may want to decide the samples to be included in the portfolio.

VIDEO- AND AUDIOTAPES

Video- and audiotapes are an excellent addition to a student's portfolio. They provide authentic evidence of growth in a student's listening and speaking capabilities in the target language. They are extremely useful for self-assessment by a student.

TESTS

Very few formal tests are given to elementary students studying a second language. A good test should provide opportunities for students to show that they have some control over the phonetic system, have memorized material used in class, and are able to say a few sentences using simple structures of the language. When tests are used, they should evaluate what has been taught in class and must use the same modality in which the material was taught. Any examination should be non-threatening to students and designed to provide them with successful experiences. Written tests should be included in the student portfolio. Oral tests can be recorded on video- or audiotapes for inclusion in the portfolio.

Student portfolios are collections of student work that allow a teacher to assess students' development in a second language over a certain period of time, all the way from several months to several years. They provide the teacher with ongoing data that can be used to assess student progress as well as to determine at what level students are in their acquisition of a second language.

Assessment, Evaluation, and Accountability: Why Bother Evaluating **FLES*** Programs?

Gladys C. Lipton
University of Maryland, Baltimore County
Baltimore, Maryland

Many people are excited about starting a **FLES*** program, even in these times of budget crises. They have followed all of the steps, set realistic goals, followed all of the suggested procedures, developed the necessary curriculum materials, set up the schedules, and hired competent and enthusiastic teachers. So, why bother evaluating the program? Because it is *essential!*

Before starting a program, a school or school community must ask itself the following questions:

1. Are our goals realistic?
2. Do we have a wide base of support that includes parents, members of the community, teachers, administrators, and others?
3. Does everyone understand the need for accountability—the need for responsibility for the program?
4. Is an evaluation design in place—one that will provide hard evidence as well as testimonials from many sources?
5. Has a pilot program demonstrated hard evidence that the children are learning the foreign language and not losing expected gains in all the other subjects of the curriculum?
6. Does everyone understand and accept the importance of starting the study of a foreign language early?
7. Is everyone involved in the program prepared, at a moment's notice, to justify the program?

It is essential to build an evaluation design into the planning stage of the program, so that there is no question about the need to evaluate, either informally or formally—or preferably, both!

Before undertaking **FLES*** program evaluation, it is essential to consider the following guidelines:

GUIDELINES FOR CONDUCTING EVALUATION AND RESEARCH ON FLES* PROGRAMS (INCLUDING SEQUENTIAL FLES, FLEX, AND IMMERSION)

1. Begin the research with an open mind: it should be conducted in an objective fashion, without bias.
2. Do not attempt to compare "apples and oranges." Make sure that you have controlled all the variables. Comparing different program models with different time for instruction and exposure is *not* a solid research design.
3. The researcher should have a research background. Action research by teachers should be carefully designed and coordinated.
4. The study should have the potential for replication.
5. We need more research studies in the United States, with varying populations and varying foreign language situations, but all the variables must be controlled.
6. The research design should include a large enough sample.
7. The data should support the findings, conclusions, and recommendations. The results should be statistically and scientifically sound and credible.
8. Conclusions or recommendations should not be based *solely* on anecdotal evidence.
9. If a test instrument is used, it should be properly validated for this specific research. Written permission should be obtained for the use of the test instrument in this specific research.
10. Acceptable, standard research procedures should be followed throughout the research and/or evaluation process.
11. Evaluation should be undertaken in accordance with the goals of the program and the national foreign language standards. (See Appendix B.)

THE FLES* SCALE FOR PROGRAM EVALUATION (A CHECKLIST)

1. All students have access to **FLES*** programs.
2. There is a foreign language advisory committee for K–12 programs.

3. The goals of the **FLES*** program are clearly stated.
4. There is provision for articulation with upper schools.
5. There is provision for ongoing informal feedback and formal evaluation (every five to seven years).
6. There is assurance that there is a continuing supply of appropriate **FLES*** materials.
7. There is assurance that there is a continuing supply of well-prepared and trained **FLES*** teachers.
8. There is documentation of the short-term and longitudinal results of studying **FLES*** and the effect on English language skills and achievement in other curriculum areas.
9. There is a written **FLES*** curriculum that indicates progress, based on national standards, in linguistic, cultural, and interdisciplinary approaches.
10. Students demonstrate their progress in **FLES*** (K–8) in a variety of ways, including progress indicators suggested by national foreign language standards committees.
11. The **FLES*** instructional program in class reflects the goals of the program through the curriculum content and the methods.
12. There is enthusiasm for the **FLES*** program on the part of students, parents, administrators, school board members, guidance counselors, and other members of the school/school district community.
13. There is more than one foreign language offered at the **FLES*** level (K–8), depending on the size of the school and the school community.

When more formal evaluation and accountability are desired, the following components should be addressed:

An Overview of Components in Formative or Summative Evaluation of FLES* Programs

1. Time frame
2. Budget
3. Personnel involved
4. Purpose of the evaluation
5. Evaluation questions to be addressed

6. Data collection
   a. Archival documentation, e,g., goals and curriculum
   b. Records
   c. Tests (classroom, standardized)
   d. Classroom observation
   e. Inventories
   f. Materials of instruction
   g. Portfolios (students and class)
   h. Analysis of oral performance in the foreign language
   i. Interviews to determine perceptions
   j. Meetings
   k. Questionnaires
   l. Other
7. Data analysis
   a. Analysis of progress in the foreign language
   b. Analysis of progress in reading, math, social studies, and other subject areas as compared with control classes
   c. Analysis of questionnaires, interviews, meetings, materials of instruction
   d. Other
8. Report
   a. Audience
   b. Format
   c. Completion of report

STUDENT ASSESSMENT

The following activities can be helpful in assessing student progress:

Oral/Written
- Make a list of terms in a category (e.g., colors).
- Respond to questions about a theme or situation.
- Express preferences.
- Ask questions about a theme or situation.
- Describe a familiar object or person.
- Tell about an experience.
- Describe a meal plan for one meal or for the whole day.

- Design a menu.
- Record a message.
- Write a letter, a fax, a poem about . . .
- Tell how to do something.
- Make an announcement on the public address system.
- Enter an e-mail message.
- Create questions for a quiz.
- Prepare questions for a guest speaker.
- Tell a folktale.
- Plan a travel itinerary (with maps).

Creative/Performance
- Make a collage on a specific theme.
- Record an ad for radio and TV.
- Draw and label a cartoon on . . .
- Create a "Concentration" game.
- Plan, in groups, for a class party.
- Make a calendar (weather, activities, sports, etc.).
- Role-play shopping in a specific kind of store.
- Sing authentic songs.
- Create the family tree of a famous person (real or fictitious).
- Create a poster about . . . (themes, culture, stories, etc.)
- Create directions for a class treasure hunt.
- Make a shopping list for a specific purpose.
- Create a language game.
- Create a greeting card.
- Role-play a cultural/historical skit.

Additional Activities
- Draw and label vocabulary.
- Ask and answer questions.
- Follow directions.
- Match words/phrases and pictures.
- Complete sentences.
- Present a conversation.
- Write dictation.
- Create a family tree.

SELF-EVALUATION

For the reflective teacher, self-evaluation is every bit as important as program evaluation and student assessment. The following checklist can be helpful to **FLES*** teachers who wish to assess their own effectiveness.

BE A REFLECTIVE FLES* TEACHER:
A SELF-EVALUATION CHECKLIST

How do you know when you've taught an effective foreign language lesson? Ask yourself the following questions:

1. Are all students actively participating in the foreign language, either individually, in small groups, or in whole-class activities?
2. Are the youngsters given the opportunity to use the foreign language in functional situations during the lesson?
3. Are students able to use the language (depending on the goals of the program) in all four abilities of listening, speaking, reading, and writing? For higher-order thinking skills activities?
4. Have I planned a variety of activities in short segments?
5. Do I plan review and reinforcement activities as well as the presentation of new work in each lesson?
6. Do I use a wide variety of auditory and visual materials of interest to young children? Do I sometimes plan a surprise?
7. Do I try to motivate each lesson and each part of the lesson?
8. Is there ongoing evaluation for purposes of diagnosis of problems as well as for grouping?
9. Are cultural topics woven into each foreign language lesson?
10. Is the textbook adapted and modified to suit the curriculum and the ability of the students?
11. Do I have effective classroom routines so that everyone is on task during the entire lesson? Is every minute used?
12. Do I explain the new homework clearly? Do I check the homework (if any) each class session?
13. Do the students and I use the foreign language? Do I only very briefly explain something in English (and only when necessary)?
14. Do my students appear to look forward to the next foreign language lesson?
15. Do I look forward to the next foreign language lesson?

Making the Grade: Continuous Evaluation in the **FLES*** Classroom

Maureen Regan-Baker
Stonington, Connecticut

On the surface, evaluation in the foreign language classroom does not appear to be easy. Most of us juggle schedules and space allocations that would make a grown person sit on the edge of the curb and cry his or her eyes out. The majority of us still write our own materials or adapt existing texts and readers to meet the configuration of our school systems, our communities, and our students. We recognize that accountability is crucial to the continuation of our programs, yet we believe we lack the time to test. The answer may lie in the perception that testing or evaluation and its eventual by-product, accountability, are continuous. Testing and teaching may need to become working partners, rather than worker and monitor. "Making the grade" in the eyes of our foreign language colleagues and the rest of the educational community does mean offering proof of a certain quality and quantity of learning.

The intent of the suggestions that follow is to offer some ways and means to that end. As a prelude to those suggestions or in preparation for their application, we might seek answers to the following questions:

- How do we define testing and evaluation, and what is their relation to accountability?
- What are the chief obstacles to testing in the **FLES*** classroom? Lack of time to test? Lack of time to prepare test materials? Lack of appropriate commercial instruments?
- What is the purpose of testing? To convince others of the efficacy of **FLES***? To determine what students are retaining and using? To grade ourselves as teachers?

However we define testing, it is not synonymous with evaluation, the former being a subset of the latter. *Evaluation* is the broader term. Without demonstrable evaluation of our students' language ability (and this includes both paper-and-pencil and oral tests), we cannot account for our place in the total curriculum. We do need test scores, point systems, and records of parental feedback to justify our *raison d'être*. However, traditional tests designed for the older student do not allow **FLES*** students to demonstrate their real strengths.

Time is a very real problem. We must think of ways to get greater evaluative value out of both the minutes we spend testing and the tests we use. When commercial instruments seem to fail us, perhaps they need to be used for other purposes.

General Suggestions

1. *Give tests often, but keep most of them short*—no more than one to two minutes. Use a stopwatch.
2. *Make tests serve multiple purposes.* A test of oral comprehension may later be used as a test of writing. The text of what the teacher "says" during an oral exam can be later "seen" to test reading, spelling, or knowledge of the sound system. What one student "writes" may be "read" by another. Reuse a student's answers on a previous exam as new test items.
3. *Use existing teaching materials as tests.* Photocopy pages from readers, catalogues, and phone books. Use song sheets, posters, maps, and classroom articles.
4. *Reuse commercial tests, but in different ways.* For classes in French, for example, use National French Contest picture sheets and simply target different information.
5. *Try for a more open-ended testing format.* Give students a single category or point of departure and ask them to supply what they know. Allow them to choose items from a body of material that they recognize and are able to enlarge upon, describe, or contradict.
6. *Test as you teach.* We say we believe in whole language, yet we test skills individually. We say that instruction should be student-centered, yet the tests are always teacher-made.
7. *Adopt an evaluative teaching style.* Most teachers teach, teach, teach, and then evaluate. Rather, try for an approach that simultaneously teaches and evaluates. Constantly allow students the opportunity to tell you what they know and to demonstrate ways in which they use what they know, their level of comprehension, and their vocabulary. Then give them "visual grades" for their achievement in the form of points on a chart located within full view of the class. Ideally, these charts should cover one week's work at a time. They should contain columns in which a student's progress in a particular skill can be recorded. Remember that, depending on the testing activity, a student may exhibit a variety of skills, even within a single answer.

8. *Allow students to prepare or have input into their tests.* What do they think they should know? Which pictures would be used on a test? Let them suggest the categories for testing.
9. *Use the report card as an evaluation device.* Write the text of the report card in the form of a letter from the child to the parent. The child says/writes: "I know my numbers, my colors, how to say ____, how to read ____. Just ask me!" The child is then tested by the parent. Or, for the older child: "*Madame/Monsieur/Señora/Señor* asked us about what we had learned and we said ____." This provides the opportunity for the student to share and elaborate. Space should be provided for the parent to comment on the child's background in language to that point. Transfer the accumulated points from the chart in the classroom to the report card.
10. *Share test results widely and often.* Tell other teachers about that day's mini-tests. Show paper-and-pencil tests to the principal, parents, and upper-level colleagues. The message sent is that this is serious business; **FLES*** students, like all students, are held accountable.

Examples of Specific Types of Tests and Test Questions

Continuous In-Class Informal Evaluation

Note: The following may appear to be activities, but they are actually tests for the students and for the teacher.

1. *Teacher:* Choose a letter, any letter, of the alphabet. (The class selects a letter.) Give as many words as you can that begin with that letter and I will write them on the board. (The class calls out words, and the teacher, noting who responds and what kind of lexical, grammatical, and cultural spread he or she is getting, writes the words on the board. As each word goes on the board, it is coded with a number or a letter.)

   Teacher: I'll say one of the words as written. You come to the board, point to the word, and then read it back to me. Tell me what it means. Then erase it.

   Teacher: Now that the board is all erased, would anyone volunteer to try to put one of the words back?

   The variations are limitless. For example, rather than asking students to choose a letter, ask them to choose a number and to supply mathematical combinations that result in that number. Ask them to name small things, things of a certain color, things to see in a famous city, etc. Because their responses are labeled with numbers or letters, you can use them in a written test, such as, "Write the numbers of the words you hear." The words, originally supplied by the students themselves, can be presented alone or embedded in a phrase. Working in reverse, give the numbers and ask that the words be translated, expanded upon, or used.

On a large grade chart, visible to the class, give the student credit for each demonstrated skill: translating, writing, comprehending, speaking, demonstrating proper usage, reading, or other abilities.

2. Give each student a 5" x 7" card as he or she enters. On the card, a verb form has been written. Ask the student to write another verb in the same person beneath the one already there. The student signs the card and hands it in and the teacher grades it. The next class, the card is returned to the student and he or she is asked to make the form negative, interrogative, or both. In each case, the student will share orally, with the class, what was written on the card after it was handed to the teacher.

Again, the variations are multiple. The card may contain any kind of information that the student is asked to expand upon, in some way alter, or contradict. Perhaps the card contains a picture to be labeled, or words describing something in the room that the student must find and match.

3. The teacher dictates five words, using the second-language alphabet to spell each one. The students write what they hear—actually, the names of five famous people, numbering the names one to five or sixty-three to sixty-seven, or whatever numbers the teacher wishes to highlight. When the dictation is finished, a group of six sentences, until now hidden from view, are shown on the board. These sentences are labeled with letters. Five of them describe the five people whose names were just dictated to the students. The students read the sentences and record the appropriate letters of the alphabet next to the names. The written descriptions may illustrate a grammatical point, a particular sound-letter correspondence, or cultural information. Note the following generic example:

68. Martha	a. The Prime Minister of Canada
69. Louis	b. Lafayette's daughter
70. Mulrooney	c. George Washington's wife
71. Pablo	d. Marie-Antoinette's husband
72. Virginia	e. Dali's mustache
	f. Paloma's father

Collect the tests and repeat the same procedure orally. Have students read the matching sentences and spell the names aloud.

In Conclusion

Continuous evaluation and/or an evaluative teaching style is less threatening for students. It judges more fairly because there is less risk of catching a student on a "bad" day. It reveals misunderstandings or teaching misdirections before they become insurmountable. It saves time because teaching and testing are combined. It can provide plenty of grades, point accumulations, and other numerical evidence of a child's progress that make reporting easier for the teacher. Such recorded data motivate children and give substance to the **FLES*** program.

He or She That Tooteth Not His or Her Own Horn . . . That Horn Goeth Untooteth

Elizabeth Miller
Crystal Springs Uplands School
Hillsborough, California

As foreign language teachers, we need to learn to "tooteth" our own horns more! **FLES*** teachers already have their energies drained to the limit; tooting the language horn to be heard by administrators and by the community is far down on the priority list. It cannot stay there, though, because our programs risk extinction if we don't become (I hate this word) "proactive."

It is not in my nature to be a self-"horn-tooter." Like my **FLES*** colleagues, I teach many levels of French in my elementary school, and for many years I raced between two and sometimes three schools to keep their French programs alive. When I wasn't in the car or in the classroom, I was drawing posters, sewing puppets, scrounging for realia, inventing language games, creating new activities for the students, and plowing through French textbooks to find appropriate tidbits for the elementary level. Who had time to publicize the successes of our work? Who kept the importance of what we were doing under the noses of school board members and state superintendents? Not my job, I thought!

First of all, each of us in the **FLES*** classroom is doing the most important part of **FLES*** publicity: We are turning on a whole new generation to the excitement of language learning. Our students themselves are our strongest advocates. By transferring our enthusiasm to them, we ensure the existence of our language programs for years to come. We will not be eliminated in our schools if our students are happy and productive. Their appraisals of our classes go directly to parents and the appropriate administrators will be informed.

The secondary schools our **FLES*** children attend are the next "horn-tooters" for us, requiring us to do nothing more than maintain quality programs. If we have given our elementary students a solid foundation and established a love for the language, they will continue at the secondary level and excel in their language studies. Many studies support the theory that early exposure to languages permits students with various learning problems to succeed; whereas waiting to start languages in high school is an invitation to failure for those students. If the students have had a sufficient number of successful experiences in **FLES***, their confidence will carry them into secondary school. By starting before the age of seven, a child with learning challenges becomes more comfortable with the language learning procedures, and more readily accepts the linguistic patterns for their communication value in context rather than as isolated patterns. All **FLES*** successes push secondary schools into expanding their programs to accommodate those excited language learners.

I have had the good fortune to have letters written to my own principal, thanking me and our school for sending them such highly qualified French students and forcing them to restructure their language courses to create adequate challenges. As a result, many of my former students have graduated from high school not only with competency in French, but also with competency in a second foreign language—something quite normal in European schools but uncommon in the United States. If you are reluctant to toot your own horn, you might consider contacting the schools your **FLES*** students attend to document your students' subsequent language success. This investment of a little time provides invaluable justification of what we do. Many administrators see **FLES*** programs as only slightly more serious than recess! Here is tangible documentation of our worth!

Thirdly, bring parents in whenever you can. If they see and hear the product of our efforts, they will audibly toot that horn! Children love to perform and parents love to bask in the glory of the performance of their offspring! A skit or modified fairy tale or songs interspersed with some humorous commercials in the target language provide entertainment that reflects positively on our programs. A few simple props and a trip to Goodwill for costumes are all you need. If you are insecure about writing your own skits or unhappy with what is published, get copies of the collections of tried-and-true skits and a second edition with new creations created by **FLES*** teachers, available from the National **FLES*** Commission of AATF.

If a performance is more than you can handle, invite parents for *un petit déjeuner français*. The students learn how to *mettre le couvert* while learning everything on the table. The menu can remain simple: *du chocolat chaud, des croissants, du beurre, de la confiture*. It provides a simple cultural activity in addition to giving people outside the classroom a chance to see what you are doing. The students can be the waiters by learning some simple phrases, such as, *Vous désirez, Madame?* and *Voici l'addition*. Have the children make menus, and, if they also make pretend French money, the copy machine can provide everyone with plenty of cash to spend. I can guarantee it will toot a horn for your classroom.

Our school has developed a pen pal program over the years that has really flourished. It is a perfect example of an automatic horn tooter. Our fourth, fifth, and sixth graders have discovered that French is not an isolated subject of study, but a very real tool for communicating with children in another part of the world. It is a way to learn about school and family life in another country, and a bridge to valuable friendships. Many schools have made contact through the Internet and carried on similar pen pal exchanges with a more modern format.

We have been able to expand the letter exchange into a student exchange and, for several years, have hosted a group of elementary school students from France. This is a perfect opportunity for public horn tooting. We brought our French guests to a town meeting to present a gift from their town to our mayor. The activities were photographed and written up in both the school and the local papers, and the credit for this unique opportunity, both linguistic and cultural, went directly to the language classes! All participants benefited from the experience, even those students who were not in French classes. Such experiences teach patience, cultural sensitivity, and a tolerance that cannot be transmitted through a textbook. A global coexistence in peace can be started from just such small building blocks of friendship. This is worth a horn toot.

Lastly, there is one annual way to toot the horn of your students' successes: the National French Contest. As national director for the **FLES*** level, I have tried to create ways to ensure more community recognition to honor those very enthusiastic language learners. Students from grades 1 through 6 are eligible to receive both national awards and local AATF awards, and in recent years we have instituted *le Tableau d'Honneur*, which recognizes the highest-scoring student in each school for every division: Division 1A (grades 1–3), 2A (all grade 4 and grades 5 and 6 in strictly oral programs), 2B (grades 5 and 6 with some grammar), 3A and 3B (for immersion and partial immersion programs, and for students with some additional French experience). This is an impressive horn to toot because the students prove their competence alongside students from all across the country. School administrators, as well as our communities, need to be aware of these successes. We encourage all participating schools to contact their local newspapers and list names of winners. Every school will have at least one!

FLES* teachers do not have the time to do a great deal of horn tooting, but in a society where foreign language programs are becoming the first victims of budget reductions, we have to be prepared to show that we are indispensable to the total educational formation of our children. The students themselves, if happily engaged, will speak on our behalf. The parents invited to see their children perform will support us. Secondary schools, if we send them excited and capable students, will reap the benefits of committed language learners at the middle and high school levels and will demand that it continue. The community, if given the opportunity to see the children hosting foreign students or receiving national awards, will be convinced that early language learning is a viable phenomenon. Too many school administrators at local, state, and national levels were educated at a time when foreign languages were not offered at the elementary school level. We need to show them in as many ways as possible that this is not an educational whim, but the only realistic way to conquer the sad reputation of Americans as monolinguistic and culturally insensitive.

In a world where technology has achieved an almost magical erasing of distances, our instant contact all over the world demands stronger language competency from all of us. We need to keep **FLES*** thriving. Toot those **FLES*** horns!

Celebrating the Successes of **FLES*** through Evaluation

Deborah Wilburn-Robinson
*The Ohio State University
Columbus, Ohio*

In the final analysis, valid testing is the only reasonable basis for defining and evaluating goals, methods, and results. To the extent that it is valid, testing is just an independent vantage point that defines and measures how well we are doing.

J. Oller, Jr.

INTRODUCTION

This article celebrates the successes of individual and broad-based initiatives targeting **FLES*** program outcomes. The first part of the article reviews the field's arrival at consensus about expected student competencies. The author then explains the need for a comprehensive evaluation program of student performance and reviews the traditional and alternative forms of assessment that have served us well to date. These assessments lay the foundation for the broad evaluation agenda that is already being addressed at the national, state, and organizational levels. Through collaboration, valid and reliable tests of student performance will soon be more widely available. The article concludes with an examination of two other critical factors in any discussion of successful **FLES*** programs: teacher evaluation and program evaluation.

BACKGROUND

The field of early language learning has experienced growth and increased recognition since its decline in the late 1960s. The national standards (National Standards in Foreign Language Education Project

1996) have provided a shared vision of what is possible in terms of early language education extending through grade 12. Progress indicators at grades 4, 8, and 12 measure students' proficiency as they progress through sequential programs.

Given the emerging consensus on **FLES***, "the challenge now is to make the Standards a viable influence in every classroom and to develop the kind of performance criteria and assessment measures needed to provide evidence of their effect" (Wing 1996, 50).

To meet this objective, state departments of education have begun to construct model curricula based on the standards. In turn, national and state-level documents provide vision for developing all types of early language programs. These models help districts formulate program-specific outcome statements that can then be assessed. Programs and assessments will be heavily influenced by local policy. Time and intensity are two of the most critical factors. Other issues that affect programs include who will teach, administration, and funding. The field needs situationally relevant evaluation based on local program goals in order to begin a serious effort at documenting the many successes of **FLES***.

Pesola's Framework for Curriculum Development for FLES Programs (Foreign Languages in Elementary Schools) (Curtain and Pesola 1994, 62) has been instrumental in providing early language educators with an efficient tool from which to build FLEX and Sequential FLES curricula based on best practices from Immersion education. Although the framework addresses assessment, she and her coauthor contend:

> Assessment of student performance receives far less time and attention in many methods classes and methods books, on conference programs, and in teacher in-service sessions than do techniques for motivating students, planning curriculum, and managing the classroom. Methods for measuring student achievement within the communication-oriented classroom have not kept pace with methods for presenting materials and for giving students the opportunity to use language in communicative ways (Curtain and Pesola 1994, 217).

Rosenbusch (1995) concurs, encouraging teachers who develop local authentic assessments to share their efforts through workshops. In the present author's view, this sharing will help move early language evaluation out of the realm of cottage industry into the twenty-first century.

The Need for a Cogent Program of Evaluation

Early language educators have many means at their disposal to formally and informally assess students. To bring **FLES*** to the forefront of the American education agenda, however, valid and reliable proof is needed to answer pressing questions for our varied constituencies. Questions involve both evaluation- and assessment-related issues. Evaluation allows us to answer the question "What have we gotten and at what cost?" Assessment, on the other hand, allows us to track student progress and make informed curricular decisions. Parents, administrators, boards of education, funding agencies, and colleagues in other content areas all require varied information based on their own agendas.

Curtain and Pesola suggest that the emphasis in assessment be changed "from *making judgments to gathering information* . . . to recognize and celebrate progress, identify areas for more intense effort, and describe levels of proficiency for the benefit of planning and articulation" (1994, 221). Elements of both evaluation and assessment are evident in their statement.

Oller concurs with trying to find a means to better articulate language instruction. Although he does not specifically address costs and benefits, he nonetheless emphasizes the need for program accountability. We must find ways to allow students to progress through the stages of language development without false starts. According to Oller, "it is not always overtly mentioned that a critical missing ingredient, perhaps the factor most directly responsible for better articulation where it exists, is testing" (1989, 100).

Evaluation and assessment, then, allow us to do the following:

- To be able to describe the communicative abilities of students
- To measure student achievement
- To document attitudes about programs
- To better place elementary school foreign language learners into the traditional secondary sequence
- To provide evidence to the greater community about early language learning
- To provide teachers and curriculum planners with information to revise instruction

A Scorecard of Current Evaluation Practices

What is generally tested in early language programs? It is most appropriate to assess students' listening and speaking skills in FLEX and Sequential FLES programs. If the goals of the program have included reading and writing, these areas should also be assessed. Most programs also have some means of checking students' cross-cultural perceptions. In Immersion programs, knowledge of the content from the core curriculum is the focus of most evaluation. Students in Immersion programs are tested via standardized achievement tests in English, although part or all of their instruction has occurred in the target language. Target language proficiency is also the object of Immersion testing.

Given the disparity of early language programs in terms of time, intensity, and situational factors, where should we begin to conceive a coherent evaluation initiative based on current practices? Lipton maintains, "The central idea in planning any evaluation of all varieties of **FLES*** programs is the matching of the goals and objectives to the evaluation procedures" (1992, 56).

Along these same lines of thinking, Curtain and Pesola similarly support beginning with local goals: "Well-written outcomes contain or imply an assessment strategy, and the first step in structuring any lesson is to ask the twin questions, 'What do I expect students to be able to do as a result of this instruction?' and 'How will I know if they have met this goal?' " (1994, 221).

Lipton offers specific testing formats for listening, speaking, reading, writing, and cultural awareness. Seven questions guide assessment:

- Does the youngster understand the foreign language?
- Is the youngster communicating in the foreign language?
- Does the youngster get meaning from the printed page?
- Is the youngster communicating in writing?
- Does the youngster understand differences and similarities between the cultures?
- Does the youngster make connections and comparisons?
- Is the youngster able to use the foreign language in real-life, functional situations? (1998, 256).

Lipton's chapter on evaluation and assessment also includes references to evaluation measures in relation to aptitude, achievement, and program differences.

Curtain and Pesola offer two guidelines for student achievement testing:
- **Guideline 1:** Use the achievement test as an opportunity for children to discover how much they know, not how much they still have to learn.
- **Guideline 2:** Test what has been taught in the way it has been taught (1994, 226-227).

If the teacher has already conceived student-oriented objectives, the groundwork has already been laid for the activities that will be a part of assessment: "The best source of ideas for assessment are the activities and contexts used in daily class sessions" (227). Curtain and Pesola offer many testing formats for achievement testing by skill area (listening, speaking, reading, writing) for those who need further inspiration.

Kennedy, Barr-Harrison, and Guarrera Wilmeth (1994) give specific recommendations for testing students in FLEX programs. The authors indicate that, as with other program models, tests should reflect the specific objectives/outcomes for each individual program. They further list item types, such as recall, true-false, completion, multiple-choice, short answer, and essay, that are possible for FLEX program student evaluation. Similarly, they provide examples of how to use oral language samples and alternative assessments, such as projects, to assess student performance.

Oller (1989) promotes the idea of using pragmatic tests to inform the curriculum and assess students' proficiency. He recommends the following formats for testing: elicited imitation, oral interviewing, dictation, cloze procedure, controlled essay tasks, and reading comprehension tests.

Short's manual (1991), although specifically designed for a content-based Limited English Proficient program, suggests several types of informal assessments that give a more complete picture of a student's competence than the use of standardized content-area tests alone. Given the preponderance of content-related elementary school foreign language programs to date, her ideas enrich the possibilities for assessing language majority students as well. Among the alternatives described by the author are the following:

- Performance-based assessment
    Following directions
    Demonstrations and illustrations
    Writing prompts
    Lab practicals
    Technology-related tasks
- Portfolios
    The author describes how pieces should be selected, criteria for assessing portfolios, how to review portfolios to inform instruction, and how to construct a final portfolio that demonstrates growth and follows the student to the next grade.

    Short's criteria for assessing portfolios are perhaps more widely accessible in *Languages and Children: Making the Match* (Curtain and Pesola 1994, 224). Curtain and Pesola offer updated suggestions on portfolio contents as well (for example, drawings that children explain or describe; written products based on language experience stories, poetry, expressive writing, letters, invitations, greeting cards, photographs, or slides of performances such as skits, puppet plays, or simulations; journals; audio- or videotapes of oral participation on an individual or group level; and visual products such as maps, charts, and displays).

- Journals
    Short talks about how student development in language proficiency, critical thinking skills, and in-depth content knowledge can be tracked through journals. Short includes suggestions for directive and nondirective tasks.
- Language-related content assessment
    Citing the work of Hayden and Cuevas (1989), Short provides several examples of using cooperative learning to measure knowledge of prealgebra concepts, using writing and illustration to assess the students' skills in applying definitions, using listening comprehension activities to measure student knowledge of the language of mathematical operations, and encouraging students to design their own problems.

Curtain and Pesola (1994) also promote the use of performance and authentic assessment in this era of outcomes-based education. The authors contend that these alternative forms of assessment more effectively match the goals of curricula in the 1990s. They cite Wiggins' (1992) work on designing tasks for performance assessment, consolidated below:

- Give the task a context.
- Design meaningful tasks that may or may not be immediately relevant or practical.
- Design performances that require students to put knowledge together with good judgment.
- Refine the tasks by going backward from models and scoring criteria.

Curtain and Pesola also offer helpful suggestions on scoring written work. They provide a scoring guide from Milwaukee Public Schools (pp. 225-226) and explain the process of using holistic scoring rubrics by choosing an anchor paper that best represents the standard and conferring with colleagues until agreement on scoring is reached. The rubric addresses the following criteria:

- Clearness of communication
- Organization
- Individuality
- Appropriate word choice and usage
- Sentence structure
- Errors in capitalization, punctuation, and spelling

Beyond performance and authentic assessments, achievement and proficiency testing, Curtain and Pesola urge **FLES*** educators to reward student participation. Similarly, they recommend collecting data gleaned from observation and anecdotal record keeping to inform the picture of each student's complete abilities.

A recent publication attempts to reconcile obtaining a thorough picture of children's linguistic abilities in the second language with providing more rigorous evidence of the test's reliability and validity. Tucker, Donato, and Antonek (1996) discuss setting realistic oral proficiency expectations in a K–5 Japanese Sequential FLES program. The article reports on the children's emerging Japanese language abilities and the teacher's reflections on student progress. Two task types are explained. The first is a twenty-item Japanese picture vocabulary test. The second is a prochievement oral interview with a variety of elicitation tasks, such as greetings, describing or answering questions related to a picture, making grammaticality judgments, forced-choice questions, and repetition items. The elicited sample is subsequently rated on comprehension, fluency, grammar, pronunciation, and vocabulary.

Beyond the description of tasks and the statistical manipulations of data, the authors urge others to document the utility, appropriateness, and psychometric characteristics of their instruments. Only with full knowledge of whether the test is appropriate in a new situation may tests be adapted by others.

Thompson (1996) describes the efforts behind the compilation of K–8 assessments resulting in *K–8 Foreign Language Assessment: A Bibliography* (1995). Although this compilation does not address issues of reliability and validity, it nonetheless offers an excellent point of departure for K–8 educators. The first part introduces readers to traditional and alternative testing formats. The following list of questions one should ask before selecting or developing tests is of paramount importance when addressing the concerns of Tucker et al. (1996):

- What are my instructional goals?
- What is my purpose for assessing my students?
- What do I want to know about my students?
- How will the test results be used?
- Does the instrument I am considering match the purpose for which I am assessing (e.g., progress in a particular lesson, mastery of a certain topic, placement, program evaluation)?
- Is the level or grade for which this instrument was developed appropriate for my students?
- Does the instrument measure the language skills that I wish to assess (e.g., speaking, listening, reading, writing, cultural knowledge)?
- Is the instrument designed for a program similar to mine? If not, can I adapt it for use in my program?
- If the instrument was not designed specifically for the language I want to assess, can it be adapted easily?

- Will the results of this assessment permit me to make the decision I want to make? (Thompson 1995, xvii)

A major portion of the compilation lists tests by language. Details about type of program and level of student are also provided. Following the bibliography are several other worthwhile tools, ranging from scoring guides and assessment resources to commercially available tests.

If early language educators would use this resource or their self-made tests and keep track of data when assessing their individual students, the process would move forward for developing a coherent evaluation for **FLES***. It is the responsibility of each and every one of us to do so.

Realizing a Cogent Evaluation Initiative

Several broad-based initiatives are moving test development out of the classroom and into the board room. In 1988, the Center for Applied Linguistics (CAL) launched the COPE (Center for Language Education and Research Oral Proficiency Exam) to assess Full and Partial Immersion students' proficiency. Students engage in a role-play in which one assumes the role of an American student and the other the role of a visiting student from another country. The two must exchange information or resolve a problem. The conversation is audiotaped, and each student's proficiency is rated independently by an evaluator (Curtain and Pesola 1994; Oller 1989; Rosenbusch 1995).

In a similar vein, CAL released the CAL FLES Test. This listening and reading achievement test is based on typical topics found in Sequential FLES and FLEX programs. Pictures, diagrams, and charts facilitate students' comprehension just as they do in classroom instruction (Curtain and Pesola 1994; Rosenbusch 1995).

The National French Contest, *Le Grand Concours,* has several different versions based on grade level, program format, and whether the student is learning the language as a second language or is already bilingual. In addition to motivating students to continue their French studies, the contest is intended to raise public awareness of the "exciting language teaching that is taking place in your schools and to underline the importance of EARLY language training" (American Association of Teachers of French 1997, 4).

In a related vein, Lipton, Morgan, and Reed (1996) report the benefits of an early start for students who persevere. AP students who indicated on a separate survey that they had learned French starting in grades 1–3 performed better than students who began in grades 4 or higher. The average AP grade for the former group was 3.35 out of 5, and for the latter group, 2.95 out of 5 or below.

Thompson (1996) describes the efforts of the Iowa State National K–12 Resource Center to bring together **FLES*** educators over two summers to devise assessments based on the national foreign language standards. She reminds us that writing objectives and learning scenarios from the standards must precede test development. The article concludes with an example derived from the workshop that other curriculum specialists and test designers may follow in devising assessments based on the national standards.

Participants at Iowa State's 1997 Summer Assessment Institute received training in SOPA (Student Oral Proficiency Assessment) administration and rating. The SOPA validity and reliability research study is one attempt to respond to Oller's (1989) charge about the paucity of appropriate early language tests. Designed in 1991 by CAL to assess Immersion students' proficiency, the instrument is being adapted, along with rating scales, for use in Sequential FLES programs. The test will be piloted in clinical and regular classrooms, and data will be collected on the instrument's reliability and validity (National K–12 Foreign Language Research Center 1996).

Singer (1997) describes a theme-based proficiency test for Louisiana French and Spanish students following eighth grade. The test contains subtests for listening, speaking, reading, and writing. Teachers are using the test results to refine their overall programs, yet have expressed the need for more professional development in proficiency-based teaching and testing. The Louisiana State Department of Education has responded by conducting summer institutes for teachers and refining the tests based on state standards.

These collaborative ventures have made funding agencies, state departments of education, and school boards sit up and take notice. Clearly, the work of these groups and institutes provides working models for others to emulate as test development continues. At the same time, the results of these assessments showcase our students' abilities and give cause for celebration.

TEACHER EVALUATION

It is often the case that administrators with little or no second language proficiency are called upon to evaluate foreign language teachers. In an effort to inform administrators about what to look for during visits to elementary-level foreign language classrooms, Lipton (1992) prepared a list of questions to guide observation and evaluation. "Do You Know a Good **FLES*** Lesson When You Observe One? (A Checklist)" addresses evidence of planning, the choice of classroom activities, the nature of interaction between students and teacher, the use of the target language, error correction, and meeting individual differences.

Curtain and Pesola (1994) also provide a checklist of teaching behaviors oriented toward communicative language teaching. The checklist may be used for self-evaluation or for giving feedback to peers. The authors also suggest providing copies of the checklists to cooperating teachers, university supervisors, methods instructors, and student teachers so that common expectations and a common language for teacher development can permeate the preservice component of learning to teach in K–8 settings.

Program Evaluation

The American Council on the Teaching of Foreign Languages (ACTFL) released a description of characteristics of effective elementary school foreign language programs (1992) following consensus building over the 1989–1990 academic year. The characteristics encompass the issues of access and equity, program goals and intensity, long sequence, articulation, curriculum, instruction, material, evaluation, staffing, professional development, school and community support and development, and culture. On the one hand, these guidelines serve as a point of departure for those responsible for planning and implementing programs. On the other hand, they are equally valuable for evaluating programs on an annual basis.

In the broad sense, program evaluation provides evidence that goals are being met. Beyond classroom testing, it is also desirable to "demonstrate the impact of the program on student performance in other content areas, on self-concept, on attitudes, or on cognitive or social development" (Curtain and Pesola 1994, 219).

Heining-Boynton unveiled the FLES Program Evaluation Inventory in 1991 to address some of these other areas of impact. She continues to collect data from students, parents, classroom teachers, and administrators. Her convincing longitudinal study provides support for the necessity of program evaluation in revising curricula, assessing attitudes, and involving the educational community at large in the **FLES*** program.

Lipton offers The **FLES*** Scale for Program Evaluation (1998, 319). The **FLES*** Scale is a checklist of significant factors that can be used in evaluating the effectiveness of **FLES*** programs.

Conclusion

Now that clear expectations for **FLES*** programs exist through the national foreign language standards, state model curricula, and the many excellent individual programs around the country, it is time to consolidate our efforts on evaluation. **FLES*** educators have spent countless hours devising local assessments that have showcased the successes of their students for the local community. Many of these assessments have been compiled for others to borrow and modify, laying the foundation for a more unified attempt at a comprehensive evaluation agenda. Broad-based initiatives that address the inadequacies of our testing to date are well under way. The development of a variety of valid and reliable instruments that reflect the goals of various programs will celebrate students' accomplishments in a coherent, consistent manner.

> From our perspective, the time has long passed for spending our time describing the shortcomings of FLES programs and enumerating the things their graduates *cannot* do; rather, the time has come to describe as clearly as possible those things the students can do and the many ways in which their incipient skills will serve them in the years ahead (Tucker, Donato, and Antonek 1996, 549).

This author concurs, adding the importance of ongoing self-renewal for **FLES*** teachers through evaluation of teaching. Moreover, it is critical to continually assess programs to match goals and objectives to outcomes. Taking these three components together, we can ensure continued success!

REFERENCES

American Association of Teachers of French. Winter/Spring 1997. *Le Grand Concours.* Carbondale, IL: AATF.

American Council on the Teaching of Foreign Languages. 1992. "Characteristics of Effective Elementary School FL Programs." *ACTFL Newsletter* 4 (Spring).

Curtain, H., and C. A. Pesola. 1994. *Languages and Children: Making the Match.* 2nd ed. White Plains, NY: Longman.

Heining-Boynton, A. 1991. "The FLES Program Evaluation Inventory (FPEI)." *Foreign Language Annals* 24 (3): 193–202.

Kennedy, D., P. Barr-Harrison, and M. Guarrera Wilmeth. 1994. *Exploring Languages: A Complete Introduction for Foreign Language Students.* Teacher's Manual. Lincolnwood, IL: National Textbook Co.

Lipton, G. 1992. *Elementary Foreign Language Programs (FLES*): An Administrator's Handbook.* Lincolnwood, IL: National Textbook Co.

Lipton, G. 1998. *Practical Handbook to Elementary Foreign Language Programs.* 3rd ed. Lincolnwood, IL: National Textbook Co.

Lipton, G., R. Morgan, and M. Reed. 1996. "Does **FLES*** Help AP French Students Perform Better?" *AATF National Bulletin* 21 (4).

National K–12 Foreign Language Resource Center. Fall 1996. *Center News.* Ames, IA: Iowa State University.

National Standards in Foreign Language Education Project. 1996. *Standards for Foreign Language Learning: Preparing for the 21st Century.* Lawrence, KS: Allen Press.

Oller, J., Jr. 1989. "Testing and Elementary School Foreign Language Programs." *Languages in Elementary Schools*, ed. K. Müller. New York: American Forum.

Rosenbusch, M. 1995. "Language Learners in the Elementary School: Investing in the Future." *Foreign Language Learning: The Journey of a Lifetime*, ed. R. Donato and R. Terry. Lincolnwood, IL: National Textbook Co.

Short, D. 1991. *How to Integrate Language and Content Instruction: A Training Manual.* Washington, DC: Center for Applied Linguistics.

Singer, M. 1997. "Proficiency Testing for Middle School: Voyage à EPCOT/Viaje a EPCOT." *Learning Languages* 2 (2): 26–31.

Thompson, L., compiler. 1995. *K–8 Foreign Language Assessment: A Bibliography.* Washington, DC: Center for Applied Linguistics.

Thompson, L. 1996. "K–8 Foreign Language Assessment and the New Foreign Language Standards." In *Creating Opportunities for Excellence Through Language*, ed. E. Spinelli. Report of Central States Conference on the Teaching of Foreign Languages. Lincolnwood, IL: National Textbook Co.

Tucker, G., R. Donato, and J. Antonek. 1996. "Documenting Growth in a Japanese FLES Program." *Foreign Language Annals.* 29 (4): 539–550.

Wing, B. 1996. "Starting Early: Foreign Languages in the Elementary and Middle Schools." In *Foreign Languages For All: Challenges and Choices*, ed. B. Wing. Northeast Conference Report. Lincolnwood, IL: National Textbook Co.

Appendixes

APPENDIX A

Definitions

FLES* (pronounced "flestar") is the umbrella term for all types of elementary school (K–8) foreign language programs, including Sequential FLES, FLEX, and Immersion

SEQUENTIAL FLES: an introduction to one foreign language for two or more years, with a systematic development of language skills (listening, speaking, reading, writing, and culture) within the parameters of themes, topics, or content areas. Good theme-related fluency is expected (if scheduled five times a week, thirty minutes a day) for four or more years.

FLEX: An introduction to one or more foreign languages, with few language skills expected. Limited fluency with a once- or twice-a-week program that emphasizes limited language acquisition and extensive cultural awareness.

IMMERSION: The use of the foreign language throughout the school day (in Total Immersion) or part of the school day (in Partial Immersion) for teaching the various subjects of the elementary school curriculum. Good fluency in the foreign language is expected after four or more years in the program.

APPENDIX B

The Five Cs of the Standards for Foreign Language Learning

COMMUNICATION

Communicate in Languages Other Than English

Standard 1.1: Students engage in conversations, provide and obtain information, express feelings and emotions, and exchange opinions.

Standard 1.2: Students understand and interpret written and spoken language on a variety of topics.

Standard 1.3: Students present information, concepts, and ideas to an audience of listeners or readers on a variety of topics.

CULTURES

Gain Knowledge and Understanding of Other Cultures

Standard 2.1: Students demonstrate an understanding of the relationship between the practices and perspectives of the culture studied.

Standard 2.2: Students demonstrate an understanding of the relationship between the products and perspectives of the culture studied.

CONNECTIONS

Connect with Other Disciplines and Acquire Information

Standard 3.1: Students reinforce and further their knowledge of other disciplines through the foreign language.

Standard 3.2: Students acquire information and recognize the distinctive viewpoints that are only available through the foreign language and its cultures.

COMPARISONS

Develop Insight into the Nature of Language and Culture

Standard 4.1: Students demonstrate understanding of the nature of language through comparisons of the language studied and their own.

Standard 4.2: Students demonstrate understanding of the concept of culture through comparisons of the cultures studied and their own.

COMMUNITIES

Participate in Multilingual Communities at Home and Around the World

Standard 5.1: Students use the language both within and beyond the school setting.

Standard 5.2: Students show evidence of becoming life-long learners by using the language for personal enjoyment and enrichment.

Executive Summary National Foreign Language Standards

APPENDIX C

FLES* Teacher Competencies

(Revised by the 1996 National **FLES*** Commission of AATF)

1. Language competency
   a. Foreign language competency
      i. Functional proficiency (oral and written) for *Sequential FLES and FLEX*
      ii. Near-native proficiency (oral and written) for *Immersion* programs
   b. English language competency
      i. For all three program models, functional proficiency (oral and written)

2. Knowledge/skills regarding
   a. Rationale for **FLES***, and the ability to communicate this to members of the school community
   b. **FLES*** methodology for all three program models
   c. National FL standards and their implementation
   d. State and local FL frameworks and standards
   e. General elementary-school (K–8) curriculum and methodology
   f. Target culture(s) and how to teach culture
   g. The American elementary-school (K–8) setting
   h. Multiple intelligences of children

3. Understanding language acquisition by children in terms of
   a. **FLES*** methodology
   b. Research studies on **FLES***
   c. National FL standards
   d. Assessing student progress
   e. Evaluation of **FLES*** programs
   f. Implications of first- and second-language acquisition principles
   g. Appropriate children's literature (in the target language and in English)

h. Implications of child psychology and child development
   i. Principles of applied linguistics
4. Professional competence/skills
   a. Multiethnic, multicultural sensitivity
   b. Ability to work effectively with children
   c. Ability to teach to the different learning styles of children
   d. Ability to establish rapport with children, colleagues, parents, administrators, and others in the school community
   e. Knowledge of technology appropriate for this age level
   f. Skill in involving parents in the **FLES*** program
   g. Skill in classroom management and conflict resolution
   h. Ability to make connections with other disciplines (interdisciplinary) and other languages and cultures
   i. Conversant with resources for age-appropriate **FLES*** materials
   j. Aware of contemporary trends in foreign language (e.g., membership in FL associations and attendance at FL conferences)

Appendix D

Focus on FLES*

Planning and Implementing FLES* Programs
(Foreign Languages in Elementary Schools)

Gladys C. Lipton
Director, National **FLES*** Institute

Why FLES*?

All types of **FLES*** programs can be highly beneficial to children. Research tells us that an early introduction to foreign languages provides many advantages for them, as follows:

1. Children have the ability to learn and excel in the pronunciation of a foreign language.
2. Children who have studied a foreign language in elementary school achieve expected gains and even have higher scores on standardized tests in reading, language arts, and mathematics than those who have not.
3. Children who have studied a foreign language show greater cognitive development in such areas as mental flexibility, creativity, divergent thinking, and higher-order thinking skills.
4. Children who have studied a foreign language develop a sense of cultural pluralism (openness to and appreciation of other cultures).
5. Children studying a foreign language have an improved self-concept and sense of achievement in school.
6. Brain surgeons question why foreign language is not initiated before the age of ten, since that period of time is optimum for learning a foreign language.
7. Positive AP/**FLES*** results.

FLES* (pronounced "flestar") is the umbrella term for all types of elementary school (K–8) foreign language programs, including *Sequential FLES, FLEX,* and *Immersion.*

Choice of Program Models

There are three basic types of **FLES*** program models. A definition of terms can help to clarify these different program models, based on the "Why **FLES***?" brochure.

FLES* is the overall, or "umbrella," term for all types of elementary school foreign language programs in grades K–8. All three program models have the potential for continuing FL study.

Sequential **FLES*** is an introduction to one foreign language for two or more years, with a systematic development of language skills (listening, speaking, reading, writing, and culture) within the parameters of themes and functional topics. Good theme-related fluency is expected if scheduled five times a week, thirty minutes or more a day, for four or more years. All children can be served by this type of program.

FLEX-Exploratory is an introduction to one or more foreign languages, with limited foreign language skills expected. There may be limited fluency with a once- or twice-a-week program that emphasizes functional language and cultural awareness. All children can be served by this type of program.

Immersion (also *Partial Immersion, Content-Based*) programs include the use of the foreign language throughout the school day by teachers and students. Because of the shortage of qualified teachers, it is difficult to serve many students in this type of program. Its major goal is to provide the basic elementary school program through the foreign language. Good fluency in the foreign language is expected after four or more years in the program.

Which One Is Best?

It is impossible to say which program model is best without identifying the context of the educational community. So much depends on the needs of the school/school community, the budgetary resources, the desired student outcomes, the continuing supply of teachers, and many other important factors. The greatest overall consideration, however, should be equity: that all students have access to some type of elementary school foreign language program. It may be that a fairly large school district can afford to schedule one or more than one type of **FLES*** program model, depending on what they have decided to be their goals and student outcomes.

The following issues must be examined, preferably by a school or school district Foreign Language Advisory Committee, looking at the various options for a foreign language sequence:

1. long-range planning, commitment, and funding
2. development of a broad base of support from different members of the school or school district community, including parents and others, in the creation of a Foreign Language Advisory Committee

3. development of goals and student outcomes for the program
4. availability of fluent, trained teachers
5. development of a realistic curriculum
6. availability of age-appropriate materials of instruction
7. development of an evaluation design of the program, based on the goals and student outcomes
8. development of the rationale for the program, articulation plans, decisions concerning beginning grade, students, schedule, and other administrative concerns
9. provision for flexibility and opportunities for modification of the program, as an evaluation of the program indicates (every three to five years)

Basis for Decisions

Decisions must be made within the constraints of time, budgets, goals, equity of access, and student outcomes in consonance with national foreign language standards. Many foreign language leaders, parents, and administrators on school and university levels have supported the following guidelines for the implementation of K–8 **FLES*** programs:

1. All K–8 elementary school students should have the opportunity to start the study of a foreign language, before the age of ten.
2. All three program models (*Sequential FLES, FLEX-Exploratory,* and *Immersion*) are valid foreign language programs, provided that they fulfill their goals.
3. There is not one best way to provide **FLES*** instruction, nor is there only one best method of **FLES*** instruction.
4. All program models contribute to a K–12 foreign language sequence.

References

Boyer, E. L. 1995. *The Basic School: A Community for Learning.* Princeton, NJ: The Carnegie Foundation for the Advancement of Teaching.

Curtain, H., and C. Pesola. 1994. *Language and Children: Making the Match.* 2nd ed. Reading, MA: Addison-Wesley.

Kennedy, D., and W. DeLorenzo. 1985. *Complete Guide to Exploratory Foreign Language Programs.* Lincolnwood, IL: National Textbook Co.

Lipton, G. 1992. *Elementary Foreign Language Programs (FLES*): An Administrator's Handbook.* Lincolnwood, IL: National Textbook Co.

———. 1994. "**FLES*** Programs Today: Options and Opportunities." *French Review* 65, 1 (Oct.): 7–10.

———. 1995. "The High School Chair's Relation to the Local **FLES*** Program." In *Managing the High School Foreign Language Department*, ed. R. Klein and S. Slick. Lincolnwood, IL: National Textbook Co.

———. 1998. *Practical Handbook to Elementary Foreign Language Programs Including FLES, FLEX and Immersion*. 3rd. ed. Lincolnwood, IL: NTC/Contemporary Publishing Company.

Lipton, G., ed. 1992. *Evaluating FLES* Programs*. Champaign, IL: Report of the **FLES*** Commission of AATF.

National **FLES*** Institute. 1991. *FLES* Programs in Action* and *Study Guide*. Video. G. Lipton, project director. Baltimore, MD: National **FLES*** Institute, University of Maryland, Baltimore County.

Rafferty, E. 1986. *Second Language Study and Basic Skills in Louisiana*. Baton Rouge, LA: Louisiana Department of Education.

Rehorick S., and V. Edwards. 1992. *French Immersion: Process, Product and Perspectives*. Welland, Ontario, Canada: Canadian Modern Language Review.

"Why **FLES***?" 1994. Brochure available from AATSP, University of Northern Colorado, Greeley, CO 80639, or AATF, Mail Code 4510, Dept. of Foreign Languages, Southern Illinois University, Carbondale, IL 62901.

For additional information, contact Dr. Gladys Lipton, Director, The National **FLES*** Institute, University of Maryland, Baltimore County, Baltimore, MD 21250. FAX: 301-230-2652.

APPENDIX E

SUGGESTIONS FOR
ATTRACTING FRENCH FLES*
STUDENTS

Gladys C. Lipton

This is a project of AATF's National **FLES*** Commission,
American Association of Teachers of French

Mail Code 4510
Department of Foreign Languages
Southern Illinois University
Carbondale, IL 62901-4510

CONTENTS

	PAGE
FLES* Definitions	1
Why French **FLES***?	2
Checklist for French **FLES*** Programs	3
Suggestions for Marketing French **FLES*** Programs	4
Additional AATF Assistance and Resources	6
Basic French **FLES*** References	7

Review Committee:
Pat Barr-Harrison
Lynne Bryan
Juliette Eastwick
Lena Lucietto
Elizabeth Miller
Harriet Saxon

If there are questions, please contact the Cochairs, AATF NATIONAL FLES* COMMISSION, Dr. Gladys Lipton, National FLES* Institute, UMBC-MLL, Baltimore, MD 21250, and Dr. Lena Lucietto, Newman School, New Orleans, LA 70115.

FLES* DEFINITIONS

FLES* (pronounced FLESTAR) is the umbrella term for all kinds of foreign language programs in elementary and middle schools (K–8) in the context of national foreign language standards of communication, culture, connections, comparisons, and communities.

Sequential FLES* is instruction in one foreign language for two or more years, with a sequential development of listening, speaking, reading and writing skills, as well as the infusion of cultural content. Experts recommend that classes be scheduled five days a week, for at least thirty minutes a day, if fluency within the curriculum is to be expected after four or more years in the program.

FLEX or **Exploratory** is an introduction to one or more foreign languages. A FLEX program can be designed in a variety of formats, but the two basic models are the "exploratory" and the "limited exposure." In the FLEX-Exploratory model, students explore two or more languages, with the emphasis on building readiness for language learning as well as the relationship of languages and their cultures. Classes may be scheduled once or twice a week, or in a six- or nine-week program, or other variations.

In the FLEX-limited exposure model, students are introduced to *one* language on a once- or twice-a-week schedule through the school year. Some language skills and cultural knowledge can be acquired, but they vary in proportion to the amount of time devoted to the program.

Immersion or **Partial Immersion** is the use of the foreign language throughout all or part of the school day for teaching various content areas of the elementary school curriculum, such as math, science, and social studies. Fluency is expected after four or more years in the program.

These definitions are based on the **FLES*** definitions in the *Why FLES* brochure*, which is available from National AATF: S.I.U., Carbondale, IL 62901-4510. Prices vary according to quantity:

    200 or more .... 25¢ each   10-99 .... 65¢ each
    100-199 .... 50¢ each   1-9 .... $1.00 each

WHY FRENCH FLES*?

1. Children have the ability to learn and excel in the pronunciation of French, particularly if they start before the age of ten.
2. Children who have studied French in elementary school achieve expected gains and even have higher scores on standardized tests in reading, language arts, and mathematics than those who have not. The extensive study in Louisiana indicates these results.
3. Children who have studied French show greater cognitive development in such areas as mental flexibility, creativity, divergent thinking, and higher-order thinking skills. Many of the Canadian studies indicate these results.
4. Children who have studied a foreign language develop a sense of cultural pluralism (openness to and appreciation of other cultures).
5. Children studying a foreign language have an improved self-concept and sense of achievement in school.
6. Beginning early in French language study has a favorable effect on French studies later on in high school and college. On the 1995 Advanced Placement French Test, those students who started in grades 1-3 and 4-6 outperformed those students who started later.
7. Brain research studies indicate the "window of opportunity" for learning a foreign language is best before the age of ten.

CHECKLIST FOR FRENCH FLES* PROGRAMS

_____ 1. All students have access to **FLES*** programs.

_____ 2. There is a Foreign Language Advisory Committee for K-12 programs.

_____ 3. The goals of the **FLES*** program are clearly stated.

_____ 4. There is provision for articulation with French programs in upper schools.

_____ 5. There is provision for ongoing informal feedback and formal evaluation (every five to seven years).

_____ 6. There is assurance for a continuing supply of appropriate French **FLES*** materials.

_____ 7. There is assurance for a continuing supply of well-prepared and trained French **FLES*** teachers.

_____ 8. There is documentation on the short-term and longitudinal results of studying **FLES*** and the effect on English language skills and achievement in other curriculum areas.

_____ 9. There is a written French **FLES*** curriculum, which indicates student progress based on national standards, in linguistic, cultural, and interdisciplinary approaches.

_____ 10. Students demonstrate their progress in French **FLES*** (K-8) through a variety of ways, including progress indicators suggested by national Foreign Language standards.

_____ 11. The French **FLES*** instructional program in class reflects the goals of the program through the curriculum content and the methods that teachers use.

_____ 12. There is enthusiasm for the **FLES*** program on the part of students, parents, administrators, school board members, guidance counselors, and other members of the school/school district community.

SUGGESTIONS FOR MARKETING FRENCH FLES* PROGRAMS

1. Plan *memorable* French **FLES*** in-class activities throughout the school year.
2. Distribute a description of your French **FLES*** Program (goals and accomplishments) and the "Why **FLES***?" brochure.
3. Plan "events" that demonstrate your students' achievements in French: songs, skits, conversations, etc.
4. Plan activities where students "teach" French to other children and adults.
5. Display French **FLES*** students' work all around the school and around the school community (e.g., public library exhibit).
6. Have student announcements in French over the loudspeaker about special events, the weather, etc.
7. Invite parents and grandparents to a French **FLES*** Visitors' *Journée Française*.
8. Plan a short "French Around the World" assembly program for the school, the community, and educational, business, and government leaders.
9. Invite speakers of French to your classroom(s) to show pictures and to tell about growing up in a French-speaking country.
10. Have high school and college students who have had a French **FLES*** experience give testimonials for the Board of Education about how their knowledge of French has helped them at school and in making their future work plans.
11. Keep an Alumni French **FLES*** Journal in order to follow those students who have continued their French studies and/or who have used French in their careers.

12. Have an International French Festival with performances by French **FLES*** students.
13. Keep a French **FLES*** visitor's log, asking guests to write their comments about the French **FLES*** program.
14. Create activities for French **FLES*** students to participate in local school and community events, such as a schoolwide or county fair.

Appendix F

Basic **FLES*** Mini-Bibliography

Begley, S. 1996. "Your Child's Brain." *Newsweek*. Feb. 19: 55–61.

Boyer, E. 1995. *The Basic School*. Princeton, NJ: The Carnegie Foundation for the Advancement of Teaching, 72–74.

Brown, C. 1989. "The People Factor in the Glastonbury, CT Schools," in Lipton G. (ed.) *The People Factor in FLES* Programs*. Champaign, IL: AATF: 71–78.

Curtain, H., and C. A. Pesola. 1994. *Languages and Children*. White Plains, NY: Longman, 2nd ed.

"Focus on **FLES***" position paper (1996), available with a s.a.s.e. from National **FLES*** Institute, UMBC-MLL, Baltimore, MD 21250.

Kennedy, D., and W. De Lorenzo. 1985. *Complete Guide to Exploratory Foreign Language Programs*. Lincolnwood, IL: National Textbook Co.

Lipton, G. 1996. "Many **FLES*** Issues, Many Approaches." *ACTFL Newsletter*. Winter: 15–16.

———. 1995. "The High School Chair's Relation to the Local **FLES*** Program," in Klein, R., and S. Slick (eds.) *Managing the High School Foreign Language Department*. Lincolnwood, IL: National Textbook Co., 153–162.

———. 1994. "**FLES*** Programs Today." *French Review*. Oct.: 1–16.

———. 1994. "What is **FLES*** Methodology? An Overview" *Hispania* 77: 878–887.

———. 1992. *The Administrator's Guide to FLES* Programs*. Lincolnwood, IL: National Textbook Company.

———. 1998. *Practical Handbook to Elementary Foreign Language Programs, including FLES, FLEX, and Immersion*. 3rd ed. Lincolnwood, IL: NTC/Contemporary Publishing Company.

Lipton, G. (ed.) 1998. *A Celebration of FLES**. Lincolnwood, IL: NTC/Contemporary Publishing Company.

———. (ed.) 1996. *Attracting French FLES* Students*. Report, National **FLES*** Commission of AATF, Champaign, IL.

———. (ed.) 1992. *Evaluating FLES* Programs*. Report, National **FLES*** Commission of AATF. Carbondale, IL.

Miller, E. 1995. "A Salad of Language Learners," in Lipton, G. (ed.) *Reaching All FLES* Students*. Report, National **FLES*** Commission of AATF. Champaign, IL: AATF: 1–10.

Nadia, S. 1993. "Kids' Brainpower," *Oregonian*, Dec. 13: 7–8.

Rafferty, E. 1986. *Second Language Study and Basic Skills in Louisiana*. Baton Rouge, LA: Louisiana Dept. of Education.

Rehorick, S., and V. Edwards. 1992. *French Immersion: Process, Product and Perspectives.* Welland, Ontario, Canada: *Canadian ML Review.*

Saxon, H. 1994. "La Francofolie," in Lipton, G. (ed.) *FLES* Methodology I.* Report, National **FLES*** Commission of AATF. Champaign, IL: AATF: 37–45.

National FLES* Institute. 1991. *FLES* Programs in Action, Study/Guide,* National **FLES*** Institute, UMBC-MLL, Baltimore, MD 21250.

Why FLES?* 1994. National AATF, Mail Code 4510, Dept. of Foreign Languages, Southern Illinois University, Carbondale, IL 62901-4510.

Appendix G

Mini-Biographies of the Contributors to This Volume

Evelyne Cella Armstrong (Ph.D., Union Institute) is Director of Extended Programs at Charles Wright Academy and Professor of K–8 **FLES*** Methodology at Pacific Lutheran University, Tacoma, Washington. She has led, for over a decade, a series of Immersion day camps for children and has developed curriculum modules for various themes.

Pat Barr-Harrison (M.A., Howard University) is the current Supervisor of Foreign Languages for the Prince Geroge's County Public Schools, Maryland. She is a doctoral candidate in foreign language education at the University of Maryland.

Christine Brown (Sixth-year Administration and Supervision Certificate, University of Hartford) is Director of Foreign Languages for the Glastonbury Public Schools in Connecticut. She recently served as Chair of the K-12 National Foreign Language Standards Task Force and is a member of the ACTFL Executive Council.

Lynne B. Bryan (Ph.D., Florida State University) teaches at Macon State College in Georgia. She directed the NEH Grant: FLES with Substance. She has served on the Executive Boards of AATSP Georgia, Foreign Language Association of Georgia, and the Georgia Board of Regents Advisory Committee on Foreign Languages.

Suzanne Cane (B.A., Wellesley, M.S., Simons School, Library Science, Boston) teaches French **FLES*** at the Lincoln School in Providence, Rhode Island, and is a member of the National **FLES*** Commission of AATF.

Astrid M. DeBuhr (Ph.D., Claremont Graduate School, California) teaches fourth and fifth graders as well as levels two and advanced placement in the Clayton School District, St. Louis, Missouri, where she is implementor for an elementary school foreign language program. She is past President of the Foreign Language Association of Missouri.

Patricia R. Duggar (Ed.S., Louisiana State University), an Education Specialist, Curriculum and Instruction—Foreign Languages, from Louisiana State University, currently teaches French and serves as Department Chair at Paul Breaux Middle School in Lafayette, Louisiana.

Juliette Eastwick (M.S., University of Maryland, Baltimore County) and **Elizabeth Tomlinson** (M.A., Harvard University) have taught French at the Bryn Mawr School in Baltimore, Maryland, for the past twenty-one years. They teach a Sequential FLES program from Kindergarten through grade 5 and are longtime members of the National **FLES*** Commission of AATF.

Paul A. García (Ph.D., University of Illinois, Urbana) served as Foreign Language Supervisor for Kansas City, Missouri, implementing ten Immersion schools. He is Adjunct Associate Professor at the University of Kansas, and his publications include methodology and program planning. He is an ACTFL Executive Council member and serves on the AATG Student Standards and Minorities committees.

Virginia L. Gramer (M.A., Indiana University), as a teacher and coordinator in Hinsdale, Illinois, has worked actively on local, state, and national committees to develop curriculum. She has assisted many districts in initiating sound elementary school foreign language programs.

Dora F. Kennedy (Ph.D., University of Maryland, College Park) is Adjunct to the Graduate Faculty at the University of Maryland, College Park, in the College of Education. She was formerly Supervisor of Foreign Language for the Prince George's County Public Schools, Maryland.

Philip Korfe (M.Ed., University of South Dakota) is a fifth-grade teacher in Sioux Falls, South Dakota. He teaches French to his students twenty minutes a day. The curriculum is composed of a variety of teacher-prepared mini-units and field trips in the community.

Katherine C. Kurk (Ph.D., University of Kentucky) is Professor/Coordinator of Languages at Northern Kentucky University. A member of the AATF National **FLES*** Commission since 1990, she published the *Calendrier perpétuel* in 1994. Her co-author, **Hilary W. Landwehr** (Ph.D., University of North Carolina, Chapel Hill) is Associate Professor of Spanish at Northern Kentucky University.

Gladys C. Lipton (Ed.D., New York University) is the Director of the National **FLES*** Institute at the University of Maryland, Baltimore County. She is the author of numerous articles on **FLES*** and two books, *Practical Handbook to Elementary Foreign Language Programs, including Sequential FLES, FLEX and Immersion Programs* and *An Administrator's Guide to FLES* Programs*. She is National President of the AATF (1998–2000).

Lena L. Lucietto (Ph.D., University of Chicago), who has taught **FLES*** in various settings, currently teaches French and Spanish **FLES*** classes at the Isidore Newman School in New Orleans. She is Co-chair of the National **FLES*** Commission of AATF.

Elizabeth Miller (M.A., San Francisco State University) is the Director of the AATF National French Contest for elementary schools. She has taught French for more than twenty years, from preschool to advanced placement literature classes, fiercely supporting the belief that communicative language classes are appropriate for all types of learners.

Peter Negroni (Ed.D., Fairleigh Dickinson University), a longtime educator, has held positions at every level of teaching and administration—the last twenty years as Superintendent of Schools in Springfield, Massachusetts. A language teacher by training, he is committed to second-language learning at every level of the curriculum.

Maureen Regan-Baker (Ph.D., Indiana University) has been a teacher for forty years, forever a **FLES*** supporter, author, filmmaker, methodologist, change agent. "Children are our nation's greatest treasure and we, their most influential intellectual guardians."

Kathleen Riordan (Ed.D., University of Massachusetts, Amherst) is Director of Foreign Languages in the Springfield, Massachusetts, public schools. She is past President of ACTFL and has served on the Executive Council of ACTFL.

Harriet Saxon (B.A., Montclair State and University of Grenoble) teaches French in the elementary schools of Rutherford School District, New Jersey. She is an advocate for early language learning and has received national and state recognition for the development of curriculum. She was a recipient of the New Jersey Governor's Award for Excellence in Education.

Rebecca M. Valette (Ph.D., University of Colorado), Professor of French at Boston College and past President of the National AATF, has published widely in the field of language methodology and testing. She is a co-author of *French for Mastery* and *Discovering French*.

Alan S. Wax (M.Ed., University of Illinois) teaches French with **Lydia Hurst** (M.Ed., St. Xavier University) at McGugan Junior High School. **Kathleen Durkin** (M.Ed., Northern Illinois University) and **Diane Merenda** (M.Ed., St. Xavier University) are teachers of sixth grade French. All are within School District 123 Oak Lawn-Homewood, Illinois. The French program has been in existence for over thirty years, having earned, along with its faculty, many top awards and honors at the international, national, regional, and local levels.

Deborah Wilburn-Robinson (Ph.D., Ohio State University) has taught in high school, junior high, FLES, FLEX, and Immersion settings as well as in community college and university foreign language classrooms. She is currently a teacher-educator in the Foreign and Second Language Education Program at Ohio State University and President of the Ohio Foreign Language Association.